P9-CLK-018

# The Crisis in the Working Class and Some Arguments for a New Labor Movement



by John McDermott

South End Press Boston, MA

First Edition



Cover design by Michael Prokosch
Publishing and production work
done by the South End Press

Typeset at Just Yer Type in Amherst, MA
Printed by the workers at Banta Company in Menasha, WI
They are represented by: C-417

ISBN 0-89608-014-5 paper
ISBN 0-89608-015-3 cloth
Library of Congress Card Number: 80-51437

**South End Press, P.O. Box 68, Astor Station**
**Boston, MA 02123**

# Dedication

***To* A.E.**

**About the Author:**

John McDermott is currently the director of a training program for the United Hospital and Health Care Workers (AFL-CIO) that assists workers in college preparation and is also professor and coordinator of labor studies, College of Old Westbury, New York. He is a long-standing member of the American Federation of Teachers (AFL-CIO) and is secretary of the Long Island Workers' Institute. Formerly he was editor for the *Viet Report* and has a long history of writing on social questions, technology and U.S. involvement in Viet Nam.

# Acknowledgements

I would like to acknowledge a big debt to some of the those who played a creative role in the genesis and production of this book and its ideas though in some cases they don't entirely agree with them. To the women and men of the South End Press collective for their hard work and especially for their commitment to a people's press. To the work and example of I.F. Stone and of the late C. Wright Mills. To Juliet Shor, Steve and Margaret Nelson, Manny Granich, Barbara Beltrand, Len DeCaux, Leonard Liggio, Beanie Baldwin, David Cherry, Stan and Cyn Israel, Mr. Patrick Gallagher, Francis Mark, Jeremy Brecher, Evelyn Dershewitz, Mike Pyros, and Ed Greer. I took inspiration and more from the work of Richard Boyer, Herbert Morais and Samuel Yellen.

For over a decade I've taught and worked on projects with workers going to school. Way, way back it was with mostly younger workers at what we called the S.E. Massachusetts University in Exile. But mostly with a more varied group of workers, night students, at the State College at Old Westbury in New York. I'm afraid to list names for fear I'd leave someone out but at point after point old comrades will recognize lessons they taught the teacher. More than that. The intelligence, the breadth of outlook, the class loyalty, the idealism and the militance of these working men and women, which I see day by day in a thousand contexts have convinced me that educated opinion, even (and especially) on what is called "the Left" is mostly just plain wrong when it talks about workers. I hope this book gets a little closer to the truth.

*John McDermott*
*Bayville, NY*
*May, 1980*

# TABLE OF CONTENTS

# CHAPTER ONE: WHY TRADE UNIONS FAIL

## Introduction

What's wrong with the trade unions? Why are people so unhappy with them? Why aren't they better?

Business thinks the unions are too unrestrained in their demands. Government "me toos" that idea, as do the press and t.v. But right now, the sharpest questions are coming from union members themselves. The criticisms are harsh and bitter. "The unions are hand in glove with the bosses. They prevent workers from doing what's necessary to protect our interests. They block walkouts, sit on grievances, come down on critics. They're run by big-shots, lawyers and accountants who are out for the main chance and don't care about the members. These so-called leaders talk a good fight but when push comes to shove they sit down with the companies and sell us out."

Not every worker is this critical of the unions. But generally, workers are so much unhappier with their unions than the bosses are that it should give us pause for thought.

It's best to begin with basics. Unions are in the business of power. You have a union, you want a union, because you're trying to force somebody to do something he or she doesn't want to do.

The boss doesn't want to pay you more money and you are after the power to force him to do it. The politician doesn't want to vote for a minimum wage law and you need the power to pressure him. The editor doesn't think it's wrong to push workers around (after all, he's a boss too) and you need power to change his mind.

Next time you're downtown, look and see if they have a statue of Justice on the courthouse. If so, check her out. She may or may not be blindfolded. She may or may not have a scale in her left hand. But it's near certain she'll have a sword in her right. Justice unarmed is justice defeated. That's the first basic.

The second basic isn't much more complicated. It's about tools and what you want to use them for and how well designed they are for their purposes. A union is a tool to get and wield power for workers, on the job and out in society. The argument of this book is that today our unions are dangerously weak because they are poorly designed to do what we want them to do. They were made to be used against an old form of economic and business organization; they're not designed to deal with the corporate system. In the last analysis, most of our problems stem from this. We are badly organized to protect our interests in society and on the job. Because we're weak in this basic, everything else goes haywire too—bad leadership, no action on grievances, sweetheart contracts, lack of democracy. But it is the basic that is the source of the trouble. Fix that and we can solve the other problems. Ignore it and nothing can be done.

The first part of the book, chapters 1 and 2, shows how and why the present day trade union movement became a blunted tool. In the second part of the book, chapters 3, 4, and 5, we'll follow the efforts of our grandparents as they created the labor movement we now have. We'll see how they united the workers of their day into a single working class, what sort of organizational tools they tried to build, and the ideas they worked out about the sort of world they wanted. We have similar tasks ahead of us and we can learn a lot from that older generation.

The third part of the book, chapters 6 and 7, examines the different classes of the present day U.S. Mainly, it's interested in how the arrangement of the different classes keeps our class divided and holds it back. There we'll see that the corporate system divides us into four different working classes, plays one against the other and holds each captive.

The fourth section of the book, chapters 8 and 9, talks about the goals of a revived workers' movement. We'll discuss socialism—both the rotten kind and the kind that the working class has always fought for. I will argue that the classless society is needed right now, and is a practical possibility. The final section, chapters 10, 11 and 12, has some proposals on how to organize and unite all workers, some practical goals, and some strategies for how to begin working for them.

## Trade Unions in Decline

What kind of tool are the unions? A good trade union militant would probably answer along the following lines:

> Workers organize on the job to raise their pay, improve working conditions and win dignity. Through their unions they act in the political field in the interests of all working people, organized or not.

That sounds nice but hides a lot more than it reveals. Try it again—being a little more careful this time to cross the "t" 's and dot the "i" 's.

> About one in four U.S. workers is in a union, organized either by trade or industry. By and large, it is the prosperous areas of the economy which are organized. The others are not. By threat of strike and with help from the government these workers alone have usually been able to keep their wages a little ahead of inflation.
>
> Unions are federated locally and nationally, usually through the AFL-CIO. For all practical purposes, the AFL-CIO is part of the Democratic Party. It has a middling power position there; on the one hand, on certain issues, the Democrats can't ignore it but on the other the AFL-CIO is too weak to actually control the Democratic Party.

Only a minority of workers, and a small minority at that, belong to unions. In 1974, out of a civilian labor force of 93 million (#569, see Note), about 21.5 million or 23% belonged to unions (#620). For anyone who is concerned about the well-being of all workers, you have to be skeptical of a tool which is effective for only one worker in four.

To be honest, these government statistics distort th picture since they refer to the percentage of the whole civilia labor force, which includes *all* 'employees.' If we leave out th Vice Presidents of big corporations and their straw-bosses, w find that about 29% of *workers* belong to trade unions.

However, the situation is even more serious, on the othe hand, because the percentage of organized workers has bee declining for about 20 years now. In 1956, about 25% of the labo force was organized. There has been a slow but steady declin ever since. This argues that trade unions have been gettin weaker for 20 years now. As you'll see, the argument will hold u as we look at different kinds of evidence later.

There is an odd pattern to trade union membership in ou country. The prosperous industries are organized; the poor one are not. That is, where capitalists can afford higher wages, th workers are organized. Where industries are poor and marginal the workers have no unions and earn less.

My fellow trade unionists would like to argue that it i because industries are organized that they pay higher wages an are *therefore* prosperous. The reverse however is true. Wher industries are prosperous and can pass along higher costs the accept unions. Where they aren't prosperous and can't pass o their costs, they resist unions tooth and nail.

This can be seen in a general way, for the moment, by lookin to see which industries are organized and which are not. The bul of organized workers are in four areas of the economy—truckin and allied industries, construction, government, and the monc poly corporate sector.

† NOTE: Wherever possible, I'll take statistics from the Statistica Abstract of the U.S., 1977 edition, published by the Federal Govern ment's Commerce Department. It is available at most libraries and i very handy to use. #569 is the table number from which I got th civilian labor force. Generally, I'll write the table number just next t the statistic. Other sources will follow that style. #431,74 will mean it' from Table 431 of the 1974 edition and HS677 will mean it's fron Table 677 from the current Historical Statistics of the United State also published by the Commerce Department.

Trucking is a key industry in the U.S. Hundreds of millions of shipments of all kinds of industrial items criss-cross the country in rhythm with the demands of rigid, high-speed production schedules. It takes a great deal of money to grease all those wheels and get everything to where it belongs, when it's needed. Big companies which use the trucking industry are willing to pay a lot of money for its services, because they understand that money is what makes it go. For all their good militancy and class consciousness, the relative prosperity of 1.9 million Teamsters rests on this economic foundation.

Unionized workers are also concentrated in public construction—highways, courthouses, schools. These unions are largely dependent on government, a fact which they show themselves when they get into trouble. Then, along with the contractors, banks and realtors, they run to Washington, D.C. or the state capital or city hall and demand public works. Government, as we know only too well, has been willing to pass its higher costs along to the rest of us through higher taxes. And that's the basis for the relative prosperity of 3.6 million organized construction workers (#622).

The relative prosperity of the 2½ million organized government employees (all levels of government, 1974 again [620]) also rests on this pass-along-the-costs-foundation.

The last major group of organized workers works for the largest corporations. Consider the following big unions:

Steelworkers (USW)
Auto Workers (UAW)
Machinists (IAM)
Meat-Cutters
Communication Workers (CWA)
Paper Workers
Rubber Workers
Electrical Workers (IUE & UE)
Textile and Clothing Workers
Oil, Chemical & Atomic Workers (OCAW)

These 6.5 million workers (1974, #622) are typically employed by companies like US Steel, GM, Armour, RCA, GE, or Gulf Oil. They receive relatively good wages because their bosses can and do pass wage costs along in higher prices.

If we got very fancy, filled up several hundred pages with facts, arguments and counter-arguments; considered in detail not only these 14.5 million organized workers (1.9 plus 3.6 plus 2½ plus 6.5 millions), but the other 7 million as well; put in a hundred "however" 's and a thousand "but" 's, the conclusion would remain. Organized workers are in the prosperous-it's-easy-to-pass-along-the-costs industries.

On the other hand, take a look at fly-by-night industries, seasonal and sweat-shop industries, industries like fast-food with lots of part-timers and students, and industries that don't have to pay the federal minimum wage. There you'll find that unorganized workers predominate. Farm workers—pickers and other stoop labor—provide a good example. There never was a time in the history of the U.S. working class when farm laborers didn't try to organize themselves. Our grandparents built up the Industrial Workers of the World with these workers and were crushed during and after WWI. Our parents tried it in the thirties and were defeated (the film and novel *The Grapes of Wrath* talk about farm laborers' organization). For about two decades now the United Farm Workers, led by Cesar Chavez and receiving aid from the AFL-CIO, have made only the slowest headway against the growers. Why? Farm workers are less militant than auto-workers? No—they are more militant. Growers are bigger S.O.B.'s than GM? Talk to an auto worker about who is and who isn't the world champion S.O.B. The answer is that fruit and vegetable growers are not (yet) in a position to pass along their higher costs. They feel they must resist worker organization in order to survive.

All this leads to another devastating conclusion. Our trade unions only work where the economic opposition of the boss is weakest and the economic position of the worker is best. As a class, we are now unable to help two out of three of our members, the two who are in the worst economic position.

I'm not saying that bosses give us unions. Everyone knows that unions are built on struggle. What I am saying is that the boss can afford to lose that struggle in certain situations but can't afford to in others. If he can pass his new union costs along he may give up the fight and we may win a union. If not, he'll never give up and, odds are, no permanent union can be built.

We could add complexity to our conclusion by talking about

how higher wages in organized industries help push up wages in industries which aren't, about how political action by the organized leads to economic gains for the unorganized. That's true. The mere existence of the trade unions helps the unorganized because union wage gains tend to spread, albeit slowly, throughout the economy. That's why a worker has to be a bit of a jerk to totally oppose unions. But on the other hand, nobody who understands the meaning of class solidarity, of uniting our strength to help out the weakest and least fortunate, will be much comforted by adding complexity to the bitter truth. We have unions only where employer opposition is weak.

## Unions and Inflation

The press and T.V. din it into our ears that unions are too powerful. They cause inflation by forcing pay increases which aren't deserved on the basis of increased productivity. Maybe everyone knows that, but it is false. In fact, the unions are so weak that unionized workers barely keep up with inflation. Today they earn just about what they earned ten years ago. As for improved productivity, all the rewards of that are going to someone else, not to workers.

I think the average worker suspects something like that is true. Anyone who goes shopping knows that our wages, while they seem high, buy less and less. However, suspecting it's true and knowing it's true are two different things. To prove it, what's required is that you become what the old time labor movement called a W.P.E., a Workers' Professor of Economics. All you need is common sense, some solid facts, and less arithmetic than it takes to do your taxes . . .

Manufacturing is the most heavily unionized sector of the economy and has the most powerful unions—Steel, Auto, Electrical, Rubber. We can use manufacturing wages to tell the general story of union wages. In 1967 the average weekly wage for a manufacturing worker was about $115 (#355, 71). Ten years later, in April, 1976, the average wage for the same worker was about $197 (#606). To compare them you have to look at inflation and you have to look at productivity.

Inflation isn't that complicated. Here's pretty much the whole story: in 1967 the government assigned the number 100, meaning 100%, to the prices of the time. Any changes since the are given as percentages of the 1967 prices. In May, 1976, fo example, the Consumer Price Index was 169.2 (#708), in othe words 69% higher than ten years earlier. It's as if the Governmen went shopping 1967 and spent $100 on what they imagined typical family would buy. So much on food, so much on housing so much to the doctor. Then they went out in May, 1976, an bought the same amounts of the same things. The bill came t $169.20.†

Let's look at the wage situation. On the basis of inflatio alone the average worker should be earning 69.2% more than h or she was earning in 1967. The average wage in 1967 was $115

| | | | | |
|---|---|---|---|---|
| 1967 wage ....... | $115.00 | OR | 1967 wage ....... | $115.0 |
| times | | | times | |
| inflation since then | | | Price Index | |
| 69.2% | .692 | | (169.2%) | 1.69 |
| multiplying gives | 79.58 | | | 194.5 |
| add original wage | 115.00 | | | |
| thus | 194.58 | | | |

The way they put that is to say that someone earning $115 i 1967 dollars would be earning $194.35 in 1976 dollars. In thi case, since the average worker was actually earning $197 in 1976 he or she was ahead by

$197.00
less 194.58
$2.42

† I have trouble believing the government's inflation figures. Fo example, according to other government figures, food prices are u 80% in the same time period, housing 77%, fuel up 146%, medical car 82% and services up 78%. Only a few things, like clothes (up 47%) ros at a lesser rate. How do you figure a shopping list which combines a that into a 69% average increase? Government productivity figures ar also suspect: the government gives 1.3% a year for the period 1967 1975 though normally productivity increases are twice that. Howeve we can use bad statistics if we keep in mind which way they ar distorted. In other words, the conclusions we get from these statistic understate reality and cover up just how badly the government i managing the economy.

That $2.42 doesn't come to much, about 24¢ added to the weekly wage for ten years. Not extravagant, but a gain.

We have to take account of productivity too. To do that you have to have a Productivity Index. They're set up the same way the Price Index was. In 1967 the Government assigned 100 to what manufacturing workers produced in an hour, week, or year and you can compare that with what they are producing later, again by using percentages.

I don't have a 1976 productivity figure but already by 1975 the productivity index in manufacturing was 112.4 (#598). That means that on the basis of improved productivity workers are entitled to 12.4% more than they got in 1967. If they are earning more than that you could blame them and their unions for the inflation. But if they are earning less than the 12%, you just can't do it. And anyone who does blame them is either misinformed or is trying to put something over on someone. The calculation goes like the previous one:

| | |
|---|---|
| inflated 1967 wage (1967 wage in 1976 dollars) | 194.58 |
| Productivity Index (112.4%) — times | 1.124 |
| | 218.74 |

In other words, if you start with the 1967 wage, correct it for inflation and add on new productivity, the average manufacturing worker should be getting around $219. But he or she isn't. The actual wage was only $197.

| | |
|---|---|
| | $218.71 |
| less | 197.00 |
| | $21.71 |

That difference, that $22 per week, didn't disappear. Someone else is getting it. And it's a lot of money, coming to over a thousand dollars per year for 15 million manufacturing workers.

So far we've been dealing with the average this and the average that. To convince yourself of what's happening, or to convince a fellow worker, you can figure out this inflation and productivity stuff using your own, or the other worker's, actual wages. It's easy to become a W.P.E. if you take it step by step.

Start by figuring out what you earned in 1967. Yearly is probably easiest since it will be on your old tax form, but you can use hourly or weekly provided you stay with it. Common sense says you need a comparable figure. If you put in lots of overtime that year, try to reduce the amount to what you would have earned in a normal year. A strike or a layoff in a year means you have to add to the figure to compensate.

I'll make up an example down the left side of the page. You just use your own figures down the right hand side. The latest Consumer Price Index I have, from the newspaper, is for January 1977. I'll use it here.

$111.00 . . . . . . . . . . . . . . . . . . 1967 wage . . . . . . . . . . . . . . . . .
times
1.753 . . . . . . . . . . Jan, 1977 index (175.3%) . . . . . . . . . . 1.753
$194.59 . . . . . . . . . 1967 wages in 1977 dollars . . . . . . . . .

That takes care of the inflation. Productivity is just as easy to figure. A conservative rule of thumb would be to add 1.5% for every year, or 16.5% for the period of 11 years, 1967-77.

$194.59 . . . . . . . . . 1967 wages in 1977 dollars . . . . . . . . .
times
1.165. . . . . . . . . estimated productivity index. . . . . . . . . 1.165
$226.70 . . . 1967 wages plus productivity plus inflation . . .

My calculation gives me $226.70 as what I should be earning on the basis of my 1967 wages if I take inflation and productivity into account. Almost . . . .

You're not an average worker. The average worker exists only in the imagination. That's why he or she doesn't get older year by year like the rest of us. For the same reason the average worker doesn't build seniority on the job. But you do. And it should be taken into account. Here's how.

Find out what a starting worker in your line of work gets right now. I'll use $175 for the example but you should try to get the actual figure. Find out also what a worker in your industry gets at the peak of his or her earning power, and how long it takes to get there. I'll say $240 a week and that it takes 20 years to get there. Twenty years on the job adds $65 to the weekly pay check or about $3 for each year of seniority. Since we're dealing with a period of 11 years that comes to $33. In the table

$175.00. . . representative starting wage for newcomer. . .
$240.00 . . . . . . . . . . peak wages after 20 years . . . . . . . . . .
$ 65.00 . . . . . . . . extra wages based on seniority . . . . . . . .

$65/20. . . . . . . . . . . . dividing by the 20 years. . . . . . . . . . . .
$3.00 . . . . . . . . annual increase from seniority . . . . . . . .

Then

$ 3.00 . . . . . . . . . . . . yearly seniority increase . . . . . . . . . . .
11 . . . . . . . . . . number of years since 1967 . . . . . . . . .
multiplying
$ 33.00 . . . . . . . . . . total increase from seniority . . . . . . . . .
$226.70 . . . 1967 wages plus inflation plus productivity . . .
adding
$259.70 . . . . . . . . . what I should be earning now . . . . . . . .

My number comes out to $259.70, rounding, to $260. What does yours come out to? Your number represents what you should be earning when you add together inflation, productivity and years on the job. What's the difference between what you earn and what you should be earning? Who has that money? What did they do to earn it? And the final question—if you are in a union, did your union keep your wages abreast of what you should be earning, based on inflation, productivity and seniority? Our average manufacturing worker, probably unionized, was out about $20 a week. The conclusion is inescapable. Unions are too weak to protect their members' incomes.

## WORKERS' PROFESSOR OF ECONOMICS

You've been reading and using statistics. And you have to use them, all the time. Statistics is the easiest stuff in the world—as long as you keep three things in mind:

1) Statistics is a collection of data; for example, the weights of a group of people;
2) It combines the data to get some "typical" result; for example, averaging those weights to an "average" weight.
3) It compares that result with another typical result, for example, comparing the average weight of U.S. adults with those of other countries.

To understand statistics means nothing more than looking to see if all three steps make sense.

Was the data collected good data? Common sense is a good guide here. If you ask people about their sexual performance common sense says that some will lie one way from boasting and others the other way from embarrassment or secrecy. The data is sure to be distorted. If the census taker asks a worker about his or her income, it is probably inaccurate for the same reasons. Internal Revenue data is better there because it comes from withholding slips. All income figures on rich people are biased to the low side because they have so many ways of hiding their income. Common sense can usually tell if the data is good data and which way, if at all, it will distort the picture.

What about a "typical" result? Does it make sense? The summer temperature in the Gobi Desert is about 120°. In winter it's minus 10°. That makes the average temperature 65°. Very comfortable in a dry climate. Look to see what "typical" is being used. Here it's an average temperature and averaging is nonsense in this case. Applying common sense to the Gobi Desert example shows we need a summer average *and* a winter average.

The other point about typical results is just that, that they are typical, not specific. People who quarrel with statistics about the "exact" figure are misleading themselves. Statistics are for when you don't have the exact figure and can't get it. Thus you use an approximate type. Actual cases will vary on either side of the type. Keep that in mind and judge accordingly.

The last thing to remember about statistics is to look at the final step comparing the two typical results. I could add the average productivity increase from 1967 to the 1967 wage to see what was produced in 1975. I couldn't add average length of service since average worker at the average wage already included the average length of service.

If you keep in mind this three step way in which statistics are gathered and used, you'll only be fooled occasionally, which will put you in exactly the same boat with the fanciest of fancy statisticians.

## Back to Trade Unions

The workers' movement, the trade unions, are getting politically weaker, less able to defend us in other areas besides the paycheck. That situation is hard to pin down but I think it is obvious to anyone who will look around.

They say that when a pike or a bluefish attacks a school of baitfish, it has an uncanny knack of spotting the weak or injured one, the one that can't swim so well. Economists are not as fierce and powerful as bluefish but they'd like to be. They try to imitate their habits. They too have an unerring instinct for the weak or injured ones, the ones who are having trouble keeping up. I often think of that when I see them on tv talking about unemployment or read what they say about it in the papers.

In 1946 we passed a law that ordered the President and Congress to maintain full employment. In Kennedy's time, the economists said they'd by happy with, the country would be well off with, 2½%, maybe 3% unemployment. Now they talk about 5% unemployment as a *target* for the indefinite future. They hardly grumble at the 6 and 8% we suffer though they know better than the rest of us that a more realistic figure would set it at 11 or 12 or 13%.

You see they know, like that bluefish on the prowl for a meal, that if they attack the working man or woman, if they say that we've got to accept lots of unemployment and high profits in order to prime the economy, then honor and rewards will come their way from the rich and powerful. And they know that the workers' movement, unable to maintain its strength, is less and less able to punish those who attack it and reward those who defend it. Justice has no sword.

Consider two stories from the newspaper: From a Charlestown, W. Va. U.P.I. dispatch of Aug. 1975: Federal Judge K.K. Hall fined the United Mine Workers $500,000, jailed one union leader and warned that others will be arrested if they don't force their members who are striking in a series of wildcat protests against the contract back to work. From the *NY Times*, same month, 1975: charges that the Shell Oil Co., Exxon, and Amoco illegally rigged gasoline prices and made an (unknown) bundle of money during the gas crisis, are dismissed by State Judge Burton B. Roberts. The court and the oil company lawyers sat down and worked out an eight page agreement in which the oil companies—*while not admitting any wrong-doing*—promised they wouldn't rig prices in the future. The court order prevents future criminal or civil charges from being brought by anyone against the oil companies for those "alleged activities." The companies agreed to pay $45,000 each, not as a fine, but to cover the expenses of the legal proceeding.

## A Little Play, Author Anonymous

Scene: Courtroom with judge, clerk, etc. Coal miner, holding a smoking shotgun walks in, accompanied by his lawyer.

Judge: "You've been wildcatting illegally, you've blown up a coal company truck, and you've put a load of bird-shot in the behind of the scab who was driving it. What have you got to say for yourself?"

Miner: (blowing smoke from the barrel of the shotgun) "Ahem! My lawyer is now ready to sit down and work out eight pages of whereases, however's and know ye all men's whose general drift, purport and intent is, more or less, ipse dixit, that we will . . . fine print, fine print, fine print, fine print . . ."

Judge: (reading) "I can't quite read the print in this here eight page agreement."

Miner: (hurt) "Well, as between gentlemen, (whispers to Judge) Buzz, buzz, buzz!"

Judge: "Of course." (signs agreement)

Coal Company Executive (running in, breathless, holding twisted steering wheel, still smoking) with scab (holding his behind, still smoking): "Your Honor, we're here for justice. We've been illegally wildcatted, lost money, been dynamited and shotgunned by that vicious miner. Help us! Give us justice!"

Judge: "You're out of order. I won't have you speaking of my fr . . ., er, this gentleman in that rough and uncouth way. Moreover, according to this here legal agreement (waves paper) all that alleged stuff is ancient history and to raise it now places my distinguished fr . . ., er, this gentleman in double jeopardy. So, buzz off. (To the miner) Where were we? Yes, the amount you should pay to cover the court costs. Let's check for the going rate. Let's see now, Exxon Company made profit of 3 billion, 142 million dollars in 1974, and paid court costs of $45,000. According to precedent, the rate is . . . (calculates, scratches his head, tears up first calculation. Court clerk leaps to rescue, shows judge the figure). The rate is .00143% (calculates again, clerk helps out again). Since you only made $6,000 this year, at the same rate, you should pay 8 and 6/10 cents to cover the costs of the hearing."

Miner does so. Leaves, whistling "Solidarity Forever."

* * *

What amount of political and economic power would working people have to have to make that little play happen in real life? That's the amount of power business has in our country right now, because that scene occurs in court rooms, legislatures and government agencies every single day, just as it did in that N.Y. courtroom. When you reflect on things like this, when you see it in the paper and on t.v. every day, you realize that in spite of talk about democracy and equality, the working man or woman, alone or collectively, is in a dangerously weak state in this country. Trade unionism is not working.

Some people may say, "Well, it would be worse without the unions." True, but does that end the discussion or should we go on and try to understand why it's not working? Any sane person is going to opt for the second alternative. So ask yourself, why are trade unions declining in effectiveness? Why are only a minority of workers members? Why only in prosperous industries? Why do they have so little political power? To answer these questions in a useful way we'll need some further economic analysis.

# CHAPTER TWO: THE ECONOMIC ANALYSIS OF FAILURE

The key to the declining power and effectiveness of the trade unions is that they no longer have any decisive economic power. In a nutshell, the trade union as we know it has been economically outflanked by capital and made more or less obsolete in its present form. Strong statements, yes, but they reflect a harsh reality. That conclusion is implicit in the 20 year decline in trade union membership, the 10 year decline of workers' purchasing power, and the low esteem in which judges and others hold trade unions and workers. What remains to be shown is how and why trade unions have been outflanked.

In what follows I want to describe the economics of trade unionism in the production of two commodities, one from a large corporate industry and one from a more or less competitive-type industry. I'll use automobile manufacture and tobacco harvesting. Then we can compare the two situations and see why trade unionism can't be effective in automobile and therefore isn't bitterly opposed and can be effective in tobacco harvesting and therefore is resisted to the death. The argument is fairly long but not very complicated, especially for a W.P.E.

## Corporate Sector Workers

In 1972, the General Motors Company had a solid year—good but not spectacular. It sold over $30½ billion worth of goods and made a profit of over $2 billion on an investment of about $11½ billion, which depreciated by almost $1 billion. GM paid out over $8½ billion in wages and salaries to 760,000 employees and $2 billion in taxes. One of the best ways to grasp all these magical billions is to break down those amounts into the average wholesale price of an automobile.

In 1972 the average wholesale price of a car was $2622 (#988). The breakdown for GM would look like this (in millions):

| Materials and Miscellaneous | Depreciation of Plant and Machinery | Salaries and Wages | Net Income | Taxes | Sales (total inc.) |
|---|---|---|---|---|---|
| $16,806.8 | + 912.4 | + 8668.2 | + 2162.8 | + 2059.8 | = $30,610 |
| | | or, in approximate percentages | | | |
| 54.9% | + 3 | + 28.3 | +7 | + 6.7 | = 100% |
| | | and for one auto, rounding off a bit | | | |
| $1440 | + 78 | + 743 | + 185 | + 176 | = $2622 |

GM would explain these figures more or less in the following way: Our stockholders invested $11½ billion in our business, or about $15,000 for each employee. We laid out expenses of $1440 in various materials, and used up $78 worth of machinery. That $1518 was turned into a car worth $2622 at wholesale prices. The difference between the two, or $1104, is the value added by the manufacturing process. Our employees, the stockholders, and the government shared that *value added by manufacture:* $743 went to our employees, $185 to our stockholders and $176 to the government, since we too are good citizens and pay taxes like everyone else.

What about management? They worked for free? Obviously not. GM's Annual Report for 1974, from which I took the GM figures, doesn't break down its employees into management employees and production employees. However, in 1972, in the auto industry as a whole, production workers totalled 83% of all employees (#1234,74). That would mean that GM had approximately 630,000 production workers; the other 130,000 employees were classified as management—supervisors at all levels and upper technical staff.

How much did the production workers get paid? Again I lon't have GM's figure but industry-wide figures are available. In 1972, in the automotive industry as a whole, production workers vorked 1,388 million hours and were paid $7,421 million That iverages out to about $5.30 per hour (overtime is averaged in ince the base rate was somewhat lower). Those workers *added a alue by manufacturing* of $22,213 million. Since they were paid 7,421 million, they received about one-third the value add- d(#1234,74). Applying this to our representative GM car, the vorkers got about one third of the $1104, or about $369.

If a representative car has $369 worth of production worker ours at an hourly rate of $5.30 per hour, that means there are bout 70 hours of labor in the car. The figure checks out since Ford Vice President told *Automotive News,* in late 1970, that here were about 60-70 hours of labor in an average modern utomobile.

In addition to wages, the average U.S. worker received arious supplementary benefits such as sick pay, vacation pay, nd employer contributions to Social Security, Unemployment nsurance, and pension plans. These came to about 14¢ additional per dollar of wages (#612,77). On this basis, the auto vorkers received an additional $51 in bennies for a total wage of 420. The remainder of the money paid as salaries and wages, 323 (— 743 − 420) went to management and upper level echnicians and professional employees. Much of it was not paid s straight salary but was tied to various formulas based on the ompany's profits for the year. I'll continue to talk of 'salaries' ut you should keep those bonuses and stock options in mind.

Looking again at our representative car we get the following reakdown:

| Materials & Miscellaneous | Depreciation | Wages to Workers | Salaries & Bonuses to Mgmt. | Profits | Taxes | Sale Price |
|---|---|---|---|---|---|---|
| $1440 | + 78 | + 420 | + 323 | + 185 | + 176 | = $2622 |
| 54.9% | + 3 | + 16 | + 12.3 | + 7 | + 6.7 | = 100% |

he figures represent a simplified but reasonably accurate stimate of the costs of making a car in the U.S. in a solid but not spectacular year.[†] All the information about GM comes from it Annual Reports for 1974 and 1975 so that if any of the origina figures are finagled, the finagling is probably to the corporation' advantage.

## Fair Shares

GM would say that the $420, $323, $185 and $176 represen the shares of the worker, the manager, the stockholder and Uncl Sam in the value added by the work of the company. They woul say that the $420, $323 and $185 represent the contribution o labor, management and capital as determined by the laws o economics. They'd argue that the laws of supply and deman work out so that each factor in the production process—worker manager, owner of capital—is rewarded to the degree to whic each contributed to the final product. No human hand distri butes these rewards; it is done by the "invisible hand" of th market. If workers want more, they have to work harder an contribute more to the process. In other words, be mor productive. Otherwise they're looking to take more than their fai share.

Right about now, I smell a rat. As we've already seen in th previous chapter, workers have been more productive—but the don't get the rewards of it. And those managers, look what they'r making .There are about 130,000 of them. They receive abou 43% of GM's salary and wage bill, or $3768 million. Simpl arithmetic shows that these 130,000 managers, supervisors professionals and upper-level technicians averaged abou $28,900 apiece for the year. GM's workers, 630,000 of them, spli $4900.2 million among themselves, which comes to an average o less than $8000 apiece.[†] Does that mean that each worke

[†] I say only "reasonably accurate," partly because we had to plug ir industry-wide figures for GM's specific situation, and partly becaus GM does over one-fourth of its manufacturing overseas.

[†] Our figures distort workers' wages downward, partly because lowe paid overseas workers are averaged in and partly because of layoffs. A representative GM worker in this country who put in a full year in 1972 would have earned somewhere around $11,000.

contributed or was only a third as productive as each manager? And how about the owners of GM? They didn't do a lick of work in 1972, or in 1971, or in any other year. Yet for every car produced, they get $185. That's in a good year. In a great year it might be $300, and even in a bad year it's at least $100. It's true they didn't work, but their money did. That's why $185 is their just and fair share according to the laws of economics.

It's self-serving on the part of GM's owners and management to credit their way of looking at the process to "laws of economics." I'd guess that if they got $5.30 an hour instead of $185 off the top, or if they only got the $5.30 while the workers pulled down $28,900 per year, they wouldn't be so happy with "laws of economics." The plain fact is that the owners own and the managers manage the company. They make the rules and they divvy up the value added, so much to this one and so much to that one. Consequently, the amounts into which the money is divided up represent—crudely—the power of each party in the whole process. The $420 represents the power of the working class. The $185, the power of the owning or capitalist class. The $323 is the power of that part of the capitalist class that's in top management, plus the supervisory, professional and technical people associated with them.

This way of looking at it is supported when you look at the role of the government. It got $176 from each car, mostly through the corporate profits tax. Later it will get some of the salaries, wages, and profits in the form of sales, excise, and personal income taxes. But for the moment let's concentrate on that $176. The government's share is tied to corporate profits. If they go down, it gets less. For example, the government got $1118 million from GM in 1975—a so-so year. but it got only $700 million in 1974, a bad year, and $185 million in 1970, a terrible year. In our year,1972, it got a whopping $2059 million and even better, $2115 in 1973.

Liberal economists point with pride to the corporate income tax as a leash on the corporations held by the Federal Government. But which end of this leash is the government really on? If profits go up, then the government gets more. If they go down, it's less. Clearly, the government wants more money to spend and it has an interest in higher profits, of which it will get its "just" share.

Now you can see the score. On one side are the owners, the managers and the government. What each of them gets is tied to profits. They have a community of shared interest. If the company is prosperous, it means big profits and *therefore* big dividends, big salaries and bonuses and big tax returns. On the other side are the workers and their unions. What they get, the managers, owners and government don't. Consequently, manager, owner and government have an interest in holding wages down.

Corporate economics creates a large class of highly paid managers—one in five of its employees. It links their interests directly to the owning class through profits. These people vote and are otherwise politically active. That, plus the tie-in between profits and the Federal Government's tax returns, brings the government over to their side. Of course, the government is staffed by the same sort of people to begin with so it didn't take much persuasion to bring them over. These three groups—owners, managers, and government officials, each very powerful, combine to hold the workers back. That, in the last analysis, is why workers, even unionized workers, don't get ahead, and it's why judges, Presidents and NLRB's act the way they do.

The figures that we worked out for GM would differ if you went to a different company, different industry or different year. But the general relationship between the figures would not vary very much in either direction. The car you own, the tv set, hi-fi, refrigerator, the bulbs in the light sockets, everything that you own which was produced by a big corporation contains a similar breakdown. And that breakdown contains—in cellular form—the general economic relations of the larger society and the classes which make it up. Economics is not an abstract subject. In its own peculiar way it is the most concrete of all subjects. It surrounds us in the form of objects—at home, work, and school. Every one of those objects contains the labor of the working class and the power of the capitalist class and its allies.

That's my way of looking at the division of value added from the manufacture of the car. If you don't like it, fine. It's your right. What you earned from your 70 hours of work on the car is determined by the "laws of economics." You can only earn more by increasing your productivity. But you've increased your productivity, you say, and you're still earning about what you arned in 1967. Don't ask me to explain it. I think GM's "laws of conomics" are an economic superstition, contrary to the evi-lence, for lulling the working people into a we-can't-help-our-elves attitude, an it's-all-beyond-our-understanding passivity. Karl Marx said, and he's right, that those "laws of economics" are ccepted by GM only because it, its management and its overnment friends, are getting $684 (= 185 + 323 + 176) nstead of $420 for working 30-odd hours or not at all. Their laws" are a masquerade behind which their power lurks. If that loesn't make sense to you, don't bother reading on; the rest of his book will make even less sense. Throw the book away or give to a friend. If you insist, I'll refund your money or part of it. I'll ive you say, 16% of the wholesale price of the book; just like GM can't do any better. But if it does make sense to you, then the ext question you should ask is why do these class relationships old? Why, in particular, is the working class, organized in trade nions, unable to improve the workers' portion of these shares? Ve have to look at the relationships of various costs and prices to nswer those questions.

## he Critical Eight

In the automotive industry, as in any other, the relationship etween the various costs and the final price has to be analyzed n the light of eight critical factors of the productive process. hey are:

#1 the amount of wages paid out.
#2 who does what job and how; that is, the organization of the work.
#3 the kind and amount of machinery.
#4 the amount produced per worker.
#5 the price paid for material.
#6 the quality of the product.
#7 the selling price of the product, and
#8 the amount of profit.

Unless you control almost all of these Critical Eight you ave no industrial or economic power. Trade Unionism tries to ontrol #1: the amount of wages. But a) it doesn't succeed in oing that and b) even if it did, lacking control over the other seven, any gains in wages can and will be wiped out by changes in the other seven.

Trade unions try to control the amount of wages. But they only succeed in getting some control over the hourly rate, which isn't the same thing. For example, suppose our friends in the UAW were able to up their wages by 10%. Across-the-board. That would raise the wage component on the car by 10%, to $462 (= 420 + 42). But GM can and will move to compensate for that extra cost by raising its selling price (Critical Factor #7) or putting pressure on its suppliers to cut their prices (Critical Factor #5). Or they can go after the wage component directly in several ways—reorganizing work (Critical Factor #2), substituting lower paid workers in place of higher paid workers (Critical Factor #1), speed-up and related devices (Critical Factor #4), introducing new, more efficient machinery (Critical Factor #3). And, in reserve, they have the power to cheapen the car's quality (Critical Factor #6) by cutting corners in its production—using cheaper upholstery calling something an option, using thinner steel, or fewer welds. Top management has the right to manage: *i.e., to vary the Critical Eight to compensate for changes in the wage rate.* If all else fails, Critical Factor #7 is their out. They can just raise the price of the car to compensate for wage increases. They do that so often it's become a habit for them.

Take our example. Suppose GM responds by raising its final price by 10% (". . . . forced by higher labor costs . . . regret regret . . ."). The situation would look like this:

| Material & Deprec. (as before) | Wages To Workers | Sal. To Manag. | Profits | Taxes | Extra | Sale Price |
|---|---|---|---|---|---|---|
| $1518 | + 462 | + 323 | + 185 | + 176 | + 220 | = $2884 |

Workers still only get about 16% of the sale price, but inflation has yielded GM a $220 bonus.

Make sure you see what's happening here. The workers got a 10% raise, going from $420 per car to $462 (= 420 + 42). To "make it up," GM raised prices by 10%, from $2622 to $2884 (= 2622 + 262). But the company only had to pay $42 of that extra $262 out in higher wages; the other $220 (= 262 - 42) is an extra bonus.

Some of the bonus will be paid out in taxes, but most of it will be left to GM to divide among the managers, supervisors and stockholders. Normally, that money will be used to strengthen GM's hand by providing money for new machinery and more intense managing. That again will tend to lessen the number of hours of labor in the car so that soon only 66 or 67 hours will be needed. This is a saving of roughly $16 to $21 (three or five hours at $5.30 per hour). So over the long run, the workers' share in the final cost of the car slowly drops to 16%, 15½%, 15%, 14½%.†

Feeling the pinch, the auto workers go out for higher wages again. They get an increase, GM applies the Critical Eight, including a rise in prices. When the dust settles this time, as before, the workers' share in the care has gone down again 14%, 13½%, 13%. The worker, meanwhile, has been speeded-up. Friends and relatives have been laid off because of the new machinery. The union is smaller now than before and the membership is pissed off at its inability to defend them. GM, ever alert for such things, steps in again, this time forcing more work changes, more speed-up, and more lay-offs on the weakened workers and their unions. They try to resist with strikes. But strikes are harder now. Because of the huge amounts of money that flow in, GM has been able to maintain and pay one supervisor for every four workers (130,000 out of its 760,000 employees, and at very fancy salaries: $28,900 average). Routine maintenance can go on; pitching in, the supervisors can even keep some subsidiary production going. In fact, in many industries—telephone, chemical and oil refining, for example—the number of supervisors to workers is so large, that normal production can be maintained for several weeks or even months when production workers are out on strike.

Stepping back a bit, when management saw the strike coming they started to put on more overtime which the workers welcomed as the extra money would bide them over the weeks when they'd have no paycheck. But they were so productive that their overtime created a huge stockpile of cars. That stockpile

†That's been the case in U.S. history. The table on the next page tells the story.

put GM in a position where it could negotiate tough, stretching out the strike.

Meanwhile, as we saw, the government now has a large stake in things. It gets $176 from GM for every car. So it puts on

The Workers' Share of $100 of
Value-added (in dollars)

| | |
|---|---|
| 1849 — 51.28 | 1931 — 35.97 |
| 1859 — 44.44 | 1933 — 35.34 |
| 1869 — 44.44 | 1935 — 39.37 |
| 1879 — 48.07 | 1937 — 40.16 |
| 1889 — 44.44 | 1939 — 36.76 |
| 1899 — 40.32 | 1947 — 40.65 |
| 1899 — 40.82 | 1954 — 38.17 |
| 1904 — 40.48 | 1958 — 35.09 |
| 1909 — 39.22 | 1963 — 32.36 |
| 1914 — 40.32 | 1965 — 32.05 |
| 1919 — 40.28 | 1967 — 31.06 |
| 1921 — 43.29 | 1968 — 30.67 |
| 1923 — 41.32 | 1969 — 30.67 |
| 1925 — 38.91 | 1970 — 30.49 |
| 1927 — 38.31 | 1971 — 29.67 |
| 1929 — 35.59 | 1972 — 29.76 |
| | 1973 — 29.23 |

Note: There was change a in the system of reporting in 1899 so two figures are given for that year.

The table is built up the following way. Suppose a worker manufactures something which wholesales for $425. Let's say he or she used up $325 worth of materials, energy, machinery (depreciation) to do so. The $100 difference is called the value added by manufacture. The table shows how much of that $100 the worker got. The remainder of each $100 went to the owners to be shared, in our day, with the manager and with government officials. Thus, in 1973 we got 53¢ less than in 1972. That means the other side got 53¢ more.

Source: 1849-1954, HS409; 1958-1971, #1217; 1972, #1234; 1968, 71, #1130; 1969, #71,1141.

the pressure to shorten the strike. It comes on as a neutral party, representing the "public interest." Sure, it's neutral! Every car which isn't produced costs it about $176. So the government is interested in short strikes and high production. But as we've seen, short strikes aren't effective anymore. Its "holier than thou we stand for the public interest and above the fray" attitude is just a fig leaf.

Is there any need to go on? the situation is pretty clear. The auto workers and their union are playing a losing game. No matter which way they turn, they get hit. They're like a lone man fighting against a crowd. Every punch he throws at one of his opponents just provides an opening for the others to get even harder blows in at him. If he's very tough and has a lot of heart he'll stay on his feet for awhile and keep punching. But the outcome of the fight is never in doubt.

Pretty much the same case could be made for the situation of any of the other big industrial unions I listed earlier, and their members. Construction workers, government workers or Teamsters too. Their production process is a little different, the numbers don't come out exactly the same, but they're all players in the same losing game. The harder they work and the harder their unions fight, the more they strengthen the owners, managers and government. And the weaker they get.

On the face of it then, what I said earlier is a fair and accurate statement. The unions are outflanked. The trade union as we know it is obsolete. That's a nasty conclusion and we can't leave the matter there. We'll come back to it again and again to see what openings there are for making them effective again. But, for now, let's deal with an economic situation where today's type of union could be effective.

## Workers in the Competitive Sector

The situation for the non-union worker, in a competitive industry, is very different. For example, tobacco is grown and harvested with hand-labor and is generally sold at auction, which means the grower has to take pretty much whatever price is offered. Government price supports and other devices guarantee him a certain minimum price but he is not in a position to jack it up, like GM does, to compensate or overcompensate fc higher wage costs.

The situation, in numbers, looks like this: In 1972, thousand pounds of average tobacco sold at about $830, or 83 per pound (#1117). It required 150 hours of human labor t produce it (#1107). That same year, southern farm laborer averaged just under $10 per day for a six day week (#1108) and by an educated guess, probably worked somewhere near te hours every day. On that basis, the labor cost to a grower for 100 pounds of tobacco was about $150. We don't need the othe figures—expenses and profit. For every thousand pounds c tobacco we can represent the situation like this:

| Expenses | Profit | Wages | Selling Price |
|---|---|---|---|
| E | + P | + $150 | = $830 |

The grower has little or no control over his selling price or hi expenses. He sells to the big tobacco companies and he hasn got the power to force higher prices on them. He also buy fertilizer from big companies, borrows money from banks, buy seed from a large seed company, and gets tractors and othe equipment from big corporations. In short, he doesn't control h expenses, as GM does. He pays the going rate.

Tobacco growing uses lots of hand labor, particularly a harvest. Each leaf is cut by hand, wrapped in a loose bundle an carried into an aging shed. Due to the nature of the work, th owner or manager of the tobacco farm doesn't have a lot of le way over most of the Critical Eight. If he buys better seed he pay more for it. If he uses more fertilizer, he pays more. The technic situation is such that he can only vary the labor process a littl bit: speed-up; long hours; sharper, better designed knive simpler knots; maybe a company store or company housing ca help him, but not much. Even with so little information you kno enough to conclude that his practical degree of control over th Critical Eight is very small, almost nil.

Consequently, if he wants more profit, it can only come fro one place—lower wages. If his workers organize a union, the higher wages can come from only one place—the farmer's profit If you mention union around this place, he's going to reach fo his shotgun.

The case of tobacco harvesting is an extreme one. But it is extreme only in that it shows most clearly what is more or less typical for businesses in competitive industries of all kinds. They have little or no control over their prices and expenses and as a result, the division of value added (selling price less materials and depreciation) has to have a loser for every winner; profits and wages come out of a fixed pile. If one gets more the other gets less.

There are other factors at work here. Businesses like these don't have the volume of a GM or a GE or an Exxon. They don't generate high profits year after year that can be used to improve labor productivity through elaborate technology and intensive management. They don't have a lot of supervisors around to get them through a strike. And so on.

These businesses have to resist unions, not as a matter of principle, but as a matter of survival. To a capitalist like this, every penny the workers get comes directly out of his profit, every day lost to strikes cuts his profits further.

Even if he doesn't actually have a union in his shop, and never had one, he has to compete with the corporations for skillful and reliable workers. Old John Tobacco Farmer can get away with paying $1.00 an hour for a ten hour day. He's way out in the country. But a businessman in a city or other built-up area has to pay higher wages to get help. He generally doesn't pay premium wages but he also knows that if it were not for the higher wage rates of unionized corporate industries, he could cut his wage rate by 20-30-40 or more percent and pocket the difference. So, he hates unions with a vengeance.

Trade unionism is incompatible with competitive industries that operate in the free market. Take our tobacco farm case. Suppose, for argument's sake, that the farmer was making $240 free and clear after paying $150 in wages. Now let's suppose the workers get organized and demand 20% more wages and are in a position to get it, perhaps because the tobacco is going to rot in the fields otherwise. In that situation if the worker has the power to get 20% more, he or she has the power to get 25% or maybe 30% more. What is the upper limit on how hard you can hit that farmer? Think about it as if you were in this situation. From the purely economic standpoint and aside from any personal factor, you can raise wages up to the last point where he'll stay in business—whatever that is.

In this situation the farmer or other businessman can take the easy way out and try to bribe the union officials. That's very common, as you'll notice if you study unions in competitive industries, which is where you'll find most union corruption. Or he can try to beat down the union by other means, fair and foul. Hire gangsters or goons, combine with other employers to break the union, pay off cops and judges to help him, use blacklists to identify troublemakers. If his workers are black, he can rev up the Klan; if the workers are very militant, the American Legion might be interested; if some of them are reds or other radical types, the Government will help. In the history of our class, those things are as common as fleas on an alley cat.

Or, the businessman can try to reorganize the business so that he can control his prices, regulate his productivity, have lots of money for reinvestment, pressure his suppliers, and get regular high-level government assistance for his labor relations. In other words, he can become a big corporation, a bona fide capitalist, not the penny ante kind. Then—and only then—can he afford to see the union as something which just might be turned to his own advantage.†

## Trade Unionism and Catch-22

The incompatibility of unions and free market economics is well-known; the fact that unions have no decisive power in corporate economics, the other side of the same coin, is less well known. Let's take a look.

One of the ways businessmen turn unions to their own advantage is by giving wage increases so they can justify price increases. In our example of the 10% increase in wages and prices, you'll earn a bonus of $220. Right off the bat! Of course, in real life all the big industries do it so that inflation will gradually eat into your $220. Normally it will show itself in high prices for raw materials and new machinery. But inflation takes time and until the price rises have rippled through the economy and come full circle to your suppliers, you can pocket quite a few $220 bonuses.

† This has been the actual historical pattern. In a real sense the corporation was evolved out of the older family company in order to create a form of business organization which economically outflanked unions and their wage demands. See Chapters 6 & 7 for more on this point.

But there is another even bigger advantage. Say the auto workers trigger a new round of price increases in cars. The steel workers, who need cars to drive to work, feel the pinch and first thing, they demand an increase. Now steel is up. The meatcutters see car prices and other steel products like refrigerators up and they find they need increases too. There go beef and pork. Now come the rubber, electrical and textile workers. Construction workers and Teamsters follow and soon after the Teachers are out with the Sanitation people and the cops. Each union feels the pressure on it to get more and the members support them. Consequently all of them are forced to accept, even encourage, price increases *for the things they produce.* But what is the net result of this? *The net result is that each union is forced to compete with every other union to keep its wage slightly better than the going inflation. But each union, by tolerating and encouraging price increases in its own industry, is attacking and defeating the wage efforts of every other union. The trade union movement as a whole is an arrangement where workers compete against each other instead of being an instrument of class solidarity.*

I feel bad writing these things. I'm a union man, a member of the AFL-CIO. I believe in the labor movement. Here I am attacking the union idea left and right. Whole passages of what I've said could be lifted out and used by labor-busting right-to-work publicity types in the pockets of the bosses. But what I'm saying is true. The labor movement has been outflanked by the corporations. It tries to strike a blow for workers, but the economic arrangement deflects the blow so it hits—not the corporation—but another worker. Union oratory about solidarity won't change it; rank and file grousing about lousy leaders won't either. For the fundamental reasons I've pointed out, trade unionism is now a means of dividing workers and opposing their interests, one to another.

There is no way out of that conclusion. Say I'm an auto worker. I need an increase. I work like a pig, in the paint shop, so that, God knows, I deserve more money. Anyway, inflation is killing me. I pressure my union to go after an increase. Given the nature of the auto industry and the economic power of the companies there is no way on this green earth that that increase is going to come out of profits and management salaries. (And it should come out of there.) They're as rich as Midas, those people, but I have no way of forcing them to do anything. So I get my raise and car prices go up; the inflation comes full circle and soon I'm working harder than ever and my money is worth les than ever. While I'm doing what I'm doing, every other unionized worker is doing the same thing. Each one is forced to demand more money, each deserves more money. They'll all end up lik me, poorer but harder working than ever.

Union leaders have a very different and, short-sighted idea of this. The steel guys want aluminum to get an increase, or the mineworkers or the truckers. It will make it easier for them to get their increase out of the company and past the government. There's no sense condemning the leaders. One of the problems of a weak labor movement is that it has no mental independence. In practice, that means that the unions hire the same kind of economists as the companies, people whose heads are filled with economic superstitions like "laws of economics," "creating a favorable climate for business," "making sure workers earn their increases with high productivity," and "wage-push inflation." They might as well believe in witches and hobgoblins. Or put it this way. If business claimed that there were witches an hobgoblins, the economists of this stripe would line up to testif that it was scientifically true. They'd probably even have witc charts and hobgoblin graphs to prove it. At any rate, the labo leadership is rife with the crudest kind of economic superstition. But, that's a symptom, not a cause of our weaknesses, so it's foolish to concentrate our fire on the leadership.

Labor unions in corporate industries are competitive wit one another. That's not true in competitive industries. There precisely because the employer can't pass on increases, an gains I make come out of his hide and not from other workers. Therefore other workers can express class sympathy with me hoping that I'll improve my lot and helping me to do so. They' help me because when my union is strong it can support their effort with money and clout. Thus, in the competitive industrie my class feelings and my daily economic needs merge into one—into solidarity with all other workers.

Not so in the corporate situation. There my sympathy goe in one direction and my self-interest in another. As a worker, feel comradely and supportive to every other worker—that's i my blood. But my interests now are different. The way things actually are, your pay gains come to me as inflation, higher prices for food, auto, rent, clothers, medicine. There's no other way you can get those increases save by your industry raising its prices; nine chances out of ten you encouraged it.

The corporate system changes the nature of trade unions, from a cooperating mechanism which unites workers into a competitive mechanism which divides them. Workers try to help themselves to improve their condition, but because the basic economic powers—the Critical Eight—are in the hands of management, this worker effort is deflected and rechannelled so that it exerts itself against other workers and not against management.

The third advantage that comes to the big companies from trade unions is related to this. Unorganized workers more or less correctly realize that inflation has something to do with union-won wage increases. They read in the paper and hear on T.V. about how this union got 5%, that one 8%. They are hazy on the details, but they do see that the union leaderships are—it's true—pretty cozy with big business. It looks to them, and it's partly true as we saw, that the unions join with the companies to encourage inflation. Unorganized workers, by definition, can't fight inflation by getting wage increases. Therefore, the unorganized workers feel that the unions gang up on them. Consequently, non-union workers often become *anti*-union. They will act politically to support anti-union politicians who, when they're in office, line up against union workers.

The unions divide us up into competing groups—auto versus steel, blue collar against white, private industry worker versus government worker, unionized versus non-unionized. Meanwhile, the corporation unites owner, manager and government. We're in a no-win situation.

# CHAPTER THREE: LESSONS FROM HISTORY

## Reasons For a History of the Working-Class

The trade union, as we know it, has been outflanked by the orporations. It fails to control any of the Critical Eight. The esult—companies get stronger and wealthier while we get veaker and poorer. The companies cooperate and the unions ompete. That's the problem in a nutshell.

"No, No," say some people. That's not the problem. Trade nions, strikes, and political action, those are fine. It's just that vorkers are confused about their true interests and lack the roper consciousness. This view of our problems is strongest mong trade union activists and labor radicals, especially those vith a touch of Karl Marx in their thinking. Poor Marx, that his evered name is attached to such views. I can picture him in my nind's eye right now. "Lack of consciousness, hah! What lack of onsciousness? American workers, millions of them, have the est consciousness of all. They know exactly what's what and act ccordingly. They know they'd be worse off without trade unions, o they support them. And they know that their unions are etting weaker all the time, so they don't set that much store by hem. What clearer idea of their interests, what better conscious- ess could you ask?"

A worker's consciousness is a real thing. It's not something that drops down from heaven or springs up from reading Karl Marx. The working man or woman sees correctly that he or she is alone in the world with very little effective help and suport from the working class itself. The working class is very divided and weak—a captive in a corporate economy it cannot control. To attack the worker for this understanding and the I'd-better-go-my-own-way behavior which follows is stupid. More than that when the attack comes from those who call themselves leaders of workers, it is self-serving. It's a way of saying, "It's not my fault it's them . . . I'm a good leader but they're bad followers."

An opposite tack is taken by those who say "Nothing can be done. The common people have always been screwed. That's the way of the world." People who say things like that suffer from a highly curable disease. It's called ignorance. The cure consists of acquainting them with some of the history of people like themselves, with the working class.

Our class is a very young class, going back only 200 years or so. As every conservative knows, it is the rowdiest, least governable, most idealistic, ornery, noisy, inventive, and disputacious class of people who've ever come over the horizon of history. They are the loving parents of every variety of fool and saint, utopian and revolutionary, philospher and quack, vague dreamer and disciplined organizer. Most classes are content to invent or borrow one or two political institutions and let it go at that—a parliament, monarchy, or perhaps, the corporation. Not workers. They've created communes, several kinds of unions mass political parties, Bills of Rights, Sons of Liberty, Conspiracies of Equals, Beneficial Societies, Corresponding Societies, soviets, consigli, factory councils, sit-downs, talk-ins democracy, secret ballot, socialism—in a dozen variations anarchism, syndicalism, communism. The list of their social and political creations is endless.

In the "good old days" when there was slavery, the caste system or feudalism, the lower orders were normally pretty docile. Maybe but once or twice in a century they'd kick up a fuss usually local. Just cut off a few heads, and things would go back to normal for another 50 to 100 years. Not that damned proletariat In the 200 years since its birth it has cut the heads off several kings, waged a score of class wars, set up a couple of governments, had them toppled, come back more determined than ever, reformed everything it touched, and come within a hair's breadth of overturning the whole shebang. Now it's getting restless again.

Unlike any other lower class in history, the working class has always harbored the arrogance that it can run society without the help of its betters. It has always harbored the view that nobles, blue-bloods, and other so-called cultivated people should do an honest day's work and live cheek by jowl with the great unwashed. And even worse, it tends to act on those views in every generation, so you've got to keep on cracking down on it or it will get out of hand.

". . . . common people always screwed . . . the way of the world." Fortunately, that is only true in the deepest and most exciting dreams of the capitalists and other fat cats.

This arrogance of the working class, this impulse to redesign society and run it for the benefit of everybody makes the history of the working class the most interesting history of all. Unlike school-book history, which can be dull at times, the history of the working class shows us people like ourselves, with deep problems, confused and divided, but people who nevertheless managed to find their way out of the wilderness and to act with intelligence and purpose.

School history is dull because it has to be. The great secret of the modern world is that it is working people who make history go forward. If the schools revealed that, instead of trying to persuade working class boys and girls that they haven't got the brains for success in this world, the School Boards would throw a fit and the federal authorities would cut off the money. So instead, the schools cast about for explanations of things which hide the history of workers from themselves. Yet it is just that kind of history which can help us in our present situation.

About 100 years ago, our grandparents and great-grandparents were in a situation somewhat like the one we're in now. The working people of the country were confused and disorganized. Vast changes were afoot in the country which threatened the well-being of the average person. There were large numbers of thoughtful workers who were anxious to band together to improve the situation.

Before going on to analyze our present situation further and bring forward some proposals to improve it, I am going to make a detour back into the history of the workers movement of 100 years ago. There are many reasons for doing so but two stick out as especially important today. The first is the obvious one—to look to see how earlier generations of workers handled their problems to gain some insight into how to handle our own.

The second reason is just as important. One of the effects of school history—school itself for that matter—is that people come to think that to be a worker is to be someone who didn't make it, a loser. If your experience of school was like mine, you quickly got the idea that the children of the better off people just had more brains than the working-class boys and girls. They were the kind of brains which helped them to do well, to go on in school, and become the successes they are today. Moreover, unless you are now in your fifties or sixties, chances are you've never seen our U.S. working class when it was something to be proud of. It has been just about 40 years since the U.S. working class last got itself together, stood up and demanded its rights, and set out to obtain them. I'm talking of the old CIO. That was the last time that the average person could just look around and experience the fact that there was more than enough intelligence, discipline, idealism and guts within the working class for it to do anything it set its mind to. Instead, most younger workers have only experienced our class at its worst—confused, divided, befuddled, cynical and with leaders to match.

We have to start now to think about how we're going to rebuild the strength and unity of the working class. One of the essential ingredients of that new strength and unity will be class pride. If our people continue to lack confidence in each other, and to think of workers as life's losers, there isn't much that can be done. But with class pride—self-respect, really—it's a different story. As you'll see, our working class has a history of struggle and achievement that is second to none. It is a history which can inspire the ordinary to do things that right now they think are beyond their abilities.

We should make that detour into our own past. From roughly the close of the Civil War until WW I our modern working class was born, grew up, and made a try at building a different, better society than we have now. As we know, our grandparents and great-grandparents didn't succeed. They were defeated. But most of the ideas, organizations, and directions that we still have n the working class and the labor movement come from that earlier time.

What did our grandparents and great-grandparents try to do?

Who and what were they fighting?

Did they have to fight?

What did they achieve?

Why didn't they achieve more?

How are things different now?

## Classes Emerging from the Civil War

You have a civil war when two classes of people fall out with one another and decide to settle their differences by force. Our Civil War was no different. Prior to the War, two classes vied for leadership in the country. They were the Southern slave-owning planter aristocracy and the Northeastern class of merchants, manufacturers, rail and canal owners and other capitalists. During the war itself, the other classes of the country lined up against the slave-owners to form the winning coalition. Its members included the middle class, which was made up of smaller merchants, professionals, and capitalists—what I'm going to call the entrepreneurial middle class. The other main classes included the workers of the Northeastern cities, the slaves of the South and, the largest class of all, the free farmers of the North and West.

The Civil War only settled the question of what was to happen to the slave-owning aristocracy. The victory of the Union Army assigned them to the historical scrap heap. But the war didn't settle the question of who was to run the country and what kind of a country it was to be. Consequently, in 1865, as the war ended, a new and much greater struggle was to develop among the victors. What class was to become the dominant class? What class would be able to dictate the future development of the country? Let's take a closer look at the contenders.

### The Capitalist Class

Before the Civil War, the U.S. capitalist class was fairly small and weak. But war always creates an abundance of two things: widows and millionaires. The Civil War was no exceptio John D. Rockefeller and J.P. Morgan were, in their own way typical of the class of super-rich men who came to prominen after the war. Both hired substitutes to avoid serving in the wa Both started their fortunes through speculation in milita supplies. (Morgan bought defective rifles from the Feder Government and sold them back again at a handsome profit Both went on to build huge fortunes by forcing smaller compet tors to sell out to them at bargain prices. And both establishe family dynasties that continue even to the present day. Othe whose dynastic origins are found in the Civil War includ Frederick Pabst, Phillip Armour, E.H. Harriman, Jay Goul Cornelius Vanderbilt, James Mellon, Henry Frick, and Augu Belmont. More names roll familiarly off the tongue one hundre and ten years later: Carnegie, Chase, Aldrich, Fisk, Hill, Dre Guggenheim, Stanford, Pullman, Hanna. The first great fortun came from opening up the west—railroads, mines, and re estate killings. The industrial fortunes immediately followe Steelmaking, petroleum-refining, meat-packing, manufacturin Then finally, at the turn of the century, finance became t source of fabulous riches. The magnates had finished gobblir up new industries and had turned to the world of finance to pu them in proper order.

It is wrong to think of these famous names as representir only rich individuals. They were founders of great family an dynastic fortunes. Until this century in the United States and i fact, since the dawn of recorded history everywhere, great wealt has always taken the form of family or dynastic wealth; that i the wealth of *several closely associated families.* When we spea for example, of the Rockefeller family, we're actually using shorthand for a group of families: Rogers, Aldrich, Payn Harkness, Flagler, Archbold. These families have been a sociated with the Rockefellers since the time of the notoriou John D. and by now are linked with them by a score of marriag and other arrangements which go back three or four generation

The reasons for the *dynastic* character of great wealth a fairly obvious. Often the original great man, the founder, ha trusted lieutenants like Flagler or Archbold, who aided him in th early going and shared in the riches that followed. Then, agai one has to have children and marry them off (otherwise th money goes to the orphans). This too, creates permanent links between wealthy families. Finally, you need allies to protect your wealth against the other rich people who would steal it if they could. Especially in the period before 1900, the economic life of the country featured a perpetual warfare among the people of great property. Each tried by any means, fair and foul, to increase his own wealth and steal away with some of the other fellow's.

I recall reading years ago of a small war between two rival groups, the Morgans and the Vanderbilts, over some choice morsel of railroad right-of-way. Though my memory of the details is somewhat hazy, at one point, the rivals fought a gunboat battle down the length of the Hudson River, followed by a siege and shoot-out in the middle of Jersey City which lasted until the frightened town authorities emerged from hiding and arranged a temporary truce. This may have been the incident fictionalized in the old movie "Saratoga Trunk" starring Gary Cooper. At any rate, unrestricted brawling between the wealthy forced many dynastic alliances. The Belmonts and the Morgans were long linked in this way as were the Carnegies and the Fricks.

Truly great wealth can never be earned honestly. It has to be stolen. The rule is that the greater the wealth the grander the scheme for stealing it and the greater likelihood that the scheme is more or less legal . . . or . . . can be made legal retroactively. Perhaps the unusual map on page 45 published some years ago by two famous U.S. historians, Charles and Mary Beard, will make my point. It shows the land *given* to the railroads between 1850 and 1871 by the government. Need one guess at the motives for such generosity? Look a little more closely and notice the swatch of shading beginning at the Great Lakes and running across the top of the country to Washington State on the West Coast. They've given away, from right to left, most of Wisconsin and Minnesota, the best part of North Dakota, Montana and Washington State. Below that, almost all of Iowa, huge parts of Kansas and Illinois. Lower down still, you can see the northern part of Florida, most of Alabama and to the left, vast tracts of Mississippi and Louisiana (it helps to win a civil war). Looking past Texas, we see a good part of New Mexico, most of Arizona and almost the entire southern half of California, plus a decent part of the northern half.

If you know something about the geography of most of those

states, you'll know that this was the best land—the riverbottoms, well-watered and fertile. Look at Kansas, as an example. Once the railroad was built the land would rise stupendously in value and be sold to the settlers who followed in its wake.

The mental outlook, or ideology of these great dynasties is called *laissez-faire.* (It is French for, roughly, let them do what they want.) They became much enamored of the writing of a man named Herbert Spencer who applied a corrupted Darwinism to human affairs. Survival of the fittest, don't interfere with nature, God has designed the struggle for life so that His Chosen Few will be revealed by their success. One could be pious and ruthless at the same time, a combination the Rockefellers have always excelled in. George Baer, a coal millionaire, spoke for his whole class when he said, while breaking a strike in 1902:

> "The rights and interests of the laboring man will be protected and cared for not by the labor agitators, but by the Christian men to whom God in His infinite wisdom has given control of the property interests of the country. Pray earnestly that the right may triumph always remembering that the Lord God Omnipotent still reigns, and that His reign is one of law and order and not of violence and crime."

The ideology and practice of laissez-faire did not of course, imply that one trusted to God's Providence entirely. As we saw from the map, one always could look for a little help from one's friends in government. I think it is fair to say, that the success of so-called free enterprise in our country rests, in the last analysis, on stealing from the public property—the common property of the people. The normal method for doing this was to bribe legislators, a prctice well developed in the 1860's, '70's, '80's, and '90's. One reformer with a nice sense of humor said that John D. Rockefeller and his Standard Oil Company did everything to the Pennsylvania Legislature except refine it.

This class of rich capitalists (a name they proudly bore) was fairly small before the war. Their size, however, depended on the economic climate, as depressions would thin their ranks and prosperity swell them again. Not all would be as famous or as rich as a Mellon or a Frick. The famous names represent only the tip of the iceberg. Every State and region boasted its super rich ıagnates. Thousands of merely rich Stevensons, Tafts, Garys ınd Sloans were added to several score Mellons and Goulds to ıake up a new capitalist class of rival families, a dynastic class hich consisted of from one to two percent of the population ıroughout the period 1870-1900.

## The Entrepreneurial Farmer

In 1870, as in the immemorial past, the largest single class in ıe country was the farmers and the various trades associated ith them. Just after the Civil War, nearly three-fourths of the opulation lived in rural areas: 28.6 out of 39.9 million in the total opulation (HSA34-5). Of a labor force of 12.9 million something ke 24% or 3 million were farmers. Add to this 3 million hired ırm laborers (HSD57-71). There was also a supporting work-ɔrce of blacksmiths, farriers, wheelwrights, welldiggers and ther trades. These people lived in tiny towns and rural areas and umbered between 2 and 3 million (HSD36-45). Thus, 60-70% f the workforce were farmers or their auxiliaries. The farmers, owever, are the key. As they go, so go the others.

A lot of unjustifiable mystification surrounds farmers in this ountry and we might as well clear it up here and now. You ill probably notice I call them *entrepreneurial* farmers. Almost om the beginning of our country our farmers have mainly not een peasants or subsistence farmers. Both those are types of ırmers who build a way of life around the land and support ıemselves largely by their own labor. By contrast, the entre-reneurial farmer is a person in the farm *business.* He grows a ommercial crop for the international agriculture market—otton, wheat, corn, cattle, wool, soybeans, or something else. He ıvests in land, tools, seed, fertilizer and farm labor. To do this, e usually borrows from a bank in the hope that he'll get a cash eturn. This is done by shipping the crop to Chicago, New rleans, Galveston or Baltimore, where it will be sold to peculators, who in turn will sell it in Detroit or Boston or send it n to Liverpool, Havana, Hamburg or Naples.

The second thing about our farm population is that we really ren't talking about the *family* farm. Already by 1880, one-ourth of our farmers were tenant farmers, paying rent, or harecropping (HS 1970, K109-53). The number of farmworkers xceeded the number of farmowners. What we're talking about is farm population, some of whom are farmers but the bulk of whom are renters, sharecroppers, hired laborers, and supportin craftsmen. Behind all that is the bank with its mortgages, interes rates and foreclosures. There used to be a saying in Kansas tha "we produce three crops, wheat, interest and rent."

Third, the way the movies always show it, there are th farmers fighting off the Indians. Life is hard. Then, in the las fifteen minutes or so the railroad arrives at the edge of towr followed by John Wayne and the cavalry. A brief scrap with th Indians, victory, smiles, a few drinks. Intimate but modes glances between Wayne and O'Hara, and Gabby Hayes, slightl tipsy, declares "Shucks, maybe I'll swap my horse for this her loco-motive."

The more common pattern (see the map) was that th government gave the land to the railroads who pressed on int the Indian territory. The cavalry accompanied the railroad an drove the Indians off, killing them or confining them to reserva tions, well away from that fertile, well-watered bottomland. The the railroads sold huge tracts to real estate agents who fanne out through the country selling good virgin farmland served by railroad. And then the settlers came, paid for their farms, an went into the commercial crop business.

After 1870, this was the way the number of farms, farmer tenants and hired hands continued to increase. They doubled b 1900 and even as late as 1920 farming continued to be the majo occupation in the United States.

The farmers had always been a dominant group in th political life of the country. Since the time of Jefferson, one of th major political parties in the country had been their spokes person and champion. However, as we'll see, the new post-civ war farmers had a chink in their political armor—they wer economically dependent on the railroads and the bankin system. Nevertheless, the farmers believed that their ove whelming numbers, their moral status as the backbone of th country, and their record of political activism would enable the to shape the course of the country as they had been shaping it fo three-quarters of a century.

## Entrepreneurial middle class

The third major group in the United States was what I ca the entrepreneurial middle class, those businessmen and profe sionals who, independent of any employer or boss, made the

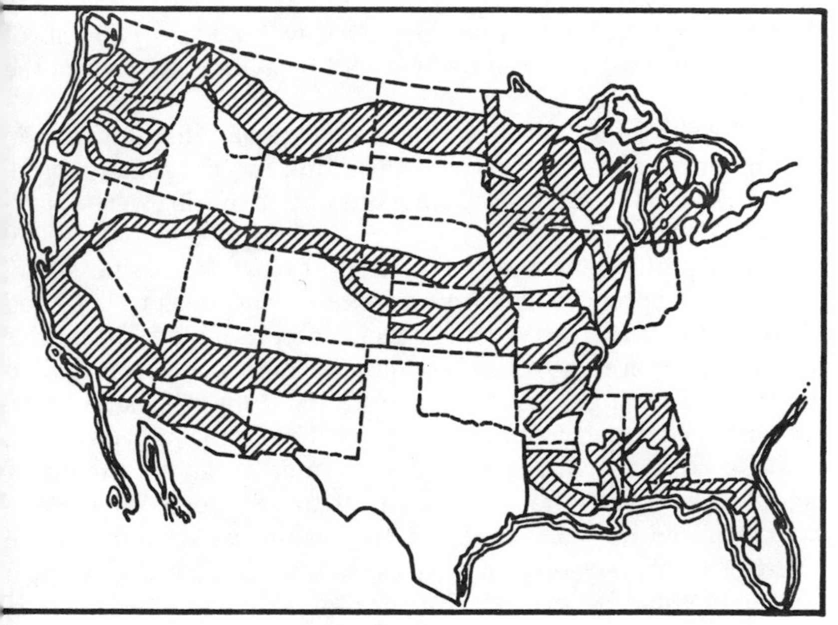

**Land given to the railroads by the Federal government between 1850 and 1871.**
Redrawn from Charles and Mary Beard, *The Basic History of the U.S.*, Blakiston Company, 1944.

living by their own wits. With their assistants and close beneficiaries, they made up about 15% of the workforce (HSD57-71). Like the agrarians to whom they were second in number, the entrepreneurial middle class saw themselves as the real America (they still do). America was the land of equality and opportunity, every American could open up his (even her) own business and prosper. This land had no hereditary rich and no political system dominated by a closed aristocracy. That was the way the country had been before the war, and since the slaveholding aristocrats of the old south were now gone, it would be even more true in the future.

Most of their businesses were small: a handful of workmen or women, a salesclerk or two. They didn't require much capital. The country was always growing and opportunities were everywhere.

The professionals were no different from the businessmen, or the more prosperous farmowners for that matter. They too were entrepreneurs. To be a lawyer, doctor, dentist, teacher or minister, required no formal training, no entrance exams and no degrees. You might arrange an informal apprenticeship to an experienced man (Lincoln did just that). You might, if you chose, go to a college or institute which claimed to know something about the subject, but it wasn't likely to be very good. What really was required for success in the professions was a quick wit, a smattering of knowledge, a bit of brass, trust in Providence and a fast horse, just in case.

The U.S. in the '70's and '80's was the land of the semiliterate professor, the quack doctor, the self-ordained minister, the travelling dentist, who sold a little elixir on the side, and the self-taught laywer.

This was the class from which the Harrimans and the Rockefellers came. It had much the same outlook as they did—*laissez-faire,* survival of the fittest and devil take the hindmost, free enterprise, and the view that success was a mark of divine favor. A familiar litany. Now, 100 years later and a shadow of its former self, this class still blathers the same sacred truths.

## Black Americans

Unlike the big capitalists, farmers, or the urban entrepreneurial class, black Americans had no designs on the direction of the country as a whole. In 1870, there were 5 million black

eople, or 15% of the population (HSA34-5). They were engaged
ı a bitter struggle for the rights won for and by them in the war. 'resident Andrew Johnson like his predecessor, Lincoln, be-.eved in a "soft peace" with the Confederacy. In practice, this lelicate phrase, "soft peace," meant allowing the leaders of the ld South to reconstruct this section as they chose without utside (i.e., Northern Federal) interference. They promptly nacted Black Codes aimed at restricting the political, economic nd legal rights won by the former slave population in their ııidst.

The character of the black population is a matter of onsiderable historical finagling in the schools and the media. 'hey teach us that the bulk of black Americans who were eleased from slavery were ill-prepared to defend their own ıterests in the hurly-burly get-rich America of 1870. On the ther hand, there was another black American, ex-slave as well s freeborn, northern and southern, and very numerous—erhaps 10 to 15% of the black population. They are, perhaps, est characterized in the life of one of the most outstanding men his country has produced, Frederick Douglass, the Liberator. 'here is no need to take my word on Douglass's stature. His utobiography is easily available and every proletarian should ead it. Douglass's story is the story of a human being who starts fe as a beast. Ignorant and fearful, with only his master's ideas bout slaves, Douglass won the struggle to become human. By is own effort, the slave becomes master of his own soul, the ;norant lout learns about the outside world. He comes to realize, ı the secrecy of his thoughts, that he should and can be free. But he real greatness in the autobiography of Douglass, in his life self, is that after all of this, Douglass dedicated his life to the reedom of his enslaved brothers and sisters throughout the ountry and the world.

Frederick Douglass was born a slave on the eastern shore of Iaryland. His master was not a particularly bad man, but as )ouglass grew, the indignity of being the property of another ıan slowly but mightily grew in him. It put iron in his soul. Slaves ere rarely taught to read for it might break the most powerful hain that bound them—ignorance. Douglass learned to read. He ıught others to read. Then, as was fairly common among the umerous slaves who had developed skills, he was sent off to work as a carpenter in the Baltimore shipyards. Working side by side with free men, white and black, his fury and despair with his enslavement grew. When the week's work closed and each free workman went off to tavern and home to celebrate his release from the sixty hours of toil, Douglass had to trudge home to his master and bow and scrape, and hand over the cash. Carefully laying his plans, Douglass fled to Philadelphia and then to New York and New England. With others of his generation, mostly black, many white, he set out to destroy slavery and free his people. A fool's quest when he started; a reality twenty years later.

As Civil War drew close and then exploded, they foresaw the need for black northerners and their friends, mostly workers and a handful of progressive middle class people, to lend strength to the ex-slaves while they developed their own. They proposed and won a Federal Freedmen's Bureau, a domestic peace corps. It helped to organize the southern poor—white too, not just black—against the old aristocracy, to teach adults and children to read, to loan or sell land and tools cheaply. By 1870 Grant was president. The Freedmen's Bureau and former slaves were holding their own in the south, helped enormously by a group of congressmen led by Thaddeus Stevens.†

† Now, right now break off reading this chapter and get hold of one of the children's American History books from school. Turn to the index and look up Thaddeus Stevens, then turn and see what they say about him in the book. Do the same with the name of John Brown. Thaddeus Stevens and John Brown are the two most famous white Americans, out of many, who cast their lot with black Americans. They fought as brothers for the rights of their fellow black citizens. Does the book you look at say just that? Does it honor them as among the salt of the earth? Or does it try to explain that while they were sort of . . . ahem, uh!!! . . . ahead of their time and of course in a certain narrow sense right . . . their methods . . . fanatics, zealots, unbalanced . . . John Brown was hanged for his efforts, Thaddeus Stevens died a natural death, but, characteristically, refused to be buried in a lily white segregated cemetary. His remains rest in a black cemetery and his headstone calls out the message of the living Stevens, that all people are created equal. Brown and Stevens were perhaps not the wisest men but they were certainly good men. Is your kids' history book willing to say that—fair and square and no if's and but's? Draw your own conclusions.

## The Plains Indians*

In 1870 the United States extended only just west of St. Louis and picked up again at the California foothills. In between, there were several foreign nations which did not recognize the laws of the United States and particularly its laws of property. These nations consisted of about two hundred thousand Indians (HSA34-5). They too had no designs on the future direction of the United States but others had designs on the prairies and mountains they roamed.

## The Working Class

In 1870 there were about two million workers or 15% of the workforce in U.S. cities. There were, as I indicated earlier, another two million artisans spread out over the numerous villages and farms of the country, but they are not properly counted in the working class since they will shortly become, the disappearing auxiliaries of the agrarian sector. In the cities the situation was very different, though in 1870 very few people realized it. Karl Marx was still a relatively unknown labor organizer exiled in London, author of some pamphlets and a few books, most of them not yet published in English. His confident assertions that the working class would grow to become the most numerous and oppressed class in society weren't likely to be accepted in the U.S. in 1870. American workers, used to high wages and intimate democratic relations with a boss who worked right alongside them, would never accept the pushing around that English and French workers did. They country was so big that disgruntled workers could go west; hence they'd never be too numerous.

*The history of the oppression and resistance of the Plains Indians is, while not directly relevant to the discussion in this volume, exceptionally important to the evolution of consciousness and social relationships in our society. Readers should consult other works to learn more about this important history. Some excellent choices are: Dee Brown, *Bury My Heart at Wounded Knee,* Vine Deloria Jr. *Custer Died for Your Sins,* and Roxanne Dunbar Oriz, *The Great Sioux Nation.* Editor's note.

Equally important, the technology of the country was located in the hand and head of the worker. Only an experienced Iron Master could peer into a flaming and bubbling cauldron of molten steel and tell whether it was ready for pouring and whether, after pouring, it would be suitable for rails or cooking pots. That was the case in every trade. Technical knowledge and industrial skill were a natural monopoly of the workers themselves. Factories employing low-skilled common labor were scarce. Factory work was often seen as women's work. In Lowell, Manchester or Fall River, it was fit work for healthy young farm girls or perhaps a dumb Paddy or Dutchman just off the boat who knew no better. Real U.S. workers for some years now had had fairly effective city-wide labor councils. The smallness of the cities, familiar relations between boss and worker, the democratic feeling of the country, an open gateway to the west, and the natural monopoly in skills all combined to create a situation in which disputes could be resolved by sitting down and talking the thing out. If that failed, the city officials, more or less equally beholden to both sides, might do a little informal arbitration and get the parties back to work. Strikes created bitterness, and interfered with God's design for a free market economy. Consequently, both workers and owners frowned upon them.

The workers would hardly have seen themselves as contenders over the future of the country. Agriculture was the major occupation of the country; commerce and industry served it. Even in the cities, commerce was the important thing. Industry served commerce and commerce served agriculture. So it had been, so it would be.

I confess I have a hard time understanding the economic ideas of the workers of the 1870's and '80's. Perhaps it was that they didn't see themselves as a decisive group in the economy. Perhaps because they saw agriculture and commerce as more important than industry, they adopted the ideas of those other segments. Like the farmers, workers in the '70's and '80's were hyped on cheap money, i.e., low interest rates. Of course, entrepreneurial farmers are always borrowing and are almost always heavily in debt. Their interest in cheap money—"greenbackism," "free silver," or "bank reform"—makes sense. For workers it looks like superstition. Certainly U.S. workers of this period lacked a clear idea of how their wages were formed in the conomy. They didn't understand the relation between their abor and the prosperity of merchants, industrialists and far- ners. This lack of an independent workers' viewpoint or ideology bout economics and class relations crippled their efforts at rganizing and defending their interests. They often lacked lirection, and for many years, despite their efforts, workers were ust swept along in the wake of the capitalists, the entre- reneurial middle class, and the farmers. Little did the tiny vorking class understand the gargantuan forces set loose by the Civil War. Little did they realize that the fate of the country had een placed in their weak and inexperienced hands.

## Capital Defeats Its Rivals

Nobody much quarrels with the general drift of events in our ountry between 1865 and say 1900. The facts are there for all to ee. The quarrel comes in trying to interpret the significance of hose facts. There is a whole historical profession which busies tself about the March of Industry, Growth of the Republic, ROGRESS IS OUR MOST IMPORTANT PRODUCT (oops, he historians probably can't use this one because it's copy- ighted), or the Age of Steel. A simpler, less grandiose inter- retation of the facts would show that capital took on its rivals nd defeated each, dispatching it to historical oblivion. Each that s but one. The working class was not so tender a morsel as it first ppeared in 1870.

Among the earliest to be defeated were the ex-slaves. Under he protection of Federal troops and with the aid of the reedman's Bureau, the poor Southerner, white and black, es- ablished Reconstruction Governments in the South. Despite vhat historians write about carpetbaggers and "gullible ne- roes," they were pretty good governments. For the first time in hat region of the country, schooling was made compulsory for all hildren; debtors prisons were abolished, and the right to vote vas extended to all classes of male citizens. But the situation was oo fragile to last. The superior economic and political power of he old aristocracy and the new railroad money began to make tself felt. The presidential election of 1876, Hayes vs. Tilden, vas the reckoning. Short of votes, electoral as well as popular, Hayes looked around for a deal. A group of railroaders, including Tom Scott of the Pennsylvania Railroad, had the electoral votes f Louisiana in their pockets. A deal was struck. Scott and his friends got some railroad rights-of-way, a promise that Feder troops would be withdrawn from the South and most importan a pledge that Southern race relations would be dealt with only b Southerners. Hayes got the votes and became President. (H had, I should point out, only a minority of popular votes.) Th new President lived up to his word; in 1877 troops wer withdrawn and Southern blacks were left to defend themselve as best they could. Throughout the '80's a great organization ( poor Southerners, black and white, called the Southern Farme Alliance, fought the good fight. But by 1890 a losing battle wa over. Klanism had won. The victorious Redeemers of th Southern Way of Life (the Ku Klux Klan) began to pass leg codes to separate the races and prevent any future political an economic cooperation between blacks and whites. Over the ne fifteen years, state after state passed these codes which wer called Jim Crow. The South had again become a prison for blac Americans.

The Plains Indians fared no better. With the end of Civ War the railroads could extend their tracks under U.S. Arm protection. The peoples of the Plains Nations fought back bu had little success. The defeat of Custer in June 1876 was a ra exception to the usual pattern. Within less than a year the Siou had been defeated and the rush westward of the railroads coul continue.

Capital took on the farmers and crushed them too. As described earlier, U.S. farming is peculiarly dependent on th broader commercial economy for its success. That broade economy was dominated in the 1870-1900 period by big capita particularly by the railroads and the banks. High interest, hig rents, high freight rates and low farm prices reaped their toll. Th percentage of tenant farmers began to climb precipitously a farm after farm reverted back to the banks: 25% by 1884, 35% b 1907, almost 40% by 1921 (HS 1970K).* The novel and film *Th*

† In those days they were called Panics, as in Panic of 1857 or Panic ( 1907. In 1929 when the bottom fell out of the economy, the powers that-be called it by a new word—"depression." That was just to prov it wasn't anything akin to those nasty old Panics *which we used to hav* In the 1957-59 "something or other" it got called "recession" and ou

*Grapes of Wrath* depict the destruction of the farmer and its aftermath in a very beautiful and moving way. It is actually set in the 1930's but could have taken place any time over the past 100 years.

The cities were growing too. Due to the enormous expansion of industrial power by big capital, the electoral power of farmers began to decline in response. The farmers fought back, with Granges, Farmers Alliances and people's parties. "Raise less corn and more hell." But they were ill-equipped to fight big capital. They too were capitalists, little ones to be sure, but capitalists all the same. They were out to make a buck; the competitive spirit dominated their whole way of life. Practical cooperation or solidarity was alien and difficult. They made attempt after attempt to cooperate among themselves—the strength and tenacity of the Farmers Alliance throughout the '80's and early '90's is a tribute to the courage and determination of these plucky little farmers. But in a contest of capital versus capital, it's the big fellow who generally wins. By 1896 the farmers' economic power was broken and in that year the defeat of William Jennings Bryan for President showed their political power was on the wane too. Consider this simple and stark fact. One hundred years ago farmers and their allies made up three-quarters of the country. Today they number less than 5% and of these 5%, two-fifths work for large agricultural companies like Ralston-Purina. The other three-fifths are among the poorest souls in the country. Their miserable farms are barely able to feed them.

Big capital against little capital. This was as true in the cities as in the countryside. The small businessman, committed as he was to the economic practices of *laissez-faire,* had only three alternatives open to him—to become a giant himself, to knuckle under to the giants, or to be driven into ruin. Henry Ford, who started his fortune somewhat later than the other great dynasts, managed the first course—he became a giant in his own right.

current "something or other" also has a new name—"stag-flation." Perhaps we should settle on a name for this "something or other" which recurs so frequently— 1837, 1848, 1857, 1873, 1884, 1893, 1907, 1914, 1921, 1929, 1938, 1949, 1957, and 1973. We could have a National Name Calling Contest and the first hundred peple who call it "capitalism" would win a carton full of old economics textbooks.

The other two fates were much more common. The three great depressions of 1873-78, 1884-87, and 1893-98 each drove thousands out of business. The big fellows would come in and buy up businesses for a song. As the size and pace of the economy quickened, many of the little fellows were simply outclassed and had to go under. But there were other methods as well. Rockefeller, when he got big enough, forced the railroads to pay *him* a fee on every barrel of oil or kerosene *that his rivals shipped.* Pious old John D. soon completed the work the Lord had assigned to him, he simply wiped out all his competition.

Carnegie, also an able and pious man, had a different approach. His main steel plant was at Homestead in Pittsburgh. The city's excellent rivers gave Carnegie a great transportation advantage. He could produce steel at a low price. But his rivals got away with paying even lower wages than Carnegie and made up the difference between shipping and materials costs. Pious old Andrew prayed, pious old Andrew saw the light. He became a public advocate of trade unionism and the darling of the country's liberal element. He encouraged the Amalgamated Association of Iron and Steel Workers in their effort to win a uniform wage scale in the steel industry. They grew, and wage scales became more even. The costs of Carnegie's rivals exceeded his own costs. They weakened, he prospered, he absorbed their business. Then, by 1892, Carnegie no longer needed the Amalgamated. He locked them out of his plants and with the help of armed thugs, the State Guard and a friendly judge or two, he managed to defeat and destroy the union. Forty-five years passed before steelworkers were again represented by a union.

The details differ from industry to industry, but it is safe to say that by the depression of 1893-98, the economic power of the entrepreneurial middle class had been broken. In politics they came to be more and more excluded from government. McKinley, the candidate of big corporations, was elected in 1896 and the next three Presidents—Theodore Roosevelt, Taft and Wilson—were, if anything, more big-capital oriented than McKinley. Every President since McKinley has talked very enthusiastically about the virtues and merits of small businessmen. They have generally been satisfied with this, to be verbally praised and economically clubbed.

So it was that the class of big capitalists, almost nonexistent efore 1860, became the dominant class of the country over the ext forty or so years. They took on and defeated each group hich stood in their way—the black people of the South, the lains Indians, the entrepreneurial farmer and the entrepre-eurial businessman. The first three fought gallantly and were efeated. The fourth died muttering the same foolish slogans hat its ghost repeats today—free enterprise, no government nterference, little business is the real America. Big capital didn't ay much but it carried a bigger stick. It had only one other rival n its quest for exclusive control of the country—let us turn now o that story.

# CHAPTER FOUR: WAR BETWEEN CAPITAL AND LABOR

I have already described some of the characteristics of the working class of our great-grandparents' generation. You might glance again at those pages (Chapter Three, pp. 35-55) in order to heighten the contrast with what was to come in the '70's, '80's, '90's and onward. Only if those workers of 1870 had had a prophet in their midst would they have understood the terrible fate that was in store for them, the explosion of change which would shatter the comfortable world they knew. Over the next thirty years (1870-1900) they would have to face a series of changes of a magnitude never before or since faced by an equivalent class of people.

## The Early Workers

The U.S. working class was very tiny in 1870, perhaps two million workers—with their families, just over six million people in all. From 1870 to 1900 almost 12 million immigrants poured into the country: from 1900 to 1920 over 14 million more arrived (#153,72). What the history books never point out is that virtually all of those immigrants went into the working class, thereby compounding its difficulties faced on other fronts. From 1870 to 1920 the percentage of foreign born in the population never fell below 13%—or one in eight (HSC218-283). That meant that during most of the period, at least 30% to 40% of the working class was foreign born. Think of the problems this posed for our grandparents. Each year hundreds, perhaps thousands, of new people came into the plant or neighborhood.

The Irish arrive first. They break strikes, they scab, they are so poor they'll live anywhere and accept any wage however low. Well you've got to make contact with them and talk it out. Overcome their fears of deportation. Overcome their resentment at the better position of the native American. A couple of years' work has to go into this and it never goes smoothly. But you make progress. Then the depression of 1873 hits. The workers go out, newly arrived Italian immigrants take their places. They have no choice. They fled from starvation at home so they'll take the lowest possible wages here. Also they're mostly ex-peasants. They have no industrial experience, so they scab. Then you have to work for years to overcome the hostility between the English-speaking and the Italian-speaking—build up class unity that overcomes national and racial hostility. Slowly you succeed. The men and women are starting to fuse into a class again. Then the depression of 1883 hits and a mass of Yiddish or Polish workers flood the plants and neighborhood, scabbing and destroying the old union. They too have little or no industrial experience: they too fled starvation and beatings at home. So you set to work. You preach the gospel of class solidarity. You try to overcome the fear and feeling of national superiority of the groups that were here earlier.

Twenty years have passed since 1870. You're making headway again, but 1892 is a depression year. Wage cuts, attacks on the union, work stoppages, strikes—and scabs. This time who are they? Chinese, Latvians, Ukrainians, Cubans, Greeks, Slovakians, Finns, Swedes. You've got to learn 20 languages and talk sense in each one of them. And so it went for 30 years, and then for 20 more years beyond that.

Part and parcel with this enormous immigration went another great change. It used to be that if a problem arose the men or women in the plant could send in a spokesperson to talk to the boss. First name basis perhaps. Human contact and old friendships could solve problems. As the size of the plant grew this became more and more difficult. At some point the boss was replaced by somebody downtown, later by somebody in Chicago or Denver. Then he was in New York, on Wall Street. It took years and years to break the workers' belief that peaceful, amicable "arbitration" was the best way to settle grievances. By then it was too late. A Beaver Falls union could deal with a Beaver Falls boss,

ut to deal with a Pittsburgh or Wall Street boss meant you had
o organize national unions. You had to convince the old time
ative Americans that their cozy little union was outmoded. You
ad to explain in Croatian and Norwegian where Wall Street was.
)elegates had to be appointed to go off to other cities and seek
ut like-minded workers, to talk to them about the need to get
ogether. That's the kind of process that takes five, ten, or even
wenty years to get going.

Meanwhile the big capitalists are not idle; they know exactly
hat's going on. Industrial detective agencies prosper: the
'inkertons and Baldwin-Felts; in Pennsylvania, the Coal and
ron Police. They spy on workers' meetings, make up lists of
ames—the black list—which is sent out to other employers. As
apital grows it gains political power. Mayors, Governors,
udges, and Chiefs of Police become more compliant. Your
elegate arrives in a new town but the railroad dicks knew who he
as from the Pinkertons. The chief is tipped off, he tells the local
aldwin-Felts. Meanwhile the delegate has found the workers
e's looking for. There's a meeting late that night but the
aldwin-Felts' goons break in armed with a warrant. The local
orkers are beaten up and carted off to jail. They'll pay a fine
arly the next day, be fired by late afternoon and be on the
lacklist for the rest of their lives. Your delegate has been taken
o some quiet spot, worked over, tarred and feathered. Or
nched. Wesley Everest died just that way on November 11,
919. He is unusual only in that we know exactly what happened
o him. Hundreds of others merely disappeared.

The habits of secrecy have to be learned; it doesn't matter
hat this guy talks a good line of class unity. Who is he? Who
nows him? He's just in from Cincinnati; you'll have to send
omeone there to check him out. Who will rent us a meeting hall?
'he saloon keeper doesn't dare, the police are on to him. We'll
eet out in the woods, post an armed guard to warn us if there's
ouble. There's a stoolpigeon in the group. The police come,
iere's some shooting in the dark, nobody hurt. Next morning the
apers are screaming: *ARMED WORKERS . . . SUSPECTED
NSURRECTION . . . FOREIGNERS PLOT.* The local respec-
ables are in high dudgeon; they demand a crackdown on
narchists, communists, trade unionists, foreigners, agitators.

There's more. The period we're talking about, especially

between 1870-1900, was a period of very rapidly changing technology, the kind that led to century-of-progress ideas, the wonders of machines and Jules Vernes fantasies. From the workers' angle the story is a bit different. Under capitalism, most technology is introduced because it saves labor. Where ten used to do the job, eight will now suffice. Economists like to point out that the new technology will cause the economy to expand so that soon there will be, say, eleven jobs where there used to be ten. Gee! that's wonderful. Except that we're not talking about jobs, we're talking about men and women. The normal pattern of such things, as I think every worker knows from experience, is that two 58 year old workers are let go, or maybe workers as young as 55 or 49 or 46, men or women earning top wages and too old to get another job. The three new jobs go to 18 or 21 year olds. They get starting pay and less of it at that. Why less? Because the two older workers realized they've had it and soon they'll take a job at any price. They are hanging around the plant gates now trying to swallow their pride and come in again at the bottom. Those three young guys had better take what's offered to them, because there are two unemployed, washed up, useless 58 year olds who will if they won't.

The second thing about the technology of 1870-1900 is even more significant. In 1870 if only the Ironmaster knew how to make steel, this was certainly not true in 1890. This is the period in which industrial knowledge and skill passed from the experienced worker to the engineer and the scientist. By 1900 science had come to the aid of capital, and steel was made under the technical direction of the chemist and the metallurgist. A whole new class of technical and scientific experts, trained in schools and institutes, not by craft apprenticeship, moved into industry. You didn't need the eye of the Ironmaster to tell if the steel was ready for pouring. Do a chemical analysis of the ore and the coke and the scrap before you start; measure the quantity carefully by machine; control the heating by means of precision measurements and so on. This went on in industry after industry. For our great-grandparents, most of this happened in a mere 20 years. The monopoly of industrial knowledge, technique, and skill passed almost completely over to management, his engineers, his scientists. The technical power of the working class was smashed and so was the economic leverage which depended upon it.

Power is power no matter what its form. As the 19th century wound into its last decades, as the power of the entrepreneurial farmer and businessman was broken and as the working class reeled from the mighty blows of immigration, radical change, and technical revolution, the power of big capital expanded uncontrollably. Its economic power overflowed its boundaries and spread into every area of politics, social life, and culture. Actually, by the late 1870's big capital already had the major voice in the national government—U.S. politics in the next 30 years is mostly a story of one victory after another as capital's enemies are beaten, routed, and finally destroyed. Every facet of government came to reflect this change in power relations in the country, from the town constable to the President of the United States, from the school board to the Senate. The Courts, which are supposedly immune to such changes, changed the most, outdoing even the press in their desire to serve the new ruler, capital. Let me give you three examples.

As a result of the war against slavery the 14th amendment to the Constitution of the United States was adopted in 1868. It declared that no state could ". . . . deprive any person of life liberty or property without due process of law." The political deal between Hayes and Scott made that a dead letter as far as the Congress and the executive were concerned. The courts followed. Surely, they said, the 14th amendment isn't intended to protect black people from violence by the Klan, only violence by state officials. So it's hands off lest we violate the rights of Southern racists to wear white hoods at night, terrorize black voters and lynch protesters.

The amendment was given a new lease on life in the 1880's when the federal courts began to define corporations as persons. Since the corporation was a person and couldn't be deprived, what were we to make of trade unions and the workers' attempts to win better wages? A union deprives a corporation of its property (money) when it forces it to pay higher wages. That, said our nation's tribunal, is clearly unconstitutional. Henceforth, the federal courts were to defend the constitution against trade unions and organized workers.

The nation's reformers were a little shocked. Big capital, by now increasingly organized in corporations, was getting too powerful. The reformers forced the passage of the Sherman

Anti-Trust Law in 1890, which forbade "conspiracies which restrained trade," i.e., monopoly and related doings. The judges set to work. How could a corporation be a conspiracy to do anything? A corporation is a person. One person: a conspiracy takes two or more persons. But a union, Aha!, a different matter entirely. Unions consist of many persons. Right! Unions try to restrain trade. Restrain trade? Yes. They try to restrain the sale and purchase of labor power by fixing wages. Right. That's it! Unionism violates anti-trust law.

But the nation's judges, in their infinite wisdom, weren't finished. Courts have the power to enjoin (or forbid) people from doing something illegal. They issue what are called injunctions. Injunctions tell what's forbidden. Let's say I'm going to testify against you in a criminal case. You come to me and threaten to blow my head off tomorrow unless I make up my mind not to testify. The court leaps in and says, "Listen buster, if you even go near McDermott, if you even say boo to him, we're going to lock you up for contempt of court and throw the key away." That's called issuing a prior injunction—an injunction against something someone is *likely* to do. Generally the injunction is pretty specific. Labor injunctions were something else.

Trade unions, by their very nature, are up to no good, said the courts. They're in the business of violating the 14th amendment, which is hallowed by the blood of our boys in the great war. They violate progressive, forward-looking laws like the anti-trust law. Isn't it clear that the minute they get involved in a dispute with capital, they *have to* do something illegal, that is, violate due process or restrain trade? Using this kind of reasoning, the courts began in the early '90's to issue prior injunctions against meetings, picketing, leafletting, planning, organizing. You name it, blanket injunctions. They were issued wholesale, not only by big, august federal judges, but by every judge down to your little whiskey-soaked J.P. in a one-horse town. Then if you violated the injunction, you were a criminal and the authorities could use force. And they did. Sheriffs, special deputies, cops, undercover cops, state guard, federal troops. It is a little strong to say it but it's essentially true: by 1895 or so, government had been turned into the "hit man" for capital and the Federal Government was the biggest thug of all.

Intellectuals and other culture makers like to feel that they tand above the petty disputes of this world. But then again, the ail probably thinks it wags the dog. At any rate the world of ulture also felt the power of capital and like the courts soon vorshipped at its feet. Herbert Spencer's ideas about the urvival of the fittest became ragingly popular among all segnents of educated society. Since the white native born Anglo-Saxon type people lived so much better, with so much more efinement, culture and delicacy than those filthy immigrants in heir warrens, surely that was the mark both of God's favor and heir own natural biological superiority. In the '90's especially, his trash flourished, and the newcomers were, accordingly, ooked down upon in spades. I once rented a furnished place in Theodore Roosevelt's home town, Oyster Bay, New York. The ouse had a library of his collected writings and I browsed most f them. In his racial ideas Teddy was representative of educated pinion of his time. He goes on and on about the natural uperiority of the Anglo-Saxon native. And the natural coarseess, brutality, and stupidity of, in descending order, the Celts, atins, Slavs, Asiatics, and Negroes. Teddy was also very vorried about the breeding capabilities of these lower specinens. He feared that they would "mongrelize" the white race (his xpression) and thereby set back the country.

Consequently, as the workers attempted to even feebly efend themselves against capital's juggernaut, respectable eople saw very clearly, they thought, that that fine talk about ecent wages and the rights of working people was just a sham. Behind it for sure, was some dago agitator out to get his hands on ny daughter, leading a roused-up mob which would never be appy till they wrecked my comfortable living room, my comortable country. Let the mob have its way and we'll all be back limbing the trees. No, by gum, we better put good men in office vho won't tolerate such goings on. And that is just what they did.

If you've been following our jumps back and forth in time, vhich can get a little confusing, you'll notice something important. Teddy Roosevelt and his ilk believed that the Anglo-Saxons were a biological race, rivalling other races—Celtic (Irish), Latin (Italians and Spanish), Slav (Eastern European), Asiatics (Chinese and Japanese), Negro (Blacks), Semites (Jews), and so on. This is exactly the period in which the beaten black and white people of the South got Jim Crow pushed on them. It's all connected. It's the age in which the big countrie gobbled up Africa and Asia. Ideas almost always *reflect* the powe relations of the world in which they move. In the period fro roughly 1890 to 1900, Anglo-Saxon racial superiority was wonderful idea: it justified repressing the labor movement in th North. It justified Jim Crow in the South, and it justified color grabbing in Cuba and the Phillipines. Ahh!, the power of an ide whose time has come (to a class that needs to clothe its greed i science, progress, and respectability).

So it was that as the working class entered the post-Civ War period, our great-grandparents were to be rocked by eigh enormous and more or less simultaneous blows:

(1) They would be repeatedly overwhelmed by large num bers of desperately poor foreigners without industrial exper ence and speaking a score of languages.

(2) Their habits, ideas, customs, and expectations would b shattered by the growth of industry and the radical changes i everyday industrial life.

(3) Force of every kind would be set loose upon them, t prevent them from organizing in behalf of their own interests

(4) Their well-being would be continually threatened by large pool of unemployed, created by technological "progress as well as immigration.

(5) Their own monopoly of technical knowledge and sk would be destroyed and with it almost all the economic levera they formerly enjoyed.

(6) They would face a legal system almost unanimous hostile to their efforts at organization and defense.

(7) They would be up against an antagonistic publi convinced that all working class activity was foreign in origi subversive in intent, and probably aimed at "mongrelizing" th Anglo-Saxon race.

(8) And finally, they would face a vigorous, new, powerfu and intelligent capitalist class with unlimited wealth which ha already destroyed its other opposition and which, in the suprem arrogance of its success, would tolerate no hint of resistance fro a filthy mob.

If you strike glass or pottery with a hammer it will shatter. you strike steel with a hammer it will get harder; strike it again will get even harder; keep on striking it, it will get very ha indeed. Our great-grandparents, though they themselves certainly didn't know it in 1870, were made of steel. It sounds corny but it's true. They didn't shatter under the eight blows. They grew harder and harder and began to return the blows with interest. But before looking a little more closely at that process, a few things should be cleared up on the question of immigration.

## An International Class

So far, my account of immigration has been pretty negative. That's the correct view of it. On the one hand, most immigrants came here because they were desperate. It's an illusion to think they came for different reasons from the black people in the 17th and 18th centuries. The whips that drove our immigrant forebearers were hopeless poverty and the chains that held them were ignorance and weakness. Their initial effect on the native U.S. working class was like that of a wave hitting a sand castle. Everything dissolved before it.

But there was another side to immigration as well. Clearly the newcomers added numbers to a tiny minority class. Soon it was neither tiny nor a minority. Equally important, you must remember that the working class is an international class. In Europe in the 1870's and onward, the French, English, Italian, German and other working classes, somewhat older than ours, were themselves growing and learning. In the holds of the immigrant ships, mixed in among the peasants from Ulster, Sicily, Galicia, and the Ukraine, were men and women from Lancastershire, Turin, Paris, Essen, Kiev, Shanghai and a hundred other cities. These were workers who had had some experience of industrial strife and political organization. In addition to their willing hands and empty stomachs, they brought something else as well. They brought their own awareness that the working class was an international class and that it was engaged in an international struggle against capital. More and more as the century progressed, this international awareness would help to overcome the provincial and the nostalgic outlook of the U.S. working class. Our class became aware that workers in other countries followed our struggles and often lent us practical aide. The effect that this would have on the morale and self-esteem of workers buried in some out-of-the-way textile mill in

New England or crowded in the slums of Chicago, would be inestimable.

And the newcomers brought something else too—practical experience of industrial struggle and how to organize it. They knew which tactics worked in which situation; what to expect from the boss, and the authorities; how to prepare and distribute leaflets, or worker newspapers. Peasants as well as workers brought essential experience. The Irish had had five hundred years of dealing with a hostile legal system, the Italians had to contend with military occupation by several armies, the Polish peasants knew their way around the Czar's Secret Police. Into the melting pot went many elements. The steel that came out was alloy steel, the toughest kind. Finally, and also of critical importance, the newcomers brought Karl Marx and European socialism with them.

Marx, the man, was very active in the German, Belgian, French, and British workers' movement, from early 1840 to his death in 1884. He made a point of being well informed about the activities of the working-class movement in each country. In 1864 he was the chief organizer of the International Workingmans Association, which soon had sections in each industrial country. He made an exhaustive study of the most advanced industrial capitalism of his day, that of Great Britain. Already in 1848, in the *Communist Manifesto,* written with his friend Frederick Engels, he had predicted the course of development of both capitalists and workers which would hold for the foreseeable future. The fact is, as anyone can see, that his forecast was amazingly accurate over the next forty years. Until the late '80's and early '90's the *Communist Manifesto* and his other writings were right on the money. Marxism blew out the opposition. Even those who hated him absorbed huge parts of his ideas. They had to. The man obviously had an uncanny knack for knowing what was going to happen.

By 1850 the *Communist Manifesto* had been published in English and had reached this country. Marxists were active here, but our own capitalist and working classes were small and immature before the Civil War, so Marxism really made no sense. Its truth was buried in the greater truth of millions upon millions of small farmers, small businessmen and skilled craft workers. But during and after the Civil War, industrial America overcame grarian small business America and its experience became nore and more akin to what Marx had predicted two decades arlier. The immigrants who came brought with them a Marxism hich embodied the economic and political experience of the hole European working class in its struggle with capital over the ast one hundred years. It was a potent view and it came to an merica which was exactly ready for it. By the middle '80's his nfluence was being more and more felt. There wasn't just a nisunderstanding between this group of workers and that boss. here was a mighty contest between two classes. Utopian rganizations for general social reform, uniting every species of reamy-eyed idealist and quack, were not enough. There had to e a powerful industrial organization of the workers. Free silver, reenbacks, and other nostrums were hopeless. Workers had to nter industrial struggles over wages—high wages built their trength, higher profits strengthened their enemies. There was o third way. Regret if you must the nostalgic U.S. of farmers, usinessmen, and craftsmen, and the easy democracy that overned their relations. But the future held only two real hoices—an America governed by Plutocrats trampling on veryone else, or the rule of the working class—the Socialist ooperative Commonwealth.

What is remarkable and noteworthy about the coming of Iarx to America is that he didn't come in the form of books and riting though, god knows, enough Marxist books and theories ave been sent and are still being sent. He travelled in steerage ith the immigrants—in their heads, not their pockets. He went ith them secretly through customs and out into the slums. Only lowly did he emerge as the immigrants began to add their xperience to that of the native workers in the great battles which ollowed.

## ormation of the U.S. Proletariat

We have now sketched in sufficient background to follow the mergence of a definite strategy of self-defense by the 19th entury working class. The most direct way to follow the evelopment of working class strategy is to outline the life the lass' most important leader, Eugene V. Debs.

Please understand that it is *not* my view that good leaders make good movements. They say that good pitching contribute 80% to winning baseball. The quality of the rank and fil member, his or her intelligence, resolution, willingness to lear from experience, his or her courage, make up—if you insist on number—99and 44/100% of the strength of the workers move ment. Debs' greatness, which I for one think is shared by only fiv or six other Americans—Douglass, King, you nominate thre others if you can find them—his greatness is mainly a reflectio of the quality of the working-class men and women of the perio who chose him as their leader. For us his life is instructiv because it shows how difficult and how long it took for a intelligent, well informed, highly dedicated worker to shed pre Civil War illusions, learn the lessons that had to be learned an set out on a winning course.

Eugene Victor Debs was born in Terre Haute Indiana, i 1855. He was fortunate in his choice of parents. Both his mothe and father, immigrants from Alsace, were active, alert peopl who supported the various progressive movements of the da His name shows that—Eugene after Eugene Sue, a progressiv French novelist of the previous era and Victor, after Victor Hug one of the great champions of the voiceless poor of the 19t century and author of *Les Miserables,* a novel popular like n other in the old working-class movement of almost every countr including ours.

In 1870, at the age of 15, Debs went off to work in the mos advanced industry of the day, railroading. Starting as a yar laborer, he advanced to Painter and finally to Locomotiv Fireman. In 1874 after a brief spell away from railroading, h helped form the first lodge of the Brotherhood of Locomotiv Firemen in Terre Haute, and soon became its full time Secretar He later extended his activities into the National Brotherhoo and in 1880 was named Secretary-Treasurer of the Union an editor of the Locomotive Firemen's Magazine.

Debs was an energetic and restless man. He was also, to us an old expression, a sociable sort of man, who liked to take drink. A friend of mine, Manny Granich, who heard him speak i New York in the early 1920's, describes him as a "skinny gink all arms and legs, with a bald head, pacing back and forth on th platform. Manny couldn't remember his voice, but he remem bered some of the things he said. That makes sense. As railroader travelling throughout the country to organize and assist the various lodges, Debs was drawn into contact with every segment of the working class. He himself commented that he helped organize every trade and calling in every sector of the country. Few men of his time were so knowledgeable about the exact state of industry and the working class.

His ideas at the time reflected those of his parents and of the infant labor movement. He was very high minded, believing in progress and human betterment. To our ears, such ideas seem vague and hazy. To an extent they were, but they contained in them a generalized love of humanity and freedom and a particular feeling of solidarity with the despised of the earth. For example, he was once offered a fancy job by a railroad executive who told him that he was the kind of intelligent, industrious fellow who should rise from the ranks. "When I rise," said Debs, "it will be with the ranks, not from the ranks." Unlike many who hold such idealistic views, Debs was an extremely kindly and generous sort of man.

Saintly, kindly old Gene Debs made lengthy old-fashioned speeches and loved to swap lies with the boys till the bottle ran dry. But he was also an able organizer, a skillful tactician in industrial disputes, and perhaps the best analyst of his day of the nature and direction of U.S. society. He was also tough. At the height of the Jim Crow Movement for example, he spoke only to racially mixed audiences. Later, 63 years old and ill, he accepted a ten year sentence to the Federal Penitentiary in Atlanta in order to speak against Woodrow Wilson's war to make the world safe for the House of Morgan.

The labor movement he entered in 1874 was small and immature. Labor organizations had existed in this country before the American Revolution but the depressions in the 1850's and the war in the 1860's had almost wiped them out. By Debs' time, there were generally two distinctively different kinds of union, and both were very weak. The workers of the skilled trades used their monopoly of technical skill and knowledge to extract certain concessions from the boss. They organized by craft, were small and were very hostile to the mass of unskilled workers being spawned by technological progress and immigration. Other workers, joined by quacks and reformers of every stripe, formed political organizations which looked to the reform of society in general. Of the latter, the most important was the Knights of Labor, founded in 1869. It was to last twenty or so years and reached a membership of over 700,000 at one point. Like so many failed workers organizations, it left a great legacy to the working class as a whole.

The Knights saw themselves primarily as an educational society. They preached the true gospel of class solidarity—the word itself comes from them. "An injury to one is a concern to all" was their motto. When they entered the scene, there was no U.S. working class—just a scattered working population with no sense of its own identity and common interests. By the time the Knights succumbed, to the quackery of the reformers and the retaliation of capital, the general run of worker knew something of his or her class and understood the necessity of class solidarity. We could use more failures like the Knights.

The working class of, say, even as late as 1880, just to pick an arbitrary date, was still too small and inexperienced to wage successful strikes. Though the workers used the strike weapon, it was not popular due to its limited effectiveness. The Knights, however, pioneered another weapon in our arsenal, the boycott. In our day it's hard to imagine how effective this weapon could be. Workers then lived in separate neighborhoods cut off from the other classes, somewhat like minority people today. So, the Knights had a neighborhood rather than a shop basis. The District Assembly, not the plant local, was the basic unit of organization. Hence, unlike the unions of skilled workers, the Knights were active among women, the unskilled poor, immigrants, and the small number of Northern black workers.

They had neighborhood power. Shopkeepers and local employers had to watch their step. My grandmother on my mother's side grew up in one of those neighborhoods and she once described how a boycott actually worked. The technique had actually been brought over by Irish immigrants but it was used here by everyone. The whole neighborhood wouldn't deal or even talk to the object of a boycott. Imagine going into the butcher shop for a bit of stew meat and the butcher saying "Mrs. So and So, I'd rather you take your trade elsewhere till your husband ceases his ill-treatment of his workers." Or going to church on Sunday and hearing a sermon on how the love of riches is the surest path to hellfires, all the while, the priest or minister, peaking directly at you. Nervously you turn around, the whole lace is staring at you. A little crude but very effective. The Knight's membership prospered on tactics like this until about 886, when the courts found boycotting highly illegal and made heir point stick by giving long penitentiary sentences to workers who practiced it. For the moment, capital had blunted the ffectiveness of working-class neighborhood solidarity. It would ot forget the episode, however, and we'll see later how the ttack on the cohesion and sense of solidarity of the working-lass neighborhood would be one of the main priorities of a later tage of capitalism. But we're jumping ahead of our story.

Debs, so far as I know, was not a member of the Knights hough he sympathized with and learned a great deal from them. t the time he joined the Brotherhood of Locomotive Firemen, owever, it was part of the craft unionism which would later lead o the AFL. In 1874 the Brotherhood was one of a group of three raft unions in the railroad industry which also included the ocomotive Engineers and the Conductors. All told they con-ained about one in ten railroad workers, the one in ten who were nore skilled and earned higher rates. The Brotherhood excluded he vast majority by means of high initiation fees. Again, there is o sense hating these workers for their policies of exclusion. lready demand for the skills of the railroad workers was in elative decline due to the size and changes of the railroad ndustry. No one in the country had ever succeeded in organizing nskilled workers *on an industrial basis.* The tactics of industrial truggle were yet to be worked out. The railroad crafts felt herefore, that by limiting themselves to workers with skill they ould have at least a little strength. This led them to take a urther step. Since they were so weak it came to be that more and nore they existed by the sufferance of big railroad capital. In a ay they knew that, so each Brotherhood more and more tried to rove to management that it wasn't radical and irresponsible like he Knights or foolish like the other Brotherhoods. So if the iremen went out, the Engineers or the Conductors, instead of upporting them, would stay on the job to prove to capital just ow reliable they were.

Let me repeat, there is no sense condemning these men. Of ourse, their policy was short-sighted. Of course, the railroad nanagement saw this and maneuvered each against the other.

But our own unions today do the same thing. The UAW combines with Ford Motors to beat back the black and young worker caucuses that spring up. The AFL-CIO collaborates with the CIA to weaken workers organizations in other countries by attacking radicals and communists. Frankly, when you are weak you have to accommodate yourself to the morals of a pimp and you try not to look in the mirror. The cure for such things is strength. Without strength, preaching isn't worth spit.

Debs came to see all of this, but not quickly. He was a slow learner, a trait he shares with the rest of us.

There certainly was enough to do in the Brotherhood. Even without the strength and experience to bargain with the Roads, the Brotherhood members had a strong interest in their own development as human beings and pursued an active program of reading, discussion and lectures. They also provided various mutual benefits to one another, such as insurance and sick relief. Debs threw himself into the work.

The year he started with the Brotherhood, 1874, was a year of—yes, what's it called?—stagflation. Panics and depressions are times when workers are at their weakest and capital presses its advantage. In summer 1877, the Railroads, starting with the Pennsylvania, began applying the meat axe—10% cuts right across the board. On July 11, when the Baltimore and Ohio Railroad ordered the same, the B&O men grumbled. Nothing new there. The Road just went ahead with its plans and began looking for scabs, just in case. On Monday morning, July 16, 40 men in the Baltimore yards refused to work unless their wages were restored to the old level. Scabs were put on. But then things began happening in a new way. Men walked off the trains in support of the 40. As the news of this travelled up and down the lines, others walked out too. In West Virginia, Washington, Missouri, Pennsylvania, New York and as far West as Denver. Spontaneously, it grew into a nation-wide strike, the first national strike ever held in our country.

The railroad men were in an ugly mood, as were the other workers in the cities. The Maryland Militia was sent into Baltimore to put them down. After a brief fight the soldiers began to fraternize with the crowd. It happened other places too.

In Pittsburgh the militia was more disciplined. The workmen fought back; they beseiged the soldiers in the railroad yard.

and set the whole yards afire. The state soldiers retreated out of the city.

The Rail Brotherhoods did not support the strike and some provided strikebreakers for the railroads as if trying to prove that a friend in need is a friend indeed. But the Roads' other friends were more significant.

The President of the Pennsylvania Railroad is a man we've met before. Tom Scott had helped arrange the deal which put President Hayes into office, which was where he still sat. Scott asked for the U.S. Army to "restore order" and break the strike. Due to the Hayes-Scott deal, Federal Troops were no longer needed in the South, the Klan would see to law and order there. And they were no longer needed in Indian territory. The Indians had finally been beaten that previous Spring and Winter. So Hayes complied. U.S. troops were brought in from West and South and for the first time used to intervene in a labor dispute. They arrested hundreds of "leaders" and broke the strike.

Debs did not support the strike. In fact he opposed it. Violence was against all his humanitarian principles. By this time he echoed the views of the Brotherhood. He did, however, draw the right lessons from the defeated strike. Several lessons in fact.

First, the Brotherhoods had to work together. If each Brotherhood continued to scab on the others hoping to secure or maintain the "confidence" of the railroads, they would be picked off one by one. Second, unemployed workers were a threat to employed ones. For practical as well as humanitarian reasons, unemployment had to be reduced. Third, the Brotherhoods were too exclusive. They had to let in more railroad workers. Again for both practical and humanitarian reasons. And fourth, the strike lacked organization. The men were undisciplined, destroyed property, rioted, and burned things. This was an invitation for retaliation from the government and the courts.

As Debs travelled around the country, these lessons increasingly grew to constitute his crusade, or program. For the next 15 years he stuck to it: cooperation of the Brotherhood and inclusion of unskilled immigrant and black workers so that strikes wouldn't be necessary.

The railroads would have to listen. Capital and labor depended on each other. All the workers wanted was a fair day's work for a fair day's pay. It was only the short-sightedness and arrogance of capital which prevented it from seeing that its best interests lay in cooperation with responsible unions.

Meanwhile, stay away from schemes for radical social reform. All you got from them was the aid of quacks and freaks. Cooperation of the unions plus friendly Democrats in government, that was what was needed. Debs became active in the Indiana Democratic Party and was elected for many, many years to the post of Terre Haute Town Clerk. He even served a term in the Indiana Legislature, again as a Democrat. He came to dislike politics. Industrial strength would have to do the job itself.

## The Eight Hour-Movement

Meanwhile, the workers of the country were going in another direction. Before the Civil War there had been widespread agitation for the ten-hour day. Gradually ten hours, six days a week, became widespread in trade and the skilled crafts. But twelve, fifteen, or even eighteen hours was still common in factory work and on the railroads. In the early '80's a powerful Eight-Hour Movement had begun mostly in and around the Knights of Labor. The workers in that movement felt that the eight-hour day would cure unemployment and provide leisure for the cultural and political development of what was coming more and more to be called, thanks to the Knights, the working class. May 1, 1886, was agreed upon as a day on which thousands of workers would hold demonstrations for the eight-hour day. Many workers decided to strike until the eight-hour day was granted. The Knights' leadership was against these demonstrations and strikes but popular sentiment won the day.

The respectable classes watched these developments closely and with some trepidation. The lower orders were becoming more and more insolent every day. The city of Chicago had become a hotbed of eight-hour agitation. For their part, the capitalists were determined not to give in.

Chicago was a peculiar city. It had anarchists. Like it or not, the anarchist's outlook makes its home in the working class. People who hold that view believe that all governments, whatever their pretenses about democracy, equality, or even socialism, are tyrannical. The anarchists obviously have a point. Even today, the governments representing the various isms rival each ther in snooping on, repressing, and imprisoning their own eople. Some people believe that government is best which overns least. The anarchists go a step further. No government. Replace it with organizations of cooperation. No organization hould have the right to compel people to do anything. Without ompulsion, compromise will have to do.

Anarchists who think the unions are germs of a society vithout compulsion are called syndicalists or anarcho-syndicasts. That was Chicago's other peculiarity. It had syndicalists in he labor movement. Lots of them.

As I say, anarchists have a point but they proverbially tend o be people who want everything done yesterday. To them, very leader is a potential tyrant, every restriction a dagger imed at the heart of workers' freedom. This makes them easily he most colorful group in the workers' movement and often the irst to understand what the broad mass of workers really want to lo.

But they're also the most dangerous group in the workers novement. Their impatience and their distrust of leaders and ong term programs have led them time after time to the bomb nd the gun. McKinley was shot by an anarchist. In old Russia, hey got scores of the Czar's officials and one of the Czars imself. Frick, one of Carnegie's associates, was badly wounded y an anarchist. The Eight-Hour Movement was made for the narchists and they prospered, especially in Chicago.

On Saturday May 1, 1886, the demonstrations and strikes egan in a festive atmosphere. All over the country, workers ame out to demonstrate for the eight-hour day. Sunday was uiet, but on Monday the 3rd, the demonstrations spread further. n Chicago, the cops, augmented by Pinkertons and by the big eterans organization of the Civil War called the Grand Army of he Republic, began to try to break up the strikes. In the course of Monday afternoon, four workers were killed and many wounded y gunfire.[†] The attacks on strikers and demonstrators con-

The Chicago Police Department has always been particularly violent nd lawless about political opposition. On Memorial Day, 1938, they antonly fired into a holiday crowd of striking steelworkers, killing n. And in 1968 they gunned down the leadership of the Illinois lack Panther Party and in the same year, beat up thousands of peace emonstrators at the Democratic Convention.

tinued throughout the next morning. A group of syndicalist called a protest meeting that evening, May 4, for the Haymarke Square. About three thousand persons attended, including th city's mayor. They heard speeches attacking the police and i support of the Eight-Hour Movement. Shortly after 10 PM, a rain threatened, the crowd began to thin. The mayor left jus about this time. There were perhaps 200 people left when 18 cops began very violently to break up the crowd. Someone thre a bomb into the police ranks, killing seven and wounding 66. Th police opened fire, killing and wounding how many we do no know.

The respectable element of the city called for law and orde Eight men—all anarchists—were indicted for murder: Augus Spies, Michael Schwab, Samuel Fielden, Albert Parsons, Adolp Fischer, George Engel, Louis Lingg and Oscar Neebe. On Augu 20 seven were sentenced to hang. Neebe was given fifteen year Lingg died shortly afterwards in prison of an explosion which th authorities called self-inflicted. Fielden and Schwab asked fo clemency and had their sentences commuted to life impriso ment. The remaining four demanded liberty or death. They we hanged in Chicago's Cook County jail on November 11, 188 August Spies, Adolph Fischer, George Engel, Albert Parsons

These men were, by any standard, foolish. They were give to bombastic rhetoric and irresponsible talk of guns and bomb and immediate revolution. They were also good and courageou men. Realizing from the start that they were doomed, the turned their trial into a trial of their executioners. Speakin clearly, forcefully, and factually, they described and documente the brutality and poverty which were the everyday life of th Chicago workers from whom they were drawn. They died wi great coolness and gallantry. Spies was already hooded with th rope fixed about his neck, when he spoke calmly. "There w come a time," he said, "when our silence will be more powerf than the voices you strangle today."

Seizing upon the momentum offered by the trial an execution, the capitalists moved rapidly to break up the Eigh Hour Movement. The employers' counter-offensive was help by the newly-formed AFL and the leadership of the Knights, w roundly condemned the eight men as terrorists and crimina The years 1886, 1887, and 1888 were years of real losses for t workers of the country.

## Beneath Appearances

The working class is a very mysterious creature. It appeared to condemn the Eight-Hour Movement and the men who died with it. Every voice was raised in a chorus of attack. In reality, just the opposite was happening. Many workers believed that the men were hanged as an object lesson to the working class. Bill Haywood, later a famous figure in the labor movement, but then only a kid in a Western mining camp, described the effect on him; how it drew him to one of the labor movement veterans in the camp, an old time Knight, and how they talked of the meaning of the Haymarket and the hanging. It woke him up. It fixed his determination and it fixed the determination of an entire generation of working-class leaders. First they set out to clear the name of the men and then, to make Spies' dying words a deadly prophecy for capital.

By this time, 1887, Debs had been in the labor movement for seventeen years, an active leader for thirteen years and a nationally known leader for over ten. His first reaction was to condemn violence of all kinds. His second reaction was to treat the whole thing, inadequately, as a civil liberties case. For him only free speech was at issue, not the general rights of the working class.

It isn't easy for people to learn things. This is particularly true of working class people and it is important to understand why.

The working class is the most conservative class in society. It is also the most revolutionary. It is both simultaneously and for exactly the same reasons. A society can tolerate almost any radical ideas or outlandish behavior from a few cranks or even a large minority, such as the students in its better universities. What matter even if some rich kids hold up banks and blow up buildings? At worst that's a damned nuisance but not a threat to really change society.

But the ruling group has to understand what's what or someone else will replace them. They know that if dissidence begins to make headway in the working class—that's big trouble. They'll crack down. Seriously crack down. That doesn't mean someone's suspension from school or diddly arrests for trespassing. Crackdown means you let the police break heads and shoot people. Crackdown means you encourage the goon element in the society, which is always present, to prey on workers. And crackdown means you look out for somebody to make an example of. The upper class may curl their pinkies as they sip tea but they didn't get there by discussing grand opera and admiring art and culture. That's one side of the street.

The other side is that a worker has to be pretty stupid not to know what the score is with the authorities. A few years ago there was a flurry of discussion over a proposed new "no knock" law which gave police the right to break into a home or apartment where they *suspected* illegal activity was going on without knocking and announcing "we have a search warrant!" The liberal press was very upset. If the law was passed, they said, the police state will come to America. I was then working politically with a group of working-class students in New Bedford, Massachusetts. I mentioned the no knock proposal at one of our discussions. We never had such fun as that night. Pete, Arlene, Irene, Buffalo, Simp, Eve, Blue and the rest simply broke up as they acted out what actually happened without the no knock law, when the police thought something might be happening in a working-class building or were just curious to know if anything was happening. Working people know that law or no law, they have very little protection against the powers-that-be. Even the most conservative, flag-waving, welfare-hating, racist, union-busting old fathead in the shop knows and watches what he or she says and thinks.

But just let old fathead know that the workers have a little strength and gumption up, he or she will sound like Mao Tse-Tung on a bender. Not all. But most. And that is because every worker, man or woman, has had to bow her or his head in front of some cop, principal, or strawboss and say, yes sir, no sir, you're right sir, not once but dozens of times. Very few of us ever forget the bitter taste of that.

Debs had this ingrained caution in him. He supported the Eight-Hour Movement, he symphathized with the anarchists—the men—not their views. He was deeply troubled by the trial and the hanging but he wasn't yet prepared to draw the real conclusion. Why? Because workers, unlike other elements of society, act on their conclusions. The Haymarket trials demanded certain conclusions. Haywood and others saw that. Debs, who was a much more thoughtful man than Haywood, hung ack, afraid of no-holds-barred class struggle, falling back into ne nostalgic view that the U.S. was different and problems could e worked out.

Meanwhile the conviction grew that Spies, Parsons, Engel nd Fischer had been hanged to serve as an object lesson to other orkers. Lucy Parsons, widow of Albert, and an important leader n her own right, set out to clear her husband's name and spread ne gospel of class solidarity. Others were similarly at work. Not nly in this country but in every industrial city in the world. To onor the memory of the men and to render support to their U.S. omrades, workers demonstrated and organized protests on very continent. The International Working Men's Association ppointed May 1st as May Day, an international workers' day in ne memory of the Haymarket martyrs. In this country an mnesty committee was formed which gathered evidence to how that the men were framed by the Chicago police. Finally six ears later the governor of Illinois, John Peter Altgeld, conucted a rigorous investigation which cleared the eight men of ny complicity whatsoever in the bomb throwing. It had been a ame. The three living men, Neebe, Fielden and Schwab were eed.

In 1972 I was in Chicago for a meeting. With a friend, I went ut to the Waldheim Cemetery where all of the Haymarket nartyrs are buried (now called Forest Home Cemetery). We new that, because of the Haymarket men, many men and women ctive in the labor movement had chosen to be buried at the Valdheim and we wanted to pay our respects to the memory of ll those good people. The cemetery staff was not very helpful. Ve asked for the location of the graves of Albert Parsons and ugust Spies. Were we relatives? No. They looked it up in a book nd told us where to walk. There is a simple monument there. pies' words are engraved on it. It was very moving to see them, ut after awhile as we began to leave—both of us were deressed. We talked about it. The cemetery staff were clearly not appy to have notorious anarchists amidst their plastic tulips nd unsold family plots. The place seemed deserted. Then a oung couple passed us. Is this the way to the Haymarket nartyrs? Yes. We walked back with them talking of the things ve recounted. Later as we left again we saw another couple, omewhat older, walking in the direction of the little monument, looking intently to left and right. Eighty-five years had passe since 1887; the hangmen had silenced the Haymarket men; thei friends had passed on. Historians wrote around the episod embarrassed to break the silence, but still a trickle of peopl went out to the Waldheim to pay their respects.

Debs now went out to Waldheim every chance he coul when he passed through Chicago. His views had been changin In his own mind, as in the minds of so many other workers of hi day, the deaths of Spies, Parsons, Fischer and Engel *had been* a object lesson. But not the lesson the executioners had intende More powerful, disciplined organization was necessary. Deb began to talk openly of and to work for a confederation of th railroad brotherhoods. He began to support, participate, an even lead strikes. He was by this time editor of *The Magazine,* th paper of the Brotherhood, and had made it into the foremos labor paper of his day. 1888, 1889, 1890, 1891, 1892. The year passed, he continued his agitation in favor of cooperation an confederation of the Brotherhoods. Some limited cooperatio did develop, but federation was more elusive.

He was a patient man but there was a limit. By 1892 Ne York State had enacted a ten-hour law. The railroads ignored i They expected twelve to fourteen hours from their workers. Th state looked the other way; things like that happened all th time in those days. Five hundred Switchmen walked out, hopin to force the governor into upholding the law. But the governc had other ideas. He sent six thousand troops to crush the strik The Switchmen put in a call for help to the Brotherhoods. Som refused. A few dillied; the others dallied. The Switchmen wer routed and Debs finally saw, after 22 years in the industry, and 1 in the brotherhood, that confederation of craft unions wa hopeless. Craft unionism, by its very nature, encouraged rivalr exclusiveness and distrust. There had to be another way t organize railworkers than through their crafts. Debs resigne from the Brotherhood of Locomotive Firemen determined t find the other way.

# CHAPTER FIVE: WAR BETWEEN CAPITAL AND LABOR (CONT'D)

## Industrial Consciousness

As already noted, Debs had an extensive knowledge of U.S. industry and its workers, often first-hand. In the winter of 1892-93 he devoted himself to a more or less systematic review of what he knew along these lines and, borrowing from some pioneering work by the Brewers and the Miners, he formulated a plan for a union that would embrace all railroad workers, regardless of their craft, and would take in unskilled workers on an equal basis with engineers and conductors, the aristocrats of the trade. It would defend not the *craft privileges* of a few workers but the *rights* of every worker in the railway industry. It would unite within its ranks a body of workers sufficient in size to take on the great rail barons and force them to pay labor its fair share. This was the birth of the industrial union in the United States.

The American Railway Union was launched in the summer of 1893 with Debs as its president. 1893 was a depression year with heavy unemployment. The Great Northern Railroad, owned by one of the most powerful men in the country, James J. Hill, slashed wages in August and then again in January 1894. A third reduction followed in March. Despite the depression the ARU men walked out. The Brotherhoods condemned the strike as unwise and scabbed just as they always did, but no ARU man anywhere would handle a Great Northern car. If a train passing through Chicago, for instance, had Great Northern cars in it either the ARU men wouldn't pass the train through or they would detach the offending cars and shunt them off on a siding. There was no violence, no burning, no mobs—just a disciplined well-thought out strike by workers who, like their leader, had an organization which allowed their experience to function in the most effective way. Eighteen days of this and the Great Northern surrendered. The U.S. railroad worker had learned how to win strikes.

Railroad workers headed for the ARU in droves, spoiling for a brawl with capital. By mid-1894, one hundred and seventy-five thousand workers had joined, almost 20% of all the rail workers. The ARU had decisively won the first round of the fight; its first year left it the country's largest single union.

Round two was a little different. Pullman cars were owned by George Pullman. George Pullman leased them to the roads. There was a town in Illinois, just south of Chicago, called Pullman. It was named after its planner, chief law enforcer, main newspaper editor, medical director, chief judge, sole employer and bishop; well, more truthfully, the man who okayed its clergymen. Company towns are fairly rare now, the lumber and the textile industries still have a few. But spurred on by the neighborhood effectiveness of the old Knights a few years before, many employers experimented with company towns as a way of getting 100% control over their workers. They wanted control over their families, what they read, what they heard in church, what lecturers came to speak with them, what associations they had, how they voted and so on. If you owned a company town you could also make a lot of money: low wages, high rents, company store. Most historians deal with them in those terms—the boss is trying to make an extra buck. I think that that's a little simple-minded. Money making and control over workers are merely two sides of the same coin. If you have one securely you get the other. If you don't have one securely you may lose the other. The capitalists of that day were very much aware of the changes coming over the working man and woman and were determined to check their rising class consciousness and develping class organization. The company town, like the Pinkertons nd the prior injunction, was a preventative measure. For capital n ounce of prevention turns out to be worth a pound of gold sorry! though corny, it's true).

Well, George Pullman had raised a whole generation of bedient, responsible workers. They had been safely insulated rom the foreign virus now spreading around. Chicago newsapers in need of a Sunday feature would often send someone own to Pullman. Amidst the lovely parks and fine buildings of he model town some passing worker would be interviewed. nvariably, he or she would express opinions on the virtues of od-fearing industrial leaders like George Pullman and the need or Principles of Cooperation between Capital and Labor. We an easily imagine the newspaper readers in those stately homes p by the Lake nodding drowsily after their Sunday roast, ontent that there were no damned foreign agitators in Pullman, ist good conservative American workers.

As James J. Hill surrendered, the responsible conservative orkers of Pullman suddenly disappeared. Their places were aken by angry and militant men and women who flocked into the RU. They too were demanding that their wages be restored. ullman refused to negotiate. The workers struck and appealed the ARU for help. Debs didn't like the situation. U.S. workers, s I pointed out, tend to be pretty mild and conservative most of he time but when they do get going they are among the most ilitant, scrappy workers in the world. Sometimes too much so. he Pullman Company was not as easy to get at as the Great orthern. Every railroad used Pullman cars. A strike against ullman put you into the position of taking on every railroad ompany at once. The ARU was still pretty inexperienced, it had lot of growing to do. Strike funds were scarce. And there were nemployed on every street corner who'd leap at the chance to cab.

The ARU met in Chicago that summer. The delegates andered down to Pullman. They came back pretty grim-faced what they saw. Beneath the veneer of the model town, Pullman n a very nasty police state. Out back, behind the pretty public uildings were slums full of raggedy women and undernourished ds. Debs tried to hold the convention in check but various orkers from Pullman came and spoke. One, a young woman named Jennie Curtis, broke open the gates with a moving description of life among the Pullman workers. The ARU voted to support the strike without stint or limit.

It was a remarkable strike in many ways. Pullman workers were not railworkers, properly speaking. They manufactured and repaired a certain kind of railroad car, diners and sleepers. The ARU, many of whose members came out of the old Rail Brotherhoods, supported them on the basis of industrial, not craft, solidarity. The ARU had no quarrel of its own going with the roads just then. Their boycott was a measure of sympathy and support to their fellow workers. An injury to five thousand workers was an injury to one hundred and seventy-five thousand members of the ARU.

The railroad companies decided to beat the boycott by running Pullman cars on their trains. The ARU workers refused to move them so that the strike grew into a national railway strike. This was not 1877. Though the ARU leadership and organizers were inexperienced in their union duties, the railworkers had been learning over the past 17 years. No looting. No burning. No threats of guns and dynamite. Orderly picketing, disciplined members, no invitation to the authorities. A national strike headquarters kept in daily contact with the various local strike headquarters. Conscious attention was paid to the regular and labor press, the former to keep it from running incendiary stories, the latter to gain support from other workers. The railroads found it harder to round up scabs and strikebreakers, and when they found them they coudn't get them to Chicago, the center of the strike.

The rail Brotherhoods were aghast. They promised to oust any member who joined the strike. The ousted workers re-organized as ARU and kept on striking. Nevertheless, Gompers and the AFL leadership, defenders of the craft principle and of Principles of Cooperation between Capital and Labor, were asked for help. They dillied and they dallied but their Chicago members prepared a sympathy strike for the Pullman and ARU workers.

ARU entered the Pullman dispute on June 26. Within a week Chicago, the rail center of the nation, was tied up. Some 25 rail companies were effectively closed down. The governor of Illinois, Altgeld was still friendly. The working class, save a few leaders, were giving important support; ARU organizing principles had the situation well in hand. There was no provocation for the national government to seize upon. Kindly, saintly old Gene Debs had a talent, it seems, for generalship. The nation's railworkers, thoroughly whipped 17 years before and beaten frequently since, had a certain talent for industrial struggle. Round two had ended with the workers on the edge of the greatest victory in their history. A victory over the nation's largest, richest and most powerful industry.

## Situation of the Adversaries

This is a good point to take stock of what had been going on in the country since the Civil War. The year is 1894. The Plains Indians, their power broken, are captives on the reservation. Black people, their power broken, are being terrorized by the Klan and milked by the sharecropping system. The entrepreneurial middle classes have ceased to be a power in the country: economically, they are rapidly being gobbled up by big capital; politically, they act as flunkies for the rich. The entrepreneurial farmers, still battling, have passed the peak of their power. Two years later, in the election of 1896, they'll make a final effort, and after that it will be all downhill.

For capital it has been a lovely 30 years. Thousands are richer than Pharoah. In the big cities the names of the great dynasties are celebrated. Some historians even refer to the '90's as the Gilded Age. The age of sumptuous new mansions on huge estates. Parties so lavish the Roman Emperors are put to shame. Private railroad carriages, private yachts, marriages with European nobility. The big capitalists run industry; they run society; they run the country. Already the U.S. is the leading industrial country of the world. Shortly our capitalists will run Cuba as well, then the Phillipines, Panama. The future is limitless.

The working class doesn't fit into this picture. A pygmy in 1865, it has been hammered by eight mighty blows over the past three decades. Yet it has grown infinitely stronger. Now it makes up nearly one-half the country, but even that figure doesn't tell the story, nor does the public record of those 30 years. The public record from 1865-1894 is a record of victories for capital and defeats for labor. You can count the number of victorious strikes on your ten fingers. The defeats require pencil and paper to tally up. The Knights and other organizations have been smashed. The blacklist probably has almost as many names on it as the union membership roles. The boycott is outlawed. The unions which remain alive, mainly the Brotherhoods and the AFL, are subservient to capital, subsisting on a few crumbs in exchange for their strikebreaking activities. The political power and social status of workers has been in continuous decline. Literally hundreds of workers and their leaders have been murdered. I don't exaggerate. For example, in 1877, 17 leaders of the Molly Maguires, a Pennsylvania miners organization, were hanged—Thomas Munley, James Carroll, James Roarity, Hugh McGeehan, James Boyle, Thomas Duffy, Michael Doyle, Edward Kelly, Alexander Campbell, John Donahue, Thomas Fisher, John Kehoe, Patrick Hester, Peter McHugh, Patrick Tully, Peter McManus, and Andrew Lanahan. Two more, Charles Sharpe and James McDonald, were hanged in 1879. Earlier, Edward Coyle, Charles O'Donnell, and Mrs. Charles McAllister, all active in the union, had been shot and killed. There were other miners murdered too but their names go unrecorded. The Molly Maguires are only a bloody instance of the general rule: every labor disturbance has shootings and hangings. Most are at night by masked men in quiet places, with unmarked graves. A few are public to set an example.†

† The Molly Maguires were hanged Thursday, June 21, 1877. The great rail strike of 1877 began Monday July 16, or 25 days later. Historians do not generally make much of the coincidence of dates. Yet the Molly Maguires mined anthracite, a type of coal commonly shipped by rail out of state and into the big cities. Their main executioner, McPartland, of the Pinkerton Detective Agency, was hired by the president of the Philadelphia and Reading Railroad, Franklin Gowen, who in the same year was actively engaged in union busting against the rail Brotherhoods. It does not seem possible that the rail strikers wouldn't have known about the Mollys or that their hanging would have left them unmoved. The more likely supposition is that the railworkers, on top of their other grievances, had recently seen a railroad president succeed in hanging 17 fellow workers and that the rail strike, especially in its violence, was tied up with the hanging. But in making that supposition you are driven to concluding that the rail strike had a *political* element, the hangings, as well as an *economic* element, the wage cuts and the

So much for the public history of the period. The true istory of working people can't be in the public record, partly ecause it is much too complicated. Perhaps you can find out ow grandma or grandpa were different from their parents but no ecord could contain all those millions of subtle changes between he workers of 1870 and 1894. But it is not just complications hat obscure the public record. From the standpoint of the apitalists, the working class is a servile class; it is a class which xists only for the capitalists. It works so that he may profit; it uild great industries so that he may own them and bask in their randeur. Its defeats are his wonderful victories. Its degradation s the price of his glory. Without the working class the capitalist is ust another guy: little, big, handsome, ugly, stupid or smart. Vith the working class, he becomes capitalist, industrialist, eader, builder of civilization, patron of the arts, ruler of the ountry, prince.

In a capitalist society, the working class is a captive class. It annot be otherwise. As we shall see later this is true today. Economically speaking, it was glaringly true in the 1890's.

Baldwin-Felts, Railroad Police, Coal and Iron Police, Speial Deputies, corrupt Sheriffs, hired Judges, bought Legisatures, croney Presidents, poverty, 72 and 84 hour weeks, child abor, illiteracy, superstition, blacklists, racism, nativism, Anglo-Saxon superiority—these were the chains that held it captive.

A captive is a person who cannot freely express his or her wn impulses. Cannot do what he or she would freely choose to ay. Often, cannot even think what he or she would freely choose o think. The impulses, actions, words, and even the thoughts of he captive are controlled by those who run the prison, own the hains, pay the guards.

The human spirit is unquenchable. Just as prisons have heir rumor mills, their grapevines, a captive class, has a life that oes on beneath the surface of the public record. Underground.

nion busting. That in turn means that the rail workers were intelligent uman beings who connected one event with another, as they should be onnected. But that's clearly impossible. Workers are dummies who nly act as mobs, never with intelligence. Consequently, there is no oint even in mentioning that these two events fall within 25 days of ach other. That is a normal practice of the historians.

It's hard to find out what goes on there. You know what you'r thinking, but what about the other hundred and fifty million o us? Workers do not own tv stations or big newspapers. The seldom write diaries and rarely leave them to libraries. The don't write novels, or philosophy, or books on economics, politic or organization. They don't have historians to write their histor or publishers to publish it. It's only occasionally, when they brea into the public record that that happens: A big strike, a famou man, a hanging with an object lesson. Even then the history often written by people anxious to curry favor with capital or b people who, thinking that what they can see is all that is ther attribute only anger or resentment or mob behavior to th workers.

The free life of the working class is underground. In th period we've been considering what was going on there is sti something of a mystery, although we do have glimpses. Deb slowly changing over a 20 year period. Lucy Parsons constant moving around the country, telling ten workers here or 25 ther in a dingy little room, about the great Eight-Hour Movement an why it failed. We know about some immigrants; we have recor of some speeches; we have a few workers newspapers. The be records are police records since police, unlike historians, wat the working class very carefully all the time, and write down wh is said. But many of those records don't exist anymore, or lik those of the Pinkerton Agency, are private property and not ope to inspection.

Most probably, the experience of Bill Haywood is typica He saw what was going on around him. He sought out an old tim and talked at length with him. He spoke guardedly to others, h made an effort to bring workers together. He kept an eye out fo other organizing efforts, and copied success and discarde failure. Over that 30 year period, hundreds of thousands of me and women were doing, probably, the same thing. Some worke were literate. They read Bellamy, Hugo, DeLeon, Marx, Kautsk Bakunin, Swinton, Most. They listened to speeches by Deb Lucy Parsons, and Mother Jones, the ideas passing among an between them.

I say probably that was what was going on. I don't know. B by 1894 something radical had certainly happened. The childr of the 1877 strikers acted very very differently. The old quac and reformers were still there. They still preached of greenbacks and money reform and universal cooperation schemes. But the railworkers no longer paid attention. The Brotherhoods were still around talking of Principles of Cooperation between Capital and Labor, but the workers went to the ARU. They were, god knows, as hungry and as angry as ever and the crazies were there—Fight the police! Burn the Roundhouse! Destroy the freight! March to City Hall! The picket lines stayed in place, hot heads were reasoned with, there was no violence. What had happened?

Hundreds of thousands of workers, perhaps millions, had radically changed. Host upon host of working men and women had absorbed and assimilated 30 years of industrial experience. The intelligence and experience of the working class itself had grown enormously. The railroad workers themselves were ready for the ARU at least as soon, and probably sooner, than Debs had proposed it. To the average worker, the industrial union idea solved the question of how to deal with the roads. Jimmy Higgins and Jenny Curtis understood that question very well. They knew what wouldn't work. They had a rough idea of what would. The ARU fit their thinking. And it was not only railworkers, but all those other workers who wouldn't lift a finger for the Carmen or the Iron Molders but who made the ARU strike their own.

The ARU represented a mental victory of the working class, a breakthrough of its collective intelligence. The idea of the ARU contained a deep understanding of the relation of forces between capital and labor, their composition, organization, and disposition, and the tactics appropriate to a winning confrontation. The ARU also represented an economic, political, and moral understanding appropriate to that strategy, that organization and those tactics. And it represented all of those things to several hundred thousand "simple" workers, not merely to the handful of their top leaders. That was why the ARU was embraced and why it became the nucleus of a successful struggle over the combined forces of the nation's most powerful industry.

In another sense, the ARU was the legacy of Spies and Parsons, the Doyle brothers, the Knights of Labor, and of all the men and women who had labored in defeat for the past 30 years.

The organization of the ARU and the disposition of its forces also had to be learned. Somebody had to learn the hard way to organize and conduct a modern strike against a powerful industry. Our grandparents were the first to do it. That took a long time and a lot of mistakes were made: they and *their* parents paid for every mistake with broken heads, jail sentences, ruined lives, sometimes death itself. But they learned.

The same can be said for tactics. As you look at labor accounts of the years 1865-1894, you will observe every possible tactic: armed rebellion; boycott; political campaign; educational drives; local, regional, and national strikes; rioting; arson; sabotage; assassination; appeals to government; appeals to the clergy; appeals to the general citizenry. Here too, much had been learned, much discarded. The tactics of the ARU toward property, public officials, police, the public, their own picket lines and other strike conduct reflected a high level of understanding.

In economic understanding the ARU foreswore the superstition of the quacks and reformers and of capitalist economics. Our grandparents had learned the hard way that the worker's wages and the boss's profits come out of the same kitty and that if you want a fair division you have to fight over that. Metal versus paper money, single versus multiple taxes, high versus low tariffs won't do it. To us, it's obvious. Because we had smart grandparents. Hundreds of thousands of them.

The political understanding involved a recognition of the *triggers* to government action. The ARU workers had shed the illusion of a "neutral" government. They knew that government had to be kept out of the strike because it would come in only on capital's side. Mail trains had to be moved regardless of the difficulties. They were. Peaceableness had to be maintained no matter what. It was. Elements of other classes had to be persuaded that the workers had a cause worth supporting. They were.

Finally, the ARU workers had come to a moral understanding which was essential. They knew that other workers who were not directly involved had to feel a powerful and compelling interest in the strike so they would lend practical support in sympathy strikes, delegations to government officials, discouragement of scabbing, provision of strike funds. By going to the aid of the relatively weak Pullman workers, the ARU had animated the moral force of millions of other workers. That too, reflected a great achievement in the class understanding of our grandparents.

An even more remarkable conclusion follows from these, nd explains the stunning industrial victory of the ARU.

Compare briefly in your mind, the two forces locked in battle ı 1894. Capital and labor, represented by the railroads and the .RU. It becomes apparent that the workers had so developed hemselves that their force thoroughly outstripped that of apital. To see this, merely run through the organization and ehavior of the railroads, keeping in mind that parallel organiza- on and behavior of the ARU. The railroads were then controlled y great dynastic families; Morgans, Vanderbilts, Harrimans, Iills, Gates, Belmonts, Stanfords. They were not highly unified. Iormally they expended a great deal of their strength against ach other—each one snarling, grappling and cheating all the thers to gain some advantage. They were united only in their pposition to the railworkers and that opposition was purely egative, save for experiments like those of George Pullman. 'hat is, they took the workers as they found them and then tried ɔ break their organizing efforts by force and fraud. Pullman was ifferent and more farsighted. He tried to create a new sub- ervient type of worker. But alone, not even he had the resources ɔ do it. The Pullman workers, you will recall, were infected from utside with the virus of resistance.

The general strategy of the rail dynasties was a matter of laying off the Brotherhoods against each other and against the norganized. Plus force. Thus, the prominence of Pinkertons and angings. The relation of the dynasties to government was ırgely one of corruption. If they wanted something they bought he public official who would give it to them. But a corrupt overnment is an inefficient and clumsy government. A com- etent government official won't accept such a situation; but will ither leave government service because of the corruption, or go ɔ where the action is, i.e., become a corporate official. That is ıost of the explanation for the importance of the Pinkertons in his period. The regular police tended to corrupt goons in niform. Police work which required a high level of professional ompetence, such as industrial spying, or keeping up a blacklist ouldn't be done by corrupt goons.

Against the dynastic jockeying and infighting of the rail ynasties, was posed the solid industrial unity of the ARU. gainst the brute force of the railroads was posed the intelligent force of the railworkers. Against the infinite corruption c railroad and government was posed the moral force of a workin class uniting to aid their weaker comrades in the town c Pullman.

For all their wealth and cunning, their ruthlessness an bloodletting, capital had been out-organized at the most fund amental level. Though they could and did hire the best brains i the land to work for them, the "simple" railworkers had learne to act with greater intelligence than their hired talent. Thoug capital controlled the moral authorities of the nation—professo press and pulpit—the moral authority of the filthy masses ha overwhelmed theirs.

All this was achieved by a class which had known nothing bu poverty, ignorance and defeat for three decades. It was stupendous human achievement, regardless of what was t happen.

## Military Counter-Revolution

As the month of July opened in 1894, the nation's capitalist awoke in their gilded palaces to the prospect of disaste Twenty-five railroads were shut down tight. Chicago, the nation' transportation center, was securely in the hands of the striker Recall that we're dealing with 1894 now, not 1980. There were n autos then, or trucks, buses, or airplanes. The railroads were th nation's transportation system and the rail companies were th largest, richest, and most powerful companies in the countr They had been solidly beaten on the industrial battlefield. It's a if, in our day, a single union embodied every worker connected t transportation and its allied industries—truck drivers, airlin pilots, railworkers, highway maintenance workers, bridge an tunnel workers, pipeline workers, inter-city bus drivers, ai traffic controllers, toll booth clerks, reservation clerks, and a the workers in the manufacturing end in auto, aircraft, rubbe and petroleum. Imagine, in our day, all those workers, joined in militant union, and out on strike in support of, say, the aut workers. What industrial or economic power in the country coul check such a huge, powerful union, animated by feelings of clas cooperation and class solidarity and enjoying the keen approv of workers throughout the country.

Put it this way. In 1937, during the organizing drives of the CIO, the victory of the auto workers against GM set off a round of organizing and strikes by several million other workers in the country which fundamentally changed the labor situation in this country. But in 1894 a victory of the ARU over the combined rail companies, far more important then than GM was in 1937, what might that have set off? An ARU victory would place the nation's key industry in the hands of workers who had already demonstrated their willingness to use their power to help other workers.

Could textiles hold when the mightly railroads had been routed? Wouldn't steel, mining, lumbering, cement, meatpacking, and manufacturing be routed if the railroads were staffed by victorious union men? Would any worker have reason to fear capital when its richest and most powerful segment had been squarely beaten? Moreover, capital was infinitely less prepared for such a defeat in 1894. In fact it was not prepared at all. The domination of capitalism itself would have been put to the challenge, with god only knows what result.

A ruling class rules because it retains the intelligence and toughness to do so. Having been out-organized, out-thought, and out-fought by the ARU, the nation's capitalists were forced to improvise a counter strategy. The outlines of the improvisation are very simple—raw military force. Later, after the destruction of the ARU, capital would radically reorganize itself and its methods of class domination. On that, more later. For the moment the capitalist class would have to depend on a military coup from the Federal Government.

The President of the United States was a Democrat, Grover Cleveland. His former law partner was the attorney for J.P. Morgan, the country's most important rail capitalist. Cleveland's Attorney General was Richard Olney, a member of the Board of Directors of two roads which were being struck—the Chicago, Quincy, and Burlington and the Atchison. Olney appointed Edwin Walker Special Counsel of the U.S. Government and empowered him to act for the Government in the strike. Walker was then the attorney for the Chicago, Milwaukee and Saint Paul Railroad, also one of the struck roads, and in fact, their representative to an industry-wide railway committee which was coordinating resistance to the strike. Olney and Walker went to Federal Judge Peter S. Grosscup, who had been appointed to the

Federal Courts through the influence of George Pullman. Olney and Walker asked for a series of injunctions which would forbid virtually all union activity—past, present and *future*—of any officer or *member* of the ARU. The Sherman Antitrust Law was cited as the legal basis for the injunction. Grosscup issued the injunction and as an added fillip, indicted Debs, Howard, Rodgers and the other leaders of the ARU. Simultaneously, Walker moved Federal Troops into Chicago, the center of the strike.

Illinois's Governor, Altgeld, protested that the state had its own troops on hand, that there was insignificant violence and that the Federal Troops were both unnecessary and would incite violence (which they did). Chicago's Mayor Hopkins protested similarly. They were ignored. Altgeld telegrammed directly to Cleveland. Cleveland replied, skirting the issue. Altgeld telegrammed again. Cleveland didn't bother to answer.

The ARU leaders were arrested and the strike headquarters was seized. Federal troops, at gunpoint, dispersed picket lines. Some 700 strikers were arrested. The Brotherhood of Locomotive Engineers furnished the railroads with lists of scabs. The other Brotherhoods also actively participated in strike-breaking activities. AFL President Gompers recommended to his members that it was "unwise and inexpedient" to support the strike. Under the protection of Federal troops, Pinkertons and hired goons began systematic assaults on strikers. Striking railroad workers were ordered at gunpoint to move trains, usually by goons, but in several cases by Federal troops themselves. Within two weeks of Walker's appointment the trains were moving. The strike had been defeated, Olney's coup had succeeded.

In a move which since has become more or less regulation, Cleveland appointed a U.S. Commission to look into the strike and make recommendations for the future. The Strike Commission deliberated. In 1895 it issued a diplomatic report of about one thousand pages, more or less regulation size for these things. It supported the Pullman workers and the ARU on every count, particularly questioning the legality of the injunction. Respectable opinion, somewhat shocked by Olney's high-handedness, applauded the progressive tone of the report. Well it could. By 1895 the ARU had been hounded out of existence. For many many years to admit to having belonged was open invitation to a

›eating or a blacklist. Debs and the other leaders had meanwhile ›een sent to prison. Since the strike was defeated and the ARU ›roken, their sentences were short: Debs got six months, the thers three. When the Commission released its report, Eugene )ebs was still in jail.

## ˀlass Consciousness

The quality of a person shows in defeat and Debs had been s defeated as any man could be. In prison with the ARU ›ermanently smashed, his friends scattered, many in hiding, and 5 years of his own effort wiped out by Olney's coup, Debs set imself the task of analyzing the defeat and rebuilding from cratch.

He didn't yield to hysteria. He saw that the ARU had ucceeded in all that it had set out to do. It had met railroad apital on the industrial battlefield and beaten it. Olney had ome at them from another direction. The industrial union rinciple was sound, but it had to be buttressed by other things.

Debs had received a magnanimous sentence from victorious apital in the person of Judge Grosscup. Why rub salt? ARU was ead. The conditions of his imprisonment were equally light. His ssociates, Howard and Rodgers, were with him. He had access › any reading material he wanted and he had extensive visiting rivileges. He began to read more systematically in economics nd politics.

The main result of his prison stay was that he discoverd Karl ˀlarx, or better, that he discovered in Karl Marx the crystaliza- on of his own 25 years of labor struggle. Reading Marx wrought ıree fundamental changes in his views. Changes which would be ecisive in Deb's activity for the next 30 years.

Debs had long believed that the differences between labor nd capital revolved around a fair division between wages and rofits. "A fair days work for a fair day's pay." That was his view, self an advance over greenbackism or "free silver," but as he ›arned now, inadequate for the workers movement. The worker ıkes materials and equipment and transforms them by his or her wn labor into a finished product worth more than the material it ontains. As we saw, $1518 worth of machinery and material are ˀansformed by 70 hours of sweat, skill and tears into a car that sells for $2,622. The 70 hours of labor have added a value of $1104 which didn't exist before. In Marx's view the division of the $1,104 is not a matter of agreeing to fair shares. The division is a matter of life and death for the working class. If its share is large, the workers will live well, bring up healthy children, and have time to consider the world and what's happening to it. They will have time to organize, economically and politically, and the wherewithal to put clout in this organization. Alternately, if capital's share of the $1,104 is large, it will be transmuted into rapid changes in machinery, salaries for strawbosses, time and motion men, company snoops. There will be lobbying money in legislatures, funds for campaigns, bribes for officials, and little presents of one sort or another for pulpit, press and professor. It will transmute itself into Cleveland, Olney, Walker and Grosscup. In short, capital's "fair" share goes to fuel its domination over labor; labor's share to fuel its resistance to capital. Economists speak blithely of this division as a division of the "pie." Sweet juicy pie is what *you* get; what the other fellow gets is an arsenal.

Debs began for the first time to understand this and to link it with his experience on the railroads. The other side of a "fair day's work for a fair day's pay" was "a fair day's idleness for a fair days profits," but those profits were not idle; they entered as new economic, political, social and moral strength for capital. Profits were and had to be a dagger aimed at the worker's heart. Many workers to this day do not understand this and it is one of the main causes of the weakness of the workers movement. Debs had come to understand it. Profits, had to be done away with, which meant in turn, that capitalism had to be done away with, that the economy and the society had to be reorganized on an entirely new basis by a different class of people, the workers themselves. Debs had become a socialist.

Debs began work in 1870 with a vague, high-minded humanitarian outlook. The early years on the job and the Brotherhood of Locomotive Firemen had changed that. He had acquired a more working-class standpoint, specifically, a craft worker's standpoint. That is, his understanding and awareness of the economic and political world ceased to be seen through the spectacles of a Victor Hugo. Now he saw things with the eyes of a working Locomotive Fireman. The problems, attitudes and well being of his craft brothers colored his mind. Later he grew beyond this. In the winter of 1892-93, in his scheme for confederation of the Brotherhoods, he pushed himself to understand things from the standpoint of railworkers. Not skilled workers, not firemen or switchmen, just plain railworkers. In prison he saw that he had not come far enough. He had so far only achieved an industrial viewpoint, his mind was still dominated by the railroad industry and the men in it he had worked with and loved for so many years.

Marx pushed him. A *class* standpoint was needed. Not a humanitarian standpoint, not a craft or crafts standpoint, not even a broad industrial standpoint. But a class consciousness. Debs had finally caught up to the viewpoint of the old Knights, but his view contained none of their economic quackery. It was grounded in the bedrock of economic fact.

If all workers share identical interests and belong to one class, industrial unions are inappropriate; a single union embracing every worker is needed. One union, one class, one united struggle against the economic power of capital. I don't know exactly when Debs made this jump from industrial unionism to *class unionism.* But by 1905, he had made it and was busy with others in forming such a union, the Industrial Workers of the World, the IWW.

Capitalism is not just an economic arrangement, as we have seen. The surplus of the capitalist is the fountainhead of a whole capitalist civilization: It creates a whole strawboss upper middle class; it creates political power; it influences Presidents; changes the law; distorts cultural and moral opinions. Within this alien civilization, the workers are captive to the capitalist. Captive to his riches, captive to their political weakness and his political strength. Captive to their social disorganization and his society. And they are captive to their low esteem and morale and his status and confidence. Debs began to see and think about this as well. His conclusion was that a worker's political party had to be organized to defend workers' interests on the political front while the class-wide union defended their interests on the economic front. This two front strategy became his life's work for the next 30 years. Most of his effort went into the working-class political party, the Socialist Party.

Socialism without workers is like a puppet without strings.

The puppet doesn t disappear, it merely collapses into a twisted heap. Such was the condition of the socialists in the U.S. before Debs came along. Such, I might add, is the condition of socialism in the U.S. today, and for the same reason. Debs brought with him into the Socialist Party hundreds of thousands of workers. As usual his views were developing parallel to those of masses of working people. U.S. socialism, previously dominated by political exiles from other countries, theoretical purists and middle class reformers, began to grow enormously and became a serious political force in the country. Debs' own election figures tell the story. As part of the campaign to spread the word on socialism, Debs ran for President of the United States on the Socialist Party ticket in 1900, 1904, 1908, 1912. He received 90,000 votes in 1900, 400,000 in 1904, a few more in 1908. Then in 1912, he got 900,000, 6% of the total vote. Yet to follow these successes of the Socialists or even Debs' later career would lead us astray.†

The Pullman Strike was the culmination of nearly 20 years of growth in the understanding and combativeness of our working class. Olney's coup had saved capitalism for the moment but deeper changes were required if capitalism was to prevent another ARU—or worse. In the ten years following Pullman, farsighted business leaders such as J.P. Morgan brought about a fundamental, even revolutionary change in the structure of business and therefore of capitalism itself. In place of rival, family firms of dynastic capital which Debs and his comrades had learned to whip there now appeared the great trusts or, as we know them, corporations, which merged the interests of the rival moguls and laid the foundation for a new and more powerful sort of capitalism. This collective capitalism would ultimately defeat Debs and his Socialists, as it would defeat the IWW and the whole labor movement. It would create new classes and would fracture the working class. It would fundamentally alter the economic, social and political face of the U.S. and eventually the world. It is this story, rather than the gallant last years of Debs that we must now follow.

† The Debs story is found in *Eugene Debs,* by Ray Ginger (earlier published as *The Bending Cross*).

# CHAPTER SIX: CLASSES IN THE UNITED STATES TODAY†

It's time now to take stock of where we are. As I indicated earlier there were two main reasons to take our detour into the labor history of the period after the Civil War. One, of course, was to show the younger worker, and remind the older worker, that the U.S. working class has been, in the past, a fighting class. There it was particularly important to show how the class could learn from its mistakes and weaknesses and figure out solutions for its disunity and other problems.

Today, to go from being weak and divided to strong and unified we too, like our grandparents, must learn some lessons and apply them. Of course, most of the things we have to learn are new and no amount of study of grandma and grandpa's day will do. Trial and error, defeat and victory, rather than armchair thinking is the ticket here. But there is at least one lesson that we can learn from those workers who've gone before us. And, in a way, it is the key lesson.

Let me put it simply. Society *is* the relation of the classes. Most people see that there are different classes in society—upper class, middle class, working class. But that's only half the story. The other half is that society is the relationships betwee the classes. That isn't so strange an idea as it first appears. Clot is its thread and their arrangement, period. A bridge is i structural members and their arrangement, period. An engine its parts and their arrangement, period. People who descrik society without understanding class arrangements are like th fellow who tried to explain how an engine works without men tioning pistons, cams, valves, carburetors, distributors and th like. I suppose it can be done but it won't help anyone learn ho to fix a faulty motor or even to rebuild it, if that's what's neede

We've already met most of the classes in today's U.S society: the big capitalists, the small businessmen. We've me that large group of salaried employees who shared with GM owners and top management the great wealth generated by GM workers. We've also met two different groups or classes o workers, those who work for small businessmen and those wh work for the big corporations. When we turn our attention to th working people of this country, we'll find two additional seg ments of the working class which also seem to be separat classes—Government (sector) workers and people who ar dependent for their living on government programs such a Social Security, Unemployment, Welfare. I am calling thes Administered Sector workers. One of the real keys to U.S society is that it splits workers into four different classes, all wit different and often opposed interests, so that we can't speak of single U.S. working class unless and until we ourselves form on On that, more later. For now we should try to characterize th different classes just as we did for those in post-Civil Wa America.

## Collective Capital†

You can't understand U.S. society until you grasp the hug changes capitalism has undergone since the time of Deb

†This and the next chapter describe, as briefly as possible, the nature o collective capital, its policies and the class arrangements which deriv from it. In the original manuscript form this section comprised severa

Capitalism has gone from a family or dynastic form of property ownership and control to a collective form. The difference is fundamental and far-reaching in its effects.

As we saw in Chapter Three, U.S. industry in the 1890's was dominated by the well-named Robber Barons and their families. The Rockefellers dominated the oil industry, Carnegie was the great steel magnate. You had Armour in meat packing, Morgan in the securities business, Guggenheim in mining, and so forth throughout the top ranks of business.

Let's look more closely at the Rockefeller Empire so as to grasp the pattern. Old John D. Rockefeller, Sr. had his fingers in many pies but the citadel of his wealth and power was the old Standard Oil Company. He ran the company and the company ran the oil industry. As he got older he planned to leave it to his son, John D., Jr. and he in turn would eventually leave it to his sons, David, Nelson, Laurence, Winthrop and John D., III. Thus the Rockefeller wealth and power would be passed down the generations the same way as titles and power were passed down the line of the Romanovs in old Russia or the Bourbons in France.

I want to make the point here that the Rockefeller family or dynasty doesn't consist only of Rockefellers. Old John D., Sr., built up Standard Oil with the help of associates—Flagler, Rogers, Harkness, Pratt—who shared in their own right in the wealth and power of the company. These were the Counts who surrounded the Kaiser, the Barons who surrounded the Tsar, linked by mutual interests, shared property and, very often, inter-marriage. This last is very important because the old way of

hundred pages and contained a description and theoretical analysis of the ideology, politics, social system, and economics of collective capital, including the important shift from commodity production to the production of products. This material will be published shortly in a companion volume.

The reader will find, in the present volume, very little discussion of the problems of racism and sexism. These subjects are taken up more thoroughly and sytematically in the context of collective capital in the companion volume.

owning property depended very much on marriages to cement alliances and children to carry the wealth and property into the future. At any rate, this pattern, a main family with a subordinate partner-families was common in the 1890's; Carnegie had Frick and Schwab, Morgan had Belmont, Lamont and Gary.

I call this pattern of capitalist ownership and control *dynastic capital.* The pattern—a central family of great wealth and power linked to allied but subordinate families—was the way wealth, and titles, had been controlled and passed down for centuries. In fact, it was a pattern which actually predated capitalism itself. And there's the rub.

For one thing, the dynasties, like the noble families of yesteryear, were always fighting one another. In the pre-capitalist world the upper class could afford theluxury of scrapping in its own ranks because their lower classes, serfs or slaves, couldn't be a real threat to replace them. But the working class is different. It has the drive to run society for itself, to become the ruling class, the only class. Alone among the laboring classes of history, it has shown the capacity to learn from defeat, to adapt to changed conditions, to grow in class intelligence and in political ability. The French Revolution, the revolutions of 1848, the Paris Commune, trade unionism, socialism—these are the halting, painful steps of a class rising from degradation toward a newer, better society, the classless society. ARU was also one of those painful steps, the most important so far in our class' history and our country's history. Before 1894, our nation's capitalists deluded themselves that American workers were different from the workers of other countries, satisfied to be ruled and ruined forever by their betters. ARU changed all that. The lesson for capital was obvious. The words of Benjamin Franklin, in an earlier, different time, can also be used here to state the problem neatly: the capitalists had better hang together... or they'd hang separately.

Even aside from the perpetual feuding, the dynastic form of property holding makes for a relatively weak, ineffective ruling class. If everyone in the family has to concentrate on keeping and expanding the family booty, lest one of the rival dynasties steals a march on you, you have no time, talent or sons to devote to the other tasks that normally fall into the hands of the very rich. Government, culture, society, will be neglected as you scrap for hat extra million. The rich didn't work in government; if a rich ynasty needed government aid, they just bribed the right fficial. If the workers got uppity and formed a union, the apitalists might come together to smash it but afterwards they'd o back to fighting and cheating each other. This attitude of "I'm oing to get mine and to hell with everyone else" was very angerous and short-sighted. The rich never make up more than few percent of society. If they don't have allied classes, people utside their own ranks who side with them in politics, econo- nics, culture, etc., they're in trouble. Another problem with these ld robber barons was that their quarrelling and cheating spilled ver to antagonize the classes who should have been allied with hem. As the century turned, the sort of behavior they used gainst Debs and ARU began to antagonize government officials who, as you'd expect, don't really like to think of themselves as ackeys for anyone else. It antagonized the small businessman who was being gobbled up by the corporation, the big farmers who were being ruined by the railroads and banks, the intel- ectuals and professionals who, getting past their first en- husiasm for capitalism, were being squeezed out too in the quest or the almighty dollar. And meanwhile, the working class was rowing and learning and becoming more confident and power- ul.

To make a long, long story very short, the capital class had to eorganize itself to get back its allies and to strengthen itself gainst the rising working class. The name of that reorganization s the corporate system.

The corporate system is less than a century old. In the years, oughly 1895-1905, a movement spread throughout U.S. busi- ess to unite rival companies into what were then called trusts. or example, in 1901, 138 different steel companies were ombined into one new company, the United States Steel orporation. After 1905 the process continued; GM, for ex- mple, was formed by amalgamation of several small auto ompanies in 1912. But the bulk of the great corporations, and ne pattern itself, were set in the earlier period in the one burst of trustification."

Even then, three-quarters of a century ago, our grand- arents and other progressive minded people saw that business as up to no good. The trusts, in the eyes of the so-called

Muckrakers, were too big, too rich, too powerful. If possibl that's even more true today. The corporations are too big, to rich, too powerful, and growing more so all the time. But ou understanding has to go beyond that formula—too big, too rich too powerful—if we're going to succeed in the task that ou grandparents failed in, namely, to win out against capitalism.

The critical, new thing is this; the corporations are th collective property of all the capitalists, and the corporation, no the rich family, is the basic unit or building block of the capitalis class as a whole. Let's take these point in order.

First, the corporations are the collective property of th capitalist class. Suppose we had a list of the names of all th people who own stock in GM, and all those that owned stock in it rival, Chrysler. Right off we'd see than many of the names are o both lists, and that situation is not unique to the car companie Many wealthy people own stock in GE and its rival, Westing house, in RCA and its rival, IBM, in Exxon and its rival Mobi The fact is that very few big outfits are owned and dominated b a single family or dynasty, as in the earlier form of capitalism Most of the big companies are owned by a broad cross-section o wealthy people and families, which means that they shar collectively the ownership of the companies and that the com panies serve to unite their interests.

Similarly, few wealthy families own stock in but a singl company. Exxon, the old Standard Oil Company, isn't th property of the Rockefeller family; thousands of families hold th stock. And the Rockefellers are not just in oil. When Nelso Rockefeller was appointed Vice President, he had to disclose hi holdings in stocks and bonds. It turned out that he had holding in oil and aerospace, real estate and banks, and so on. That's tru of most rich people. If you were rich you too would diversify you holdings thus tying your fortunes, not to the success or failure o this or that company, but to the success or failure of a whol spectrum of companies and industries and thus, to an extent, t the corporate system taken as a whole. Thus, by necessity, you ideas about what was good or bad for yourself and your famil would be drawn into harmony with those of other capitalists. Yo would go from a narrow dynastic consciousness to a broader clas consciousness. But we're getting ahead of ourselves.

Economists have very lively disputes about who really run

the corporate system and in whose interests. (When they say, "The consumer, of course, blah, blah, blah," dismiss them as fools or rogues and likely both.) Some economists say that they are run by and for their largest stockholders, others say by and for their officers, still others that they're run by and for the trust departments of the big New York banks. Probably, the most frequent situation is that a corporation is run by its officers, though the other situations also exist. All in all, as you'll see, the differences between stockholder-dominated corporations, bank-dominated corporations and officer-dominated corporations don't come to all that much.

Let's suppose you're head of International General Everything and Then Some, Inc., a typical corporation. Let's even suppose you have unusual personal influence, stature and power, even by the standards of the corporate world, that everyone is in awe of you and, in addition, you and your family are richer than Midas. What them? Even under the extreme suppositions I've made, you're still responsible to many people—not "under" them but responsible to them.

—To the other officers in the corporation. You must convince them to continue to perform in a way which wins their acceptance of your ideas and policies—and yourself. Each wants your job and while you are more powerful than any one of them, or any group of them, you are not more powerful than all of them together. That's what it means to be "first among equals."

—To the largest stockholders. You need their support and confidence lest otherwise they become a group opposed to you, a group working for your successor.

—To the big banks. The big bankers are like super-stockholders since they vote large amounts of stock through their trust departments. You have to go to them too for short term cash to make up this week's payroll or first quarter taxes. Thus the banks are a group whose support you need and whose opposition you should dread.

—To the big Wall St. investment houses. If they have confidence in you they'll help your company grow by helping you gobble up other firms. If they don't have confidence, they'll help someone else gobble you.

—To the big law firms. You need their help to keep government off your back and, most important, to smoothe the way of your relations with other big companies.

—To the big auditing firms. They have to be convinced that you're running the company in a responsible way, i.e., looking out for the interests of the capitalist class which owns it.

—To major government officials. As head of a big corporation you're liable to find that government is your biggest customer. Of course, a friendly attitude over at IRS, the Anti-Trust Division or the regulatory agency are definite assets.

The support and confidence of all these groups is needed by whoever runs I.G.E.T.S., Inc. If you're the real head, you need it. If you're only a figurehead for some wire-puller among the stockholders, then Mr. Wire-puller needs it. And if you're only a stooge for the New York banks, the heads of the New York banks need it, not only for the way they run I.G.E.T.S., Inc., but also for the way they run their banks.

You can see the situation. The actual powers-that-be of each big corporation are in the same situation. Each of the big companies has officers of *other* corporations on its Board of Directors (just as its officers sit on other Boards). Each has a large cross-section of the nation's wealthy families among its stockholders. Each deals with the same New York banks, the same Wall St. investment houses. Each use the same law firms and accounting firms. Each has to deal with similar, often the same, government agencies. Thus, every corporation is responsible to a large cross-section of the capitalist class in the shape of officers, stockholders, bankers, securities dealers, lawyers, auditors, top government officials. And part of that cross-section is part of the cross-section of other corporations, in the same industry and in different industries. So you can see my meaning when I say that the individual corporation and the whole corporate system are the collective property of the capitalist class. It's a cloth of many threads.

As indicated, the most common situation is for a corporation to be run by its officers, along with, perhaps, a small group of outside (i.e., non-officer) directors. This group is not *under* nyone but is responsible to many representatives of their own lass. Customarily they run the company the way they see fit and o long as it's profitable, grows, cheats only people who aren't apitalists, and stays out of the law courts, that group will ontinue to run it unhindered by the powerful array of lawyers, anks, auditors, etc. who watch over it from a slight distance. Thus you have a form of collective property holding among the apitalists whereby everyday authority is spread out into the nanagements of individual corporations. From the standpoint of he capitalist class this makes for an excellent situation. Having ollectivized and centralized their *interests* they can decentralize he *details* of carrying them out. Collectivization has brought the est of both worlds to our capitalists.

Now to the second point; the individual corporation, not the amily, or dynasty, is the functioning unit of the capitalist class. Thus, a *collective capital.* In a way this point really follows from he foregoing, but an illustration will give it more force. The GM Corporation and the Rockefeller family were worth about the ame amount in the early 1970's, about $11 billion (give or take a ew hundred million since we don't want to quibble).[†]

That amount of wealth makes both the head of GM and the ead of the Rocekfeller family—David, I guess—very powerful. But the Rockefellers only spend a few million a year on living xpenses and knick-knacks. GM spends roughly $30 billion a

† A billion dollars is a very elusive concept. Look at it this way. uppose that every day, seven days a week, you got a thousand dollars. n a year, you'd have roughly a third of a million and in roughly three ears, a million .Since a billion is a thousand million, it would take you nree thousand years to earn a billion dollars at the rate of a thousand a ay. (We're assuming no interest and no taxes.) Now, if at the time of hrist, someone started laying aside a thousand dollars a day to your ccount, now, 2000 years later, you'd still be shy almost one third the mount. Reflect a minute on this, and then realize that the Rockefeller amily is worth between two to twelve billion dollars (only God's ccountant knows for sure), and that there are maybe up to a dozen nore families in or near the billion dollar mark. Then ask yourself, how ould they possibly have *earned* that money in any realistic sense of *arn.* And, if they didn't earn it, who did, and how did they come to get old of it?

year, on supplies, machinery, real estate, salaries and wages. The people who preside over GM's spending determing the lives of millions, the fate of whole counties, cities, states, regions, even countries. GM's spending represents enormous immediate power. Thus, whoever heads GM and the head of the Rockefellers both have enormous influence, but the GM head has that additional power besides. There are a handful of other families in the Rockefeller class, but at least a hundred other corporations in the GM class. Moreover, all of them spend. Thus, it's the corporation where you find wealth being used in our economy, not the family. The corporation is the unit of capitalism; it integrates the families into a new, collectivized class by binding their interests together and by pursuing them in detail within the individual corporations. Let's look at these corporations to learn more about the capitalist class.

In 1971 there were 1,733,000 corporations in the U.S. Most of them didn't amount to much. But, among them, 2,800 (#778)corporations had assets of $100 million or more (#792). Together they held 68% of all corporate assets and employed about 38% of all private sector employees (#568), including roughly half the nation's union members (#590). This is the corporate sector of the economy, the home of all the familiar names—GE, GM, ATT, Exxon, Xerox, Standard Brands, Gulf and Western.

These 2800 companies average about 9,000 employees each and, by a crude but conservative estimate, require a top management team of at least a dozen men. Companies of this size simply can't be run by a single individual. The fellow in charge, President or Chairman, surrounds himself with a team of colleagues who are given real responsibilities. If they fail the top man doesn't take on their job; instead he finds himself someone new who knows how to put authority to good use.

With roughly a dozen men sharing responsibilities for each of those 2800 companies, that gives us (12 x 2800 =) 33,600 men in the corporate sector with real, everyday authority. Figure that they serve ten years each, or one third of their career in such positions. So there are three times that number, or 100,800 of them in the corporate world at any one time—33,600 at the top, another 33,600 now in middle management but destined to take over in a few years, and 33,600 more who are just starting but who'll eventually advance to top responsibility.

On the other hand, the upper class doesn't only have men of great ability. There are the dopey bluebloods to consider, those men who come from the right family and the right schools and clubs but who just aren't very good and who have to be shunted off to sinecures which don't involve real responsibility. By a conservative calculation, there are two of them for every talented blueblood headed for the top. That gives us 302,400 upper class men at any time in the top 2800 corporations who form a pool from which the 33,600 men with real responsibilities are drawn.

The upper class is not only active in the corporate sector. It also runs the big foundations, law firms, universities and research labs, and it has active representatives in the government. Again being conservative, let's say there are one of them to every five in the corporate sector. That gives us 363,000 (rounding off a little) as the pool of upper class men from which the 40,000 men (33,600 + 20%) who actively run the big corporations, the federal agencies, the foundations, banks, universities, and law firms are drawn.

Moreover, these 363,000 men have parents, wives and children so that when you add them in we're talking about an upper class of just over one million people.

The thing to note is how we got that million people.† We didn't start with wealth. We started with the men (and a few women) who actually run things. Then we built up the pool from which they're drawn and only then the families from which they come. Naturally, if you looked at those one million upper class people, you'd find that with one or two exceptions, they're the wealthiest million people in the country. That's important too, but what's most important is not *how much* they own, so to speak, but the *way* they own it—collectively, and jointly managed. There are four main results from this pattern of jointly owning and actively controlling the corporate system.

1) The upper class is no longer at war with itself as it was when it was dynastically organized. For instance, they no longer compete and cut prices on each other. Rather, they charge very

† My own sense is that the ruling class is perhaps twice this size. In the calculations above I was aiming at a *minimal* estimate of its size.

high prices and cooperatively, just pass those prices along. We'll eventually foot the bill. This provides for big profit margins to handle things like taxes and provides a steady, almost uninterrupted growth of their wealth.

2) This collectivized form of capital permits a division of labor within the upper class. If the sons of your family are hopelessly stupid, the sons of other families can run the businesses and your wealth will continue to grow. Within the upper class, meritocracy or the *rule of talent* can be encouraged, to its mutual benefit. Similarly, if young Throckwarton has a taste for public service, he can exercise it, by going into the Treasury, the State Department, or a big foundation or university, insuring that those institutions will work closely with and serve the general interests of the upper class. In the old days you had to come in and bribe government officials to do your bidding. But that makes for ineffective, resentful officials and potential public opposition. Now the upper class integrates government and corporation so that government enthusiastically, effectively and normally serves the broad interests of the upper class. The same holds for universities, t.v. networks and foundations.

3) As a result, the upper class has become a true reigning class, that is, a class which actively manages society. Furthermore, they make it work tolerably well for the majority of people. By contrast, the rich of the 1880-90s really were robber barons in that they were responsible to no one but themselves. To rule a class must normally find areas of mutual interest with all or almost all the other classes so that even while it gets the lion's share of everything, the other classes are tied in to the system enough to not rebel. By establishing a collective property interest the corporate system also creates mutual interests for other classes. The division of labor it affords allows the upper class to spread itself out and take over the running of all the activities which are essential to society—business, government, law, culture, science, education.

4) Finally, and this is related to my last point, the collectivized form of capital allows the upper class to create and maintain a very large, closely allied class of managers, technicians and professionals which act as a ball bearing or anti-friction, lieutenant class. That's much simpler than it sounds, so let me explain.

## The Middle "Element"

Conservative thinkers have always understood that you can't have a society with just two classes. Even 2300 years ago, the Greek philosopher Aristotle understood this clearly. As he said, if you have the few rich and the many poor the poor will have very little in its way if it wants to change things. The contrast in the two life styles will be clear, the poor will be in direct social contact with the rich, they will resent and envy the rich. There won't be sufficient numbers to hold the poor in check when the poor get angry and try to change things. So you need a middle class, says Aristotle, a class intermediate in size and wealth between the few rich and the many poor. Such a class will naturally link itself to the rich because it depends on their favor. There are other advantages as well. The middle group will provide overseers, assistants, and managers so the wealthy won't have to mix too closely with the poor. And instead of merely envying the rich, a poor lad can aspire to belong to the middle group. Plus the rich can recruit new blood for their own class from the middle group.

U.S. capital makes it its business to hide class identity so that Aristotle's word, "middle class," has come to be used for everyone who isn't either super-rich or on the verge of starvation. To avoid confusion I am going to use the word "middle element" to describe the group Aristotle was talking about. In our society they come in the upper 25% of those who work in the corporate sector, government and the other institutions of collective capital (less the 1-2% upper class). They usually earn a living from a salary and their normal occupations are as managers, executives and supervisors, scientists, engineers or higher-level technicians, professionals, including some (salaried) lawyers, many (salaried) doctors, university teachers, social workers, architects, etc.

The middle element has one job and only one job—to manage workers. Some do it directly as supervisors and straw bosses. Some do it indirectly by creating engineering or other technical systems which make workers more productive and lessen their control of the work. Some do it very, very indirectly by shaping and controlling the working class outside the job. The teacher who encourages the right attitude, the social work professional who keeps tabs on the poor. Directly or indirectly, two things are always true of this middle element class. The manage workers and they do so under the broad direction of th class of collective capital.

Naturally, they are well paid for their service. As we saw i the case of GM, the 20% of "middle elementers" employed b GM each earned almost three times as much as the workers- about $30,000 a year compared to about $12,000. That hold true on a national basis too. For example, in 1975, the top 20% c families received 41.1% of all reported income, while the lowe 80% received only 58.9%. To put it simply and dramatically, let' suppose a cross-section of 100 U.S. families were splitting $10 in the same proportions as their income. The top 20 familie representing mostly the upper class and the middle elemer would get $41.10 or (41.10/20=) $2.05 each. The other 8 families, mostly working people, would get $58.90 or (58.90/80= 74¢ each, or only a third as much. Those are the proportions i which income is divided in the country.

The middle element class is a new class in history. Newe even than the working class. It was created in order to blunt th growth of working class power. Near as I can make out, th technical part of this class—the engineers—was formed in th 1870-1880 period. You'll recall that at that time capital wa trying to break the workers' technological hold on industry, b taking industrial skills from the worker and putting them into th management level. This took the form of creating the moder engineering professions. The creation of the supervisory c managing part of the class began at the turn of the century, th way being led by the famous trusts (=modern corporation which were just being formed. The following table begins to te that story (HSP4,5 #1234).

Until the turn of the century manufacturing plants wer getting larger and capitalists were saving money by using fewe managers in bigger plants. But after the turn of the centur capital began using its big profits to build up the supervisor levels. As you can see above the figure doubles in the first tw decades of the century. The leading figure in this movement wa a man named Frederick W. Taylor who coined the term and th philosophy, "Scientific Management." This so-called "scientifi management" had two basic ideas. One was to take all of th thinking part of work, all the know-how and planning, away fro

Non-production Employees in Manufacturing
Per 100 Employees — Selected Years

| Year | Non-production Employees |
|---|---|
| 1889 | 10.0 |
| 1899 | 7.1 |
| 1904 | 8.7 |
| 1909 | 10.7 |
| 1914 | 12.1 |
| 1920 | 13.5 |
| 1954 | 20.9 |
| 1972 | 29.2 |

the worker and put it in the hands of management specialists. The ideal worker was a pair of hands which obeyed the manager's brain.

The second idea was to select out those workers who would work under that new arrangement. Taylor wanted healthy workers able to work at a very fast pace who would *accept* the fact that someone else did all the thinking.

We've wandered afield to talk about the middle element class, but the main points are clear enough. Collective capital, through its corporations, is able to extract immense wealth. Some of this wealth is kept as profits for the owners and top management. But there is enough of it to syphon off two huge streams of income to create social allies and control workers. In the case of GM we saw an amount of money nearly equal to the workers' share being paid out to a large group (17% of GM employees) in order to create a formidable class allied to capital. And the other large stream is the profits sent off to the government to be spent on laws, military contracts, roads, and schools and federal welfare programs.

None of this would be possible without the collective form of capital. As we saw in Debs' time, under the dynastic arrangement of capital, the existing middle group in society, the small businessman and the prosperous farmer, were being destroyed. With no lieutenant and anti-friction class to help it out, capitalism was on the verge of destroying itself. But far sighted leaders of the class, men like J.P. Morgan, saw that was a formula for capitalist suicide. They forced through changes, mainly the creation of big corporations, which by collectivizing and unifying the property and power of the rich enabled them to bring new allies to their side and weaken the workers.

## The Small Business Class

The third class we have to talk about is the small business or *entrepreneurial* middle class. These are the people who own their own businesses and make a living by their own enterprise. Today it includes small businessmen, farmers, and some doctors and lawyers. The small businessman is the backbone of the class.

Earlier we saw that there were 1.7 million corporations of which 2800 formed the corporate sector of the economy. That still leaves 1.7 million corporations and—hold your hat—10 million single ownership businesses and another 200,000 partnerships. Don't be taken in by this illusion, however. Those 10.2 million single ownership businesses and partnerships provide a living for only 5.2 million of their owners (#593), maybe 5.5 million if we include the people who own their own corporations (1970). Remember we're talking about all the businesses in the country which have assets ranging from plus $100 million to—lord knows. And that's the point. Small business doesn't do so well. The average profit of all those businesses was about $4,000. It's kept that way because any "small" business that can turn a regular handsome profit is gobbled up by the big corporations. In my youth the family grocery store was replaced by the supermarket chain, just as a few years ago the fast food diners were replaced by McDonald's and HoJo's. Right now, sporting goods stores are being crowded out by Korvettes, Hermann's, Sears. And independent auto repair shops look to be on the way out. Tomorrow it will be some other line of business. As a result, the *successful* small businessman is likely to make only as much as a factory worker. Certainly he's not up there in the moneysphere like the middle element man or women.

The entrepreneurial middle class and the middle element have different attitudes and relations to big capital. The middle element is a dependent class created by capital. Its income is losely tied to the profits of collective capital. As a rule it accepts apital's lead in politics, economics, social and cultural attitudes ecause it believes that collective capitalism is right and proressive. There are squabbles in this happy family but, generally hey're both pushing for a highly-profitable-technologically-dvanced-bureaucratically-organized society in which workers now their place.

On the other hand, the entrepreneurial middle class dislikes nd fears big capital. Mr. Small Businessman knows that he can e dinner for the Jolly Green Giant. But because he can't jack up is prices as much as he would like, he hates labor unions even nore. Big capital is a distant threat. His own workers are a resent danger. Also, he sort of admires the big capitalists. Why ith a little luck or a big killing, there goes he himself, Mr. 'hwipple, corporate mogul, advisor to presidents, hob-nobber ith Jackie O. and Frank S.

Collective capital understands this double attitude of adniration and envy versus fear and hatred. They put up with it, artly because they need and welcome all anti-working class llies and partly because the small business class has so much ower at the state and local level. In this country, local political ower rests in a dark corner occupied by construction comanies, realtors, local banks, lawyers, construction unions (someimes) and some folks in dark glasses who don't answer questions bout who they are. In fact, it is this alliance between Mr. Small usiness-man and Mr. B. Corporate Mogul which keeps the epublican Party together—the more conservative minority ing representing the small businessman, the liberal majority ing representing collective capital's alliance with the middle lement.

How big are these classes? Naturally it's hard to be exact in hese things, but as any scale model builder knows, when you're naking models of things, you can only hope to get the main parts ight.

There are about 78.6 million people employed in the U.S. of hom 66 million are employed in the private sector (#593). The 800 companies of the corporate sector directly employ about 25 nillion people. You have to add to that figure to bring in people mployed in the satellite institutions. So there are about 30 nillion corporate sector employees, of which at least 7.5 million are middle element. This leaves 22.5 million corporate sectc workers. An additional 36 million are employed in the com petitive sector, of whom about 6 million are owner-proprietor and 30 million are workers. About 11.5 million people work fo government, about 20% are middle element which leaves 9.: million workers. Putting these number all together by class, w get

.36 million — collective capital
9.8 million — middle element
  7.5 million in private sector
  2.3 million in government
6 million — entrepreneurial middle class
61.7 million — workers
  30 million — competitive sector
  22.5 million — corporate sector
  9.2 million — government

You can multiply that table out on the basis of 208 million tota U.S. population and you get, in round figures

1 million upper class
26 million middle element
16 million entrepreneurial middle class
165 million U.S. workers
79 million competitive sector
59.5 million corporate sector
27 million government sector

For some purposes that scheme would be a class structure with numbers, for the U.S. But it would leave millions o Americans out in the cold. Like the unemployed, who, with thei families, made up about 10 million in 1970, or the 20-30 millio who depend on government welfare programs.

## Four U.S. Working Classes

All things considered, the U.S. working class has fou separate components:

30 million (and dependents) who work for small businesses

22.5 million (and dependents) who work for the corporate sector, its satellites, and allied institutions
9.2 million (and dependents) who work for government
25-35 million who directly depend on government programs for their living. I call these administered sector workers.

That list should total altogether, 165 million.

I said earlier that we have to consider these as separate classes, until they form themselves into a single class. Now is the point to discuss that by considering the actual present day interests of those four groups and the class alliances they've formed to pursue those interests.

The leading group in the U.S. working class is the corporate sector working class. Roughly half of them are unionized and most receive benefits unionized workers have won in the past, such as paid vacations, health insurance, retirement beneifts, or seniority. They earn rougly 20% more than competitive sector workers and, because of their unions, they can stay nearly abreast of the inflation (#566). This is a *national* class, looking to the national government. They are heavily involved in national politics through the AFL-CIO link to the Democratic Party. What's not often appreciated is that these workers and their unions are tied closely to their industries, help them out by pushing for government contracts, government aid to corporations, and so on. Put it this way: the AFL-CIO joins with the corporation to make sure the corporate share of pie is big and juicy. Then they turn around and fight with the corporation to get their share of the slices. In national politics the Democratic Party has been mainly, though not exclusively, an alliance of collective capital and the corporate sector working class. And it makes sense, from one point of view.

The competitive sector working class is larger but much less politically active. There are few unions here and many of them are racketeer unions. These workers tend to pick up the more local, conservative attitudes of their employers. It is not a national class but a loose collection of regional and local classes. The competitive sector worker gets few if any benefits. He or she is often only a seasonal or part-time worker; unemployment (not just layoff) is more frequent. Though not generally politically active, this sector's workers tend to be more conservative—

feeling that big labor, big government and big corporations work together to soak them (as is often the case). Because they're not organized to use their collective intelligence, they often accept the line, put out by government and business, that unionized workers are the cause of inflation. They fail to see that the wage gains of unionzed workers only *compensate partly* for inflation; these unorganized workers think unions *cause* inflation. That makes many of them anti-union, an attitude which is reinforced by the prevalence of racketeer unions in this sector.

Government sector workers are a mixed breed. The 2.5 million federal government workers are nationally oriented, better paid, get decent benefits, and are generally liberal. In many ways they are comparable to the corporate sector workers. On the other hand, some of the nine million state and, especially, local government workers labor under conditions similar to those in the competitive sector—low pay, no job security, obligations to local power groups, and so on. In the nature of the case, government workers all tend to follow politics pretty closely, but here it may be only the sort of politics that affects this or that group of political cronies rather than a large group of workers.

In spite of these similarities to other workers, government workers have to be singled out as a special group for two reasons. First, their income levels, benefits, and jobs are dependent on the politics and economics of government, not the private sector. During bad times, when other workers are leaving their jobs, government workers may find opportunities expanding. Alternately, they may find hard sledding even in good times because the legislature or the Congress goes on a budget cutting campaign. And, in general, while government workers find advantage in the expansion of government activities, that isn't necessarily the case for the rest of us.

Second, most government workers, even when unionized, are forbidden by law to strike. Often the laws are very harsh—two days pay in fine for every day on strike, loss of seniority, jail for selected leaders.

To understand administered sector workers, you have to understand one of the most striking changes which has occurred in this country—the decline of the family as the primary functioning social unit. I'm not talking about love and affection here. I'm talking about everyday activities and responsibilities.

ıt one time it was large, extended families that held property, ocialized and educated the young, cared for the sick, poor or ged. As we've seen, the corporation has replaced the rich family s the property holding unit for the upper class. And this in turn as allowed institutions controlled by the upper class to replace he working class family as the socializer of workers' children and aretaker for the sick, poor or aged. You have to turn your mind ack to George Pullman to grasp the full meaning of this. ullman built his rotten little town around the idea that he imself would totally control all the aspects of the life of his orkers. In that way he thought he could keep out the diseases of rade unionism, socialism and working class independence. Collective capital has somewhat the same idea but on a grander, ational scale. The political State of Collective Capital claims hat it, and not you, must control when the children should go to chool and what they will learn there. Meanwhile, their media, specially t.v., drum their message into the children so that the arents basically lose control over what the kids think, believe nd, often, do. For adults, the only source of entertainment, ulture and, especially, news is the one or, possibly, two newsapers in town, three newsmagazines and three national netorks. In a lot of ways, and I don't mean to exaggerate, we ıcreasingly live in a great big Pullman, a national company town ı which the key areas of inspiration, ideas and organization are nder the thumb of collective capital. George Pullman would be ownright impressed.

Part and parcel of these changes is that the unemployed, oor, elderly, and sick now are much more dependent on overnment programs than they are on their families. Some of his is a good thing, an improvement over what was before. ertainly, Social Security, medicaid and unemployment inurance are. Still, the people caught up in these systems are for he most part working-class people and they're increasingly ependent on systems which control them and which they can't ontrol. Will the unemployment be extended another 13 weeks? an the family allowance be extended so that the children can pend a week or so at day camp? Will the Social Security keep ace with inflation? These are the questions that concern etween 25-35 million workers daily and, at some point, will onfront each of us. Moreover, you can't quit Social Security, strike unemployment, or pull a job action on the welfare. You ar under the administrative, bureaucratic control of the govern ment agency and you, alone or collectively, have little or no powe to influence what it does. That's why this group of workers has t be treated as a separate component of the working class so tha when we turn our minds to what can and must be done to improv ourselves, their concerns and problems can be considered on a equal basis with the other sectors of the working class.

# CHAPTER SEVEN
# HOW THE WORKING CLASS IS RULED

To understand how the working class is ruled, is kept in a weakened, ineffective condition, is to understand what the program of collective capital is and how it works. The program of collective capital, its aims and values, is threefold:

1) an expanding corporate sector
2) liberal democracy
3) a humanist social system

## An Expanding Economy

In Chapter Two we distinguished the corporate sector of the economy from the competitive sector. Now the key point about the corporate sector is that it is a planning sector.

To most people, when you talk about a planned economy, they think of the USSR or the other Communist countries. In the U.S. we don't have central planning but we do have a planned economy. It's just that it has multiple centers of planning—2800 companies in the corporate sector each of which is a planning unit.

Planning? What about competition? You have to remember that we're no longer dealing with dynastic capital where each company is a wild beast in a hostile jungle, surrounded by other equally wild beasts. For the big corporations the world is a lush meadow. Each company has the power to set its own prices and plan its own profits. The other beasts in the meadow are owned and controlled by the same collective farmer, so to speak, so that when our corporate beasts compete they do so only over that little corner of extra rich grass, or that choice bit of labor or luscious new product.

Each company does for itself what I call *fine planning.* Basing its plans on the money which flows in from a nearly guaranteed annual profit, it determines when the opportunities are best for it to grow and to prosper. The government, especially at the federal level, helps the companies along. It provides subsidies for the whole corporate sector, in the form of research expenditure, the military budget, road building outlays, subsidies to the airline and railroad industries, bail-out funds for corporations that threaten to go under, tax breaks, agricultural price supports, school subsidies, etc.

Plus, the government does *coarse planning.* By coarse planning I mean the attempt to control certain broad but critical aspects of the economy. These include the rate of employment and unemployment; the skill levels of the workforce; the rate of inflation, economic growth, and the money supply; and the relative shares which go either to profits for owners, salaries, for the middle element, and wages for workers. The distribution of the gains from productivity increases comes under this sort of planning too. In a Soviet-style economy both fine and coarse planning are done by the state. They try to get a much closer fit between the two. For instance, the amount, prices, and styles of women's shoes would be planned by the same agency which planned the rate of economic growth. But in our country there is a division of labor in planning. Government plans the coarse features of the economy, making sure the meadow is lush, well-watered and well-protected from wild beasts. But within the meadow, each company does what it wants, assured by a cooperative government that there's enough nourishing clover for all.

Here's an example. Formerly, when industry wanted to expand in a certain direction it had to pay higher than average wages in order to draw the top-flight worker with the necessary skills. Nowadays, through planning, capital can anticipate where it will need people. Through the government, foundations and schools, word is let out that such and such skills will be in demand. Students of all ages flood into those areas of study, often *paying their own way* so that when the jobs do open up there are more job-seekers than jobs. Through planning, industry gets the skills it needs, wages are kept down due to plenty of skilled job-seekers and, to top the whole thing off, the expenses of training don't come out of the pockets of industry, like in the old days.

The steady expansion of the *corporate sector* of the economy —this is the economic program of collective capital. That means the steady expansion of the size of the corporate sector, of its profits, of its ability to employ new technology and realize greater productivity, and of the big corporate and government bureaucracies. Don't be misled by the speeches that corporate leaders make when they complain about big government. What they're complaining about is that the social welfare budget is getting too big *at the expense of the government agencies and expenditures that help them.* Never a complaint will you get that the Commerce or Defense Departments are too big or about mineral subsidies, road subsidies, or the amount the government spends on interest going to the big banks.

When the corporate sector expands three things happen that strengthen collective capital's hold on the working class:

1) Their wealth and power expands and with it their ability to take on new activities, either through their companies or the government.

2) There is now plenty of money and opportunity which is used to pay off the middle element. New technology means new engineers, new products, new managers and new sales directors. High, expanding profits can be shared with the middle element in the generous fashion we observed at General Motors. So the antifriction class stays strong and prosperous—happy with the status quo and closely allied to collective capital.

3) The corporate sector working class grows and stays reasonably prosperous so that the division between corporate and competitive sector workers continues to deepen. Differences in pay, benefits and growth rates widen. Both the working class and the individual worker get the worst of both

worlds. The whole class is fundamentally divided and weakene And corporate sector workers more than pay for their ec nomically more privileged position. They are continually sacr ficed on the twin altars of “Higher Productivity” and “Changin Technology.” Speed-up turns workers into machines. Fum them, burn them, chemical them, asbestos them—whatever i needed to up production.

While corporate sector workers suffer the evils of high pr duction and Russian Roulette technology, competitive secto workers suffer the evils of low productivity and declinin industry—low pay, no benefits, seasonal and part-time wor run-away shops and no representation. The regular, norm economic program of collective capital fragments the workin class.

## Liberal Democracy

Along with this economic program is a political program liberal democracy. To understand liberal democracy we have t step back a moment and apply some ideas about groups, leader and cronies that we already know. Let's suppose you and I belon to a club of 100 members. And let's suppose that we want to ru that club. The usual way of doing this is as follows: First, we hav to go out and get a following—15-20 people who know and like u and will support us either out of friendship or because we'v promised them special favors after we get in. Now we're set fo step two. We have our two votes, yours and mine, and our friend are 15 more, which makes 17 in all. So we get involved in a election and *use the issues, any issues, in order to split the rest the vote.* You see, there are 83 people in the club who aren't in ou crowd. If we can split them in half—42-41—we can win th election 59-41. Even if we come out short in the split, say 38-4 we still will win 55-45. We can even lose the split badly, say 3 49, and we still win the election 51-49. Rule of thumb: Get following and then try to split the rest. If we've been active in you local, a club, or vestry or in local politics itself, we'll understan where *issues* come in and where they don't. Normally, we don depend on our stands on the issues to get and hold our *followin* We depend on friendship, flattery, promises. They support u because we'll use our office to *help them personally.* The other 8 support or don't support us because of how they think we'll use the office *to further the purposes of the club.* That's where issues come in. We pick any positions on the issues which are advantageous. Normally, we can forget our promises on issues after we're elected. But we can't forget our promises to our following because we want and need their support. That's the standard formula for getting and keeping office—accumulate a following and split the rest.

Let's say there's another leader around who also has a following. If it's possible, we should make a deal and combine forces. Here's why: If our rival's following is about 15 and we and our pals number 15, the election will be decided by the members and the issues, which from our standpoint means it will be decided by which brand of malarkey sounds best at the moment, ours or our rival's. It's better to make a deal. Now there will be three leaders and—the following is too big now! Too many favors. Cut it down. Come what may, we and our partner only need 15 or so assured votes to keep us in office just about forever.

That's particularly true if the club has members who don't even vote, like most clubs do. If only 60 people in all vote, we need only 13 out of 42, less than a third, to stay in office. (You and two other leaders and 15 followers gives us 18. If we get 13 more we'll have 31, a majority of the voting members.)

These are the rules of politics in a liberal democratic setup. 1) Get a following, 2) Use issues to divide the electorate, 3) Make deals with potential rivals. 4) Remember, apathy is on your side. It's cynical to say so, but also pretty true. On the other hand, liberal democracy is not the worst possible arrangement by any means. The very fact that the other 83 can vote means you've got to be careful not to rile them up so much that they'd unite against us. In addition, since they're not fools we have to do something for them while we're in office. They're wise enough not to expect much, but they do want something. If there were no elections, we and our following could do pretty much what we wanted. In a democracy there are limits and, as we know from looking at the rest of the world, that's a huge difference.

National politics in the U.S. works something like our little club. With just a few important facts we can even make a scale model of the *normal American electorate,* let's say, the presidential electorate. In our country, we have a two party system, and the two parties are evenly balanced. Since the election of Franklin Roosevelt in 1932, the Democrats have gotten a total of 359 million votes for the President, the Republican 347 million. That comes to Democrats 50.85%, Republicans 49.15%. It would be hard to come closer. In recent years, moreover, only about 60% of the electorate voted. The obvious question then is, out of every 100 eligible voters, why do 80 workers and 20 people from the other classes end up voting evenly, 30-30, for the Democrats and Republicans?

| 80 workers eligible | 20 other eligible |
|---|---|
| ? | ? |
| 30 votes Democratic | 30 votes Republican |

In any given election they don't even come out but over the long haul they do. And that's more important.

Well, we know that about 85% of the upper classes vote. That's 17. So only (60-17) = 43 workers vote, slightly more than half. Moreover, the upper classes vote tightly together—also by a measure of about 85%. They'll vote, 14-3, for their party, the Republicans. The other 16 Republican votes come from workers. Here's a pretty accurate picture of the normal presidential electorate:

| | Democratic Votes | Republican Votes |
|---|---|---|
| Workers | | |
| 80 workers are eligible but only 43 vote | 27 | 16 |
| Others | | |
| 20 others are eligible and 17 vote | 3 | 14 |
| | 30 | 30 |

In any specific election there will be a shift of a vote or so either way. But the long run balance of the electorate is more interesting and much more important. Let's look further into it. The workers vote 27-16 for the Democrats. But those workers' votes represent the votes of four different classes of workers, many with opposed interests. For the sake of the argument, let's say the vote looks like this:

| | |
|---|---|
| Corporate sector workers | 14 Dems. — 5 Reps. |
| Government sector workers | 6 Dems. — 3 Reps. |
| Competitive sector workers and Administered Sector workers | 7 Dems. — 8 Reps. |

The earlier numbers which we used are pretty accurate. hese numbers are crude estimates based on other information. hat is, we know corporate sector workers vote more often and iore liberally than any others. Using our numbers, while they iake up only about a third of the working part of the working lass, they are casting nearly half the worker votes, and they are oting more heavily Democratic (14 of 19 or 74%) than the thers. Government sector voters also vote more heavily than orkers generally, but probably not as one-sidedly. Thus they're iven 9 of the 43 worker votes and they vote only 6 of 9, 67% emocratic. Competitive sector workers and administered sector workers don't vote much and they don't vote one-sidedly.

We get the following:

| | Democratic Votes | Republican Votes |
|---|---|---|
| Workers | | |
| 80 workers are eligible but only 43 vote | 27 | 16 |
| Others | | |
| 20 others are eligible and 17 vote | 3 | 14 |
| | 30 | 30 |

here the workers' 43 votes breakdown like this:

14-5 corporate sector workers
6-3 government sector workers
7-8 administered sector workers and competitive sector workers

27 Democratic votes 16 Republican votes

For the Democrats to win the election, they have to hold ieir 14 corporate workers, 6 government workers, 7 other orkers, and 3 of the other class, plus get an extra vote omewhere. The problem, as we saw, is that the working class is ivided badly. If the Democrats do or promise something extra to ie corporate workers, to get them to vote 15-4 instead of 14-5, they may well lose a vote or more among the other classes c workers. Let's say the Democrats promise to repeal the Taft Hartley Act, which restricts unions. But that will antagoniz competitive sector workers and retired workers because man are convinced that without Taft-Hartley the unions will go craz with strikes, driving up wages, which will increase inflation eve more. So they may split 6-9 or 5-10, or perhaps one or two c those workers who don't vote at all will come out of the woodwor to save the Nation from Trade Union Bolshevism. Same thing i you steer money to the old or unemployed. That means highe taxes so any votes you pick up in one place you may lose in ar other.

The Republicans are in a slightly better position. Becaus they are in a minority, the middle element and entrepreneuria middle class who are the core of the Republicans know they ca only win by sticking together. Plus, they have to hustle 1 worker votes just to stay even. So even though the Reaganite and the Rockefellerites fight like hell in the convention they a vote together in November. Meanwhile they've mined every pos sible issue, from abortion to youth crime, to pull away ever worker they can. And they're often successful. The division c workers in the economy shows up in the election returns.

From the standpoint of the capitalist class, they're jus following the rules: 1) Get a following, the middle element, 2 Split the workers, 3) Make deals with possible rivals—the sma business class, and, to some extent with conservative workers, 4 Count on the apathy of the workers (almost half don't vote).

The Democrats get nearly all their votes from workers; 27 c 30 in this example. But look at the roster of Democrati presidents, governors, senators, congresspeople, legislator judges, and mayors. Rarely do you see a worker. Most Democrat ic big-wigs are middle element or small business people, with sprinkling of real upper class types—Kennedy, Roosevelt, Har riman. When I put down 14 Republicans—3 Democrats wit that little arrow showing 3 of the other classes voting Democrati we were also showing where all the leaders of the Democrati Party came from. *The working class is so divided that no one par of it can provide leadership for the rest.* Leaders must be draw from other classes but these other classes have a vital stake i keeping the workers divided. Thus, by means of liberal democracy, collective capital rules over us politically.

## A Humanist Social System

Collective capital strives for a humanist social system. What that means, in actual practice, is that the working class will have no independent social existence, that it will be socially and culturally captive. Think back to the time of George Pullman, whom we met during our discussion of Debs and the ARU. In that period of our country's history, as we saw, the working class was largely immigrants. For this and other reasons, workers lived apart from the rest of society, segregated into working-class tenements, not unlike the way many blacks and hispanics are segregated today. And their segregation was not just physical, but cultural and institutional as well. The schools made only half-hearted attempts to reach them. The churches, dominated by English-speaking clergy, or the previous wave of immigrants, often did little better. The government was content to limit its own contact to police harassment and an occasional arrest. But people cannot live without society. Life is much too complicated and unpredictable to be dealt with by unaided individuals or by separate families. Take children. You can't raise them from scratch. You need guidance and help to give you a general idea of what to try and what to avoid. In the same vein, your marital problems are not unique to you. Over time people have found ways to solve or live with them or, even better, to avoid them. With society, you can get the benefit of other people's experience in the form of morality, precepts, values, or examples. Then again you may be hurt, sick, unemployed. In a normal society there are ways in which others can help fill your place in terms of money, responsibility, and so on.

In the 19th century, the workers were cut off from society and denied its moral, financial, and other assistance. Their only alternative was to form their own society. By Debs' time the working class had developed networks and arrangements based on the family, the neighborhood, the trade unions and political clubs, their immigrant associations and, to a small extent, the churches. In other words, there evolved a separate society within American society.

There was a good side to this segregation. cut off from the influence of other classes, and not having to rely on their ideas, working class ideas and values began to have their own influence. Ideas of equality, cooperation, sticking together, the right of every person to share in both the goods and the responsibility to do and decide things. Socialist and Marxist ideas came in with the immigrants and like them mixed in with the native-born variety. It is this process of forming a separate society and becoming aware of that fact, that is called the formation of a class and the development of class consciousness. As we saw in an earlier chapter, the Knights of Labor deserve much of the credit for the formation of the working class in our country. For when Debs, Parsons, Jones, Swinton, or Haywood came to a working-class area and began talking politics, trade unionism or socialism, they weren't coming in to start a discussion among isolated individuals, who would hear and discuss the ideas only once, and have no chance to put them into practice. Debs and Parson were part of a *continuing* discussion, among people who were part of a separate society, a distinct class, who would continue discussing and organizing long after the speaker was on his or her way.

George Pullman tried to prevent all of this. So does collective capital today. But in order to prevent it, you have to integrate the worker into society under your rules and command. In 1894 that was the town of Pullman. Today it's the Welfare State.

Collective capital does not segregate its workers. On the contrary. In fact, it tries to integrate and control every aspect of working-class life. It has a negative and a positive reason for doing this. On the positive side, it wants to reach into the working class and pluck out some part of it—make sure it's healthy, educate and train it to create a pool from which to draw new recruits for the middle element and, most importantly, the corporate sector working class. Dynastic capital took its workers as it found them, used them up and threw them back on the ash heap. But collective capital, following Taylor's ideas, needs a more productive, reliable, trained worker to use in its high production industries. So it raises the average social productivity of part of the working classes. The rest of the class, the lower productivity folks who have lower educational and health vels, who are too old, etc., are left to the competitive sector. But n order to create that pool of available recruits capital has to ontrol the *social reproduction of the working class*. This is the ositive significance of that whole network of schools, medical nd social services, unemployment insurance, foundations, and elfare—what we call, loosely, the Welfare State.

It is here that we can see the essential humanism of the ocial system of collective capital. Capital wants the *best* of the orking population—the most trained, productive, healthy, menable people. A social system based on *hereditary* rights ouldn't do this since the qualities capital wants are found in very walk of life and level of society. To get the cream of the crop apital needs a meritocracy—where the most desired places are on on the basis of ability, or merit.

What we call meritocracy, when looked at from the side of apital, we call equality of opportunity, looked at from the side of veryone else. One can criticize this country for not having real quality of opportunity. But it is wrong not to see how equality of pportunity really is worked at by capital's social system. What lse is the point of schools, or colleges, or laws against dis-rimination, than to make sure that all of us will have to scramble or the best places? Then capital can pluck out the most uccessful scramblers, elevate them to privileged positions and uide their talents into improving the wealth, power and security f collective capital.

Now, I don't want to exaggerate the *extent* of equality of pportunity in this country, merely its *importance*. In fact, equality of opportunity" does not translate into social mobility. Iere's the actual situation:

| | Working Class | Middle and Upper |
|---|---|---|
| Present generation | 80 | 20 |
| of which | 6 go up | 6 fall |
| Next generation | 74 old + 6 new | 14 old + 6 new |

Out of every 20 upper and middle adults about 6 of their childrer fall out of their class and become workers. They're replaced by 6 workers' children. This arrangement for changing classes in eacl generation assures that:

1) the climbing part of the working class has a remote hope to get ahead (6 of 80),
2) the middle group is kept on its toes (6 of 20 will fail),
3) the talent of the middle and top (6 new faces who got there by scrambling) is constantly renewed,
4) the continuity of the upper group is maintained (14 are descended from the previous top group).

Whatever happens in each generation you'll preserve the clas system, which is most important of all. That's the positive side o capital's social system. The negative side is preventive. B moving in and controlling all aspects of working class life, yo prevent the growth of a separate society which can spawn Knights of Labor, an ARU, a Debs, Parsons or other opposition I call this effort at total control over the working-class and the individual *social taylorism.*

Here is the point to tie in two ideas we've met before and t come to grasp what I feel is the most profound and importan truth of our era. You'll recall earlier that the modern workin class is the first laboring class in history which has had th impulse to rule society. The history of the laboring people of th earth is a history filled with revolts, and attempts to revers injustice. But until the birth of the modern working class laboring people had always looked only to be ruled better b someone else—a kinder czar, an emperor who went to war less, king who demanded lower taxes. But from its beginning th working class has developed ideas of democracy, socialism, an classlessness which means they must run society themselves That's the first idea.

The second idea is this: When Debs and the America Railway Union took on and beat rail capital in 1894, they coul only be defeated by a military coup, Olney's coup, because o every other level—economic, moral, intellectual, and political— the working class had already come to be superior to dynasti capital. That's the real significance of the Pullman Strike an Boycott. It sounded the death knell for dynastic capital. Not onl here in this country. If capital was not prepared to radically reor ganize itself and change its relation to the rest of society, the workers, through their unions and socialist parties, were going to take the whole ball game away from them.

Well capital did reorganize. They started by forming the great trusts (= corporations) in the period 1895-1903. This began to collectivize their property. They used the wealth of these corporations to build up a new lieutenant and anti-friction class. And eventually a huge welfare state apparatus. From a politics of bribery and corruption they moved to class alliances which would enable them to control the essential behavior of both major parties and of society itself. What I'm saying is this: These changes had to be made to forestall the development of the working class into a rival of and successor to the capitalist class as the leading class in society. Capital understands, even if we don't, that the working class is now prepared to run society for itself. Every thrust of their civilization reveals that truth. The necessity to divide the working class by economic means into four separate classes. The necessity to ally itself with the corporate sector working class in one of the major parties in order to keep the class split. And social taylorism, the necessity, through the social system, to control the social reproduction of the working class lest some isolated segment of that class with flourishing native impulses might give rise, once more, to serious challenge to capital's domination.

## The Fundamental Truth

In all the industrial countries, the working class is now prepared to become the ruling class. This is the most significant fact of our era, a fact which is revealed in the very structure and design of modern capitalist civilization. And yet, when we actually look at the working class we see it is confused, divided, and leaderless.

It is very difficult to examine the capacity of the U.S. working class in these terms because the very thrust of the society we live in proclaims that the workers are the failed class, the group of people whose abilities and talents make them fit only to labor at mindless tasks. Within the dominant institutions of our society—the modern corporation—the three main functions are rigidly separated. Top management plans and judges, middle and lower management supervises, and workers work.

This separation of social labor: Planning and judging, supervising and laboring, is at the core of the philosophy of the corporation and permeates every aspect of collectivized capital's civilization. The three class set-up within the corporate system—collective capitalist, middle element, worker—corresponds to precisely that division of labor. As we've seen, the whole thrust of Taylorism is to remove every ounce of intelligence and thoughtfulness from the worker's work, and turn it over to different classes. The worker will not think, plan, judge, supervise or direct. Just work. Years ago the labor press published a cartoon entitled, "The Perfect Soldier." It showed a big strapping fellow, of massive size, with enormous muscles—and no head. In our time that cartoon could be called, "The Perfect Worker," because that is the way that our society views and treats workers. Those at and near the top in our country, the opinion-makers and leaders, believe we have a system of meritocracy, and equality of opportunity. But think a minute. What does it mean to be a worker where you have meritocracy or equality of opportunity? It means that you are a failure, one of those men and women who had their chance to do better but didn't measure up. To be a member of the working class means your talents and abilities fit you only to do menial work under the direction of others. This, of course, is a dirty side of capitalism, of capitalist humanism, a side which polite society people and glib liberals don't talk about. But they don't have to, it is proclaimed by the very structure of our civilization. The deepest prejudice of our society is this, namely, that workers are the failed class, the class of losers, the people whom meritocracy and equality of opportunity have relegated to the bottom. But then, in olden days, it was equally clear to everyone that the sun revolved around the earth, so clear that not even fools could deny it.

I stated earlier that the working class is now prepared to be the leading class in society. What evidence is there for that belief? To begin with you've got to realize what the working class of Debs' day accomplished, how it overcame the eight blows, how it bested capital in so many ways, and how close it came to toppling capital. So what is it about the working class today that makes it more likely to be successful than it was nearly a century ago?

First it is far larger. In the 1890's, the working class made up less than a third of the U.S. population. Today eight in ten Americans are in the working class. We are not only the largest class, we are the overwhelming majority in the whole country.

Second, the working class of Debs' day was deeply superstitious. That is, large numbers of workers had beliefs that weren't amenable to reasonableness and evidence. Religious superstition was widespread. Today one of the strongest currents we can observe is the pressure *by religious people on their own churches* to shed superstitious mumbo jumbo and contribute to the solution of the spiritual problems of modern life. In the 1890's deep racial superstitions were settling in among workers—it was the worst period of racial prejudice in the post-Civil War period. Today, I believe most workers, black and white, understand that the various peoples are and should be equal, and are willing to work at the problems that raises. Similarly with attitudes about women. Finally, the workers of Debs' day had many social superstitions about themselves, often inherited from a peasant past, at the time only a generation or so behind them. I think it's different today. Workers believe all sorts of things today, some odd, some not, some true, some false, some far out, some conservative. But the point is, they're reasonable beliefs responsive to argument and evidence.

That gets us to the final point. In Debs' day the working class movement was very, very dependent on a small corps of leaders, most of whom were not workers. That's generally been true of the workers', socialist and communist movements around the world. Marx, Lenin, Trotsky, Mao, LaSalle, MacDonald. In this country, De Leon, Berger, London and others were men from other classes, often the mercantile or rural classes. They saw their own classes being destroyed by capital and cast their lost with the working class because they were the most potent opposition to capital. But the dependence of workers on those other classes was fatal. Because when capital began to reform its own worst excesses, that old source of leaders for the working class dried up. That's one of the reasons the working class has been in the doldrums for so long and it will remain so as long as we wait for various Moses to come from the other classes and lead us to the promised land. When and as the working class movement re-emerges, events will bear me out that there are innumerable men and women, now ordinary workers, who have the mental,

moral, and spiritual capacities to assume responsibility in ever
area of human and social life. That's what I mean when I say tha
the working class is prepared to assume the leading place in
new society without essential reliance on any other class.

What sort of new society? What will it look like? How will
be run? Upon what program can we unite our class, now splin
tered by capital, to run such a society? We have to take thes
topics up in their turn.

# CHAPTER EIGHT
# WHAT SOCIALISM IS NOT!

A new society run by workers would be a socialist society. I mean working class socialism and not the other shoddy substitutes that falsely parade around under the socialist label. In fact, public discussion of socialism is so muddy that we could start by clearing up some of the confusion which surrounds the subject. Among these is the question of social incentives. After clearing that up we can talk about what socialism is *not* and then go on to talk about what it is.

## The Question of Incentives

There are people who say that society can't work unless there is a system of incentives to spur people on. Since socialism is supposed to be a system without incentives, it seems natural to these people to think that any dumb, messed up, or horrible way of doing things must somehow be connected to socialism. We should consider this question of incentives.

Under capitalism, things are set up so that only the upper class and the middle parts of society can get the incentives which are around. That word "middle" shouldn't fool us at this point since it means the upper 20% less the upper 1 or 2%. Thus in a multi-class society certain rewards are laid aside and reserved for those who are successful. The rewards include profits, big salaries, status, leisure, luxury, feelings of big accomplishment, fame, and so on. The whole point of this system of incentives is that they can go only to a minority. If the incentives were spread over the whole population, they wouldn't be incentives anymore—according to this theory. Because of our old friend equality of opportunity, everyone can get a *shot* at the incentives but not everyone can actually win them.

The idea is that only a few can be rich but if everyone has a chance to be rich they'll all work harder and we'll all benefit from the results. To most of us it sounds sensible since we all know how lazy we really are and, of course, others are lazier than us.

In fact, this is the dumbest theory ever put forward. To see why, just apply the theory to other areas. Suppose we only fed the 20% of chickens who laid the most eggs in order to give all chickens an incentive to lay more eggs. You're not going to get many eggs that way since unfed chickens don't lay them. Or suppose you only let the .300 hitters play baseball; then soon you'd have only two or three person teams.

The trouble with a so-called incentive system is that *80 out of 100 can't get the incentives.* You know that from the start. Of course, you don't know which 80 won't get them, or which 20 will. Or do you? Normally about two-thirds of the middle element kids stay in the middle element, while only about 6 in 80 working-class kids will climb into the middle element. Thus, if people know what's going on, 74 out of 80 workers should sit back on their butts because they're cut off from the incentives. They're like the chickens who aren't going to be fed. Since they're not going to get anything, why should they give anything?

Realize that there are only so many incentives. Come what may, only about 20 out of 100 people can get them. If I work twice as hard, I still may not get them, since when all is said and done, only the 20 who work hardest, get lucky, or are well born, can get the incentives. No matter what the other 80 do, they're not going to get them.

A system of real incentives would be set up so that every erson could get the incentives if they contributed to society, if hey really worked hard and did useful things. In such a setup, the umber who got the incentives wouldn't be fixed at 20 ahead of ime. If 90 put out, 90 would share the incentives. If only 70, then 0 would share and, if by chance 100 did the proper thing, then 00—everybody—would get in on the goodies. In this latter ystem, every man, woman, and child could truly say to themelves—if I do a good job, I'll be better off. And the rest of us ould be better off since nobody would really be in a position to ay—"Aw, what the hell. It's a stacked deck. They can shove their ork. I'm goin' fishin!"

The question of incentives turns on the question of classes. n a multi-class society, only a minority can get the incentives. hat, in fact, is a good *definition* of a multi-class society. Such a ociety puts everyone against everyone else, with winner take ll. It's a setup where there have to be losers—80 out of every 100 n fact. If you're going to keep them working hard in spite of this ou've got to trick them into believing falsely that they have a olid shot at winning. Socialism would offer incentives to verybody, not a shell game such as we have today.

## hat Socialism Is Not

There are other misconceptions about socialism. Many eople who call themselves "socialists" have terrible ideas about , so much so, that reasonable, thoughtful, intelligent workers orrectly will have nothing to do with "socialism." Therefore, I ant to start off our discussion by talking about what socialism sn't, to clear the decks, for discussion later of what it is.

Socialism is *not*

1. A theory—Karl Marx's or anybody's.
2. The dictatorship of the proletariat, or any other dictatorship.
3. A form of government as in "socialism, democracy and fascism."
4. Government ownership of the means of production.
5. A humane ideal.

Repeat—it is *not* any of those things. Let's take them in rder.

## 1. SOCIALISM IS NOT A THEORY—KARL MARX'S OR ANYBODY'S

When I was younger, school, magazines and t.v., got something like the following into my head: There was this scruffy bearded guy named Marx, who no sensible person could really understand, who sat theorizing and writing and was very angry. He cooked up a theory about the Thesis battling with the Antithesis to produce a Synthesis, which led him to predict that bloody socialist revolution would end capitalism and democracy one hundred years ago. All his predictions were wrong and all his ideas have since proved wrong. Even so he managed to persuade some people to his foolish ideas and he is a hero in Russia, China, Cuba, Vietnam and some other countries. All of this proves how dangerous windy theorizing can be and anyway Marx wasn't a worker and could never understand that workers want incentives.

Now if all that sounds jumbled, that's just the way it was in my mind. But in all that jumble a few things stood out: that socialism is a theory, that Marx was a big socialist theorizer, and that theories have to do with writing books. Part of that is right but very little.

Let's start with what a theory is. Normally a theory gets created this way: Someone thinks about something, writes it all down in a book. A few thousand, well-educated people read the book and like the theory and our theorist has a following. What the following has in common is that they liked the book, liked the ideas. Existentialism is a theory like this. It was thought up by Kierkegaard, a Danish writer. He put it in some books, the books attracted a following who call themselves existentialists. Evolution is a theory about nature, thought up basically by Darwin. Pointillism is a theory about painting. There are all kinds of theories, about science, about life, about art and about nonsense. Some are very popular like evolution. Some are good theories like the theory of the conservation of matter. Some are stupid like the capitalist theory of incentives. And some are vicious, like the theory of fascism or the theory of racial superiority.

Socialism is not a theory. Nobody thought it up and wrote a book. Socialist ideas and values go back thousands of years and are usually found among the poorer sort of people, the laboring people. In the 19th century, the word socialism became attached to certain ideas of the workers movement, ideas like cooperation, class solidarity, and an end to factory exploitation and the wage system. Nobody thought up those ideas and wrote a book spinning them out. These ideas grew up not among a few thousand educated people, but out of the experience of millions of mistreated, half-starved men and women who slaved like animals and who were trying to understand what was happening to them and how to change it.

That's a huge difference. A theory is thought up by someone usually more or less well off. He or she sits down in a quiet room and spins it out chapter by chapter, all very neat and orderly. Socialism is a set of ideas and values which first emerged as fragments in the minds and conversations of common people, at the bottom of a mine or next to a clanging loom. The ideas got shared and developed in snatches of guarded conversation in the tenements, taverns or jail cells. Later, much later, someone with a talent for analyzing and organizing ideas took all those scraps and pieces and tried to put them together in an orderly way to make sense out of them. That is where Marx or Babeuf or Gramsci comes in.

Socialism is the attempt by millions upon millions of laboring people, in all the countries of the globe, trying to understand their situation and to learn how to improve it. Socialism is not a theory, it is a movement. There are theories of socialism and theories to socialism but they come later, after the experiences and they represent attempts to make sense of those experiences.

Marx's writings and his life provide a perfect example of this process. In 1847 he was a reforming newspaper editor in western Germany, sympathetic to the rights of German workers whose organizations were at that time illegal and under police suppression. An underground workers organization, The German Communist League, asked him to write up their program for public presentation. This he did with his friend Frederick Engels. The result was the famous *Communist Manifesto.* The following year he participated in the wave of revolutions which passed through Germany and Europe. In fact, he was elected as the most important leader of the German revolutionary and democratic forces. Upon their defeat, he was forced to flee to Belgium and then to Paris. Eventually, because of his activities in the workers and revolutionary movement, he was exiled to London where he spent the next 34 years in exile, until his death in 1883.

During those three and one-half decades Marx divided his time between two chores. He studied the capitalist system in order to understand it and thereby find a way for the workers movement to overthrow it. Simultaneously, he plunged into organizational work for the German Communist League, and later for the International Working Men's Association, which he had founded in 1864. It was an association of the working-class organizations of each of the industrial countries. Throughout the 50's, 60's and 70's, he was in constant correspondence with workers organizations in all the countries, an activity which kept him well informed of developments in the movement.

Marx was not a worker by origin. He was from the tiny class of entrepreneurial professionals. But from 1847 to the end of his life, his only occupation was as a leader and participant in the international workers movement where he had a reputation as an extremely able organizer. His writings, even the most abstract, are disciplined and directed by this participation. As he once wrote, "The philosophers have only interpreted the world in various ways; the point however, is to change it." He certainly took his own advice. His influence on our ideas of economics, politics, society, history, or morals, is so profound, so widespread that even those who hate him most have a little Marxism in their ideas.

Many socialists and Marxists argue that Marx is important because he was such a genius. There is no doubt that he was a very able man, a giant on a par with Shakespeare, Dante, Lao-tse, Newton. But he was no smarter than them. What makes Marx so important—even as a theorist—is something very different than smartness. Marx was the first of the real giants to cross over the class lines, from the educated classes to the working class, and view the world through the workers eyes. He looked at oppression as it landed on the worker; he saw poverty as a poor man. An Adam Smith or a Lord Keynes see the world from the standpoint of the property-owning classes, from above, where things are prettied up. They address themselves to bankers, kings, statesmen, or other economists. They say, "Here is the situation as it is and here is what you should do." The people who read heir stuff, if they want to do anything, just do it—by telephonng like-minded biggies, passing a law or investing some money. 'hat's all they have to do because the whole society is, so to peak, geared up and waiting for their call, their law, their nvestment.

Marx addressed himself to a people in captivity, each isoated and powerless. It was never enough for him to say, "Do this, o that!" It would be like me telling you "Pass a law, build a steel lant, make peace with Russia." You're no senator, passing a law or you isn't a matter of saying yes or no. You can't build a steel lant by writing a check or make peace with Russia by signing a reaty.

For you or for any other worker, before you can do anything, ou have to start from scratch and talk to people. You've got to ersuade them not to be so discouraged and get them together in group. Then you've got to show them that a course of action hich you recommend will strengthen the group so that at a ertain point it can do what it wants to do. It's not easy. People nay not even know what they want until they feel their own trength and solidarity.

The difference between the two situations is enormous. Vhen you address yourself to the upper classes of society you an do so, confident that they have the instruments to act ready t hand: parties, corporations, courts, senates, or newspapers. 'hey just choose objectives and go to work. For a Marx, or me or ou, we have to build the instruments even as we pursue the bjectives. If we fail with the instruments, the objectives will emain a pipe dream. And for us the instruments are always *oluntary* organizations of people who have to be *persuaded and mboldened.* Marx couldn't have been a windy theorizer. His ooks long since would have been forgotten. His ideas became uccessful because, embodied in organizations of working peole, they help workers to understand their situation and move orward to improve it.

You may not agree with socialism but it's important to nderstand what it is. It is the historical movement of the working class. Not a theory, not an ism, not an idea. A movement. ocialism is something which was formulated by workers, eveloped by workers, tested by workers, often loved and ometimes hated by workers. Anyone who comes along spouting something they call socialism—if what they're talking about isn't of the workers, by the workers and for the workers, then it isn't socialism, no matter how socialist it sounds. And it isn't worth a damn.

## 2. SOCIALISM IS NOT A DICTATORSHIP OF THE PROLETARIAT OR ANYONE ELSE.

Until the 20th century, people who called themselves socialists were democrats; they believed in and defended what we call liberal democracy. In fact, during most of the nineteenth century socialists were the main defenders of liberal democracy against the reactionary alliance that capitalists had with thrones, aristocrats, bishops and slaveholders. But then came Lenin with his theory of the vanguard party, and the connections between socialism and democracy got a little blurred. For Lenin, the party represented the most class conscious workers and therefore the whole working class. When the party thought or wanted something—bingo—the working class thought that, or wanted that, or should think or want it. Lenin's theory, which obviously has some holes in it wasn't well-received at the time among socialists. But after World War I, when the socialists of all countries were being defeated by capital, Lenin won in Russia. As you know, success has a way of covering up for bad arguments. Since then socialism has been more or less identified with the dictatorial rule of a party which claims to represent the interests of workers. Their real interests—as opposed to the ones they only think they have. The socialists who agree with Lenin called themselves communists.

In the Soviet Union and most other communist countries they have what they call the "dictatorship of the proletariat." Whether it's "of the proletariat" there is some doubt, but there is certainly no question about the dictatorship. Since the U.S. press is very good at reporting the warts on others' faces, there is no need to go into the gory details of Soviet dictatorship.

The thing that interests me is the fact that in the Soviet Union the party is politically active and the rest of the country is politically inert. That's an important formula; the party is active, everyone else is inert. That situation is just as Lenin intended it. Lenin's defenders say that he wouldn't approve of present day Soviet practice, which I'm sure is true. But his objection would b that the party wasn't political in enough ways and in the right ways. Lenin would like more debate and differences—but only within the Communist Party.

The fundamental idea of the vanguard party is that it should absorb all the politically active people, so that all the creative political activity and leadership goes on in the party. The rest of the country just follows. This relation between the party and the people is identical to the relation between a ruling class and a ruled class—one an active monopoly of political leadership containing all political people, the other an inert mass. We see this in the Soviet Union where the party has become the germ of a new ruling class. In Lenin's day, that ruling class was pretty responsible and dedicated in its work and didn't hog all the goodies the way ruling classes usually do. I don't think that holds anymore.

It would take us too far afield to point out all the similarities between our ruling class, based in the corporation, and the Soviet ruling class, based in the Communist Party. Both are collectivized ruling classes, willing and able to create a whole civilization—economics, politics, culture, morals, the whole shebang. The Soviet system of rewarding its bosses through bonuses for reaching production goals works out exactly the way our management stock-option plans work out. The existence of this ruling class leads some people to say that the Soviet Union is or is becoming a capitalist society. That is a big question so let me duck it for now. What we can't duck however is the fact that the dictatorship of the proletariat leads right into a multi-class society and socialists should rid themselves of it.

Socialism is the historical movement for the emancipation of the working class. Always, its cutting edge has been the attack on a multi-class setup. Equality is its middle name. We've had enough experience now to see where this dictatorship of the proletariat business leads the socialist movement: if not into the cruelties of Stalin then merely the heavy-handed way of Brezhnev and his cronies.

Marx favored a dictatorship of the proletariat but his meaning is so different from Lenin's that they deserve different names. In Marx's view, present day society is a dictatorship of the capitalist class. The phrase is bombastic but its meaning is simple enough: everything is set up so that the decisive power belongs to capital. They have the edge in everything—economics, politics, society, law, manners, morals, culture, you name it. For Marx, dictatorship of the proletariat means—reverse that! He did not mean a dictatorship in the modern meaning of the term—a relation of a small ruling class over the working class. He meant the rule of the working class for itself without compromise with other classes.

Marx didn't write all that much about politics; he was more interested in history, economics and society rather than government and narrow government matters. But during his lifetime a workers government was set up in Paris and he wrote some interesting things about it.

In 1870 the German leader Bismarck goaded France into declaring war on Germany. The French under Napoleon III, nephew of the great Napoleon, were shamelessly unprepared—corruption and ineptitude being a mark of the regime. In early 1871 they were forced into a humiliating peace by Bismarck. But the workers of Paris refused to accept the defeat. They rose in arms, seized the city and organized a commune to govern themselves. Marx had been very close to the workers movement in Paris. He tried to leave England and join in the defense of the Paris Commune but was prevented from leaving by the British authorities. Denied the use of the sword, he took up his pen to defend the workers government against the lies of the respectable press. His articles on the Commune are gathered together under the title, *The Civil War In France*. They are well worth reading. For our purpose a few points will suffice to give his views on *the nature of government under the working class's so-called dictatorship.*

The Commune was governed by a council elected by universal suffrage. Frequently the council members were *instructed* on how to vote by the voters. Their terms were short and they could be removed by their constituents at any time. Marx dwells on how important this recall was for it kept the government from transforming itself from a servant of society into its master.

The Commune was not a legislative body only but a combined legislative and executive body responsible for carrying on the tasks of governing and defending Paris. Council members could not hide behind executive secrecy or legislative B.S. to isguise what they were doing. Everything they did was under he noses of the citizenry. And they had to answer for it.

The power of the police and the courts were severely estricted. For the first time the schools were open to everyone.

All public employees—including officials—were either vorkers or the representatives of workers and they carried out heir duties at workers' wages. The plan of the Commune was hat every area of France was to be self-governing.

The Commune was proclaimed on March 18, 1871. It held ut until May 28, 1871 when a French army, armed by Bismarck, orcibly re-occupied Paris. Wholesale executions and deporta-ions of the Paris working class followed. It is not clear whether he Commune was a workable model of government for a modern tate, but it is certainly clear that Marx's dictatorship of the roletariat has nothing, repeat nothing, in common with the ractice of the modern communist dictatorships.

Socialism is the movement for the emancipation of working eople from the fetters of authoritarian government. This means very kind of authoritarian government—of the left, the right, the enter; of capitalist, of communist; of church; of state; of orporation; of expert; and of zealot.

Not every group of people can be free and govern them-elves. An ignorant people cannot. A superstitious people annot. As we know, to govern even our own personal lives is not asy. It calls for wisdom, foresight, restraint, the ability to erceive mistakes before they go too far and a willingness to orrect them. It's the same with group life. In many of the non-ndustrial countries there are large classes of people who are gnorant of the modern world, superstitious and provincial in heir outlook. Notice that I say *classes*. A Nigerian peasant is just s smart as a Detroit worker. If he or she doesn't know something e or she can learn it just as quickly as you or I. But a class of easants or a class of small merchants or entrepreneurial armers cannot learn self rule. They are so infected with class ackwardness, class superstition that they'll normally fall prey to nother class which will rule them.

But in all the industrial countries, especially in the U.S., the vorking class is developed enough to govern itself. It has the bility, the experience, the reservoir of talent to govern in its own ame to win socialism. There was no earthly excuse to prevent this, leastwise the Leninist doctrine of the dictatorship of th proletariat. Socialism means working-class self-rule, or it simpl is no improvement over what we have.

## 3. SOCIALISM IS NOT A FORM OF GOVERNMEN

There are many people who think socialism is just anoth form of government or a matter of electing into office some part which calls itself socialist. But you can see already from wha little has been said about socialism, that it is a much bigger thir than a simple change of government or a new crowd in the offic

Socialism is a revolutionary movement for working class se rule. Unfortunately the word revolution is all tied up in our minc with the act of insurrection. Talk revolution to people and the think of riots, shooting, civil war. And since in any rio insurrection or war, most of the people who get hurt are worker working-class people are very unhappy with talk of revolutio Let's start from scratch on the word revolution then.

To have a revolution means to have a fundamental alteratic of society, a basic change in the class setup. Take France. Befo the French revolution, French society was dominated by th aristocracy, which shared power with the church. This rulir class encouraged a society in which the vast multitude of peop were farmers—peasants in particular. They discouraged th growth of the class of capitalist industrialists; that is, the wanted it to grow only within the limits set by a primari agricultural society, led by a land-owning aristocracy. The ma prizes—wealth, power and status—they reserved for ther selves. Finally, they kept a check on the growth of the workir class by checking the power of the capitalists. When the du settled after the French Revolution a very different arrangeme presented itself to the eye. The capitalists were now the fir class of society, they had the main prizes of wealth, power ar status with the aristocrats pushed down into second place. Tl capitalists encouraged the growth of the working class at tl expense of the peasants; after all, capitalists make money c workers, not peasants. Post-revolutionary France was industri not agricultural; cities grew, the countryside declined in impo tance. There were new values and ideas too. The aristocra thought making money wasn't terribly nice but they did like spend it, especially for show—clothes, castles, horses, wine balls and entertainment. The new capitalists made money in order to make more money—to grow their money, to invest. Their pleasures were somewhat less expensive. We in the U.S. are so embedded in a capitalist society that we don't appreciate how different a pre-capitalist or pre-industrial society really is. For us, aristocratic airs and peasant superstition are matters of curiosity. It's hard to imagine a society designed around them.

Likewise, it's hard to imagine a society without classes, the revolution which socialists have always aimed at. We just accept the fact that some classes have vast wealth, easy access to the most interesting work, lots of influence and confidence in their ability to do what they please, together or individually. What would it be like for your children to live a life where they were always consulted on important decisions? Or where the work of a sanitation worker was treated with as much respect as that of a lawyer? Hard to imagine! But two hundred years ago, capitalists were treated with disdain by the aristocrats. A merchant, even if he was rich, might be kept waiting in the kitchen until their noble lordships were ready for him to come in, bow and scrape, make himself humble, and hopefully make a sale. Nowadays we wait, bow and scrape, and hope for the favor of our masters.

The socialist revolution would change that. Our children and their children would live in a world as different as ours is from that old aristocratic world. Notice it's not a question of our children having a chance at the good things of life. They have that now, though as we've seen it's not such a good chance. With socialism our children would actually have the good things of life, not just a chance at them. That would be a revolution. Socialism is a movement for a society without classes, for a society where all the good things are not reserved for the top two percent or the top twenty percent but are more or less spread out. Incentives for all, not a few. Respect for what you do for all useful employments, not just a few.

Socialism is not a utopian view. There will be problems under socialism but they'll be different ones than now. Some workers are more key to the production of things than others. How will we prevent them from getting extra power or wealth because of it? Some parts of the country are richer in resources than others; same problem. Some work, like coal mining, is more dangerous than others; how will you get people to do it—money, regimentation, appeals to duty? Racial and gender prejudice won't die just because capitalism goes the way of feudalism. How do we eliminate it?

What socialism will really mean for us is that certain unsolvable, unimprovable situations which we now have to bear will be done away with and we'll be free to work at the real problems of a modern society. For example, under capitalism people are controlled by the machinery of production. Talk all you like about human relations in industry, your job is to produce in rhythm to the machine. If musak helps, then musak. Soft soap? Then soft soap. Harsh discipline? Then harsh discipline. The problems of boredom, overwork, dangerous conditions, lack of purpose to our work, unemployment, employment in socially useless work—these and others cannot be solved under capitalism. Two whole classes of society, the ruling class and their creature, the middle element, must keep us producing, they have no other reason for existing than that. Therefore not only can't you solve the problems of human beings in modern industry, you can't even begin to deal with them. Socialism won't solve these problems either. It will, however, allow *us* to deal with them. Then it's up to us to be smart enough to solve them. But the classes who created them will be gone.

Our capitalist society is like a bus with a crazy driver who is forever running into things—like other countries, or depressions. The driving is somewhat better than it used to be but we still always get lost. The bus is in terrible repair. There are sharp edges everywhere, the rain leaks in, the fumes are overwhelming. Recently air conditioning was put in, but the springs still pop up from unrepaired seats and the whole thing is a fire trap. Before, we didn't know how to drive, or anything about keeping machinery in repair; now we do. Throwing that wild driver off won't insure a good ride. It will only make it possible for *us* to have a try at making a good, safe, comfortable ride to new places. That's a big improvement but by no means a utopia.

Same thing in politics and in social life. There are terrible problems around in having a democratic society of two-hundred-odd million people. Bringing up kids, getting along with each other, living in cities, keeping insects down, getting wholesome food, finding a place in society for old people, defeating bureaucracy, making life fun and pleasant. Two whole classes have a ested interest in our not solving these problems and in prevent-ıg anyone else from solving them. For us, socialism means hucking these troublemakers to one side so we can have a go at olving these overdue and worsening problems.

If socialism meant instead adding the problems of, say, ussian society to ours, or creating a whole new layer of ureaucrats to sit on our heads—forget it. Anyone who wants ıat is crazy.

## 4. SOCIALISM IS NOT GOVERNMENT OWNERSHIP OF THE MEANS OF PRODUCTION

This is a complicated problem but the answer to it is simple. Ve don't want it. Nonetheless, until very recently, socialists of all izes and varieties have been for extensive government ownerhip and nationalization. Why is that and why the change?

In Debs' time the most obvious fault of capitalism was its haos and the cause of the chaos was the savage competition etween the capitalist families. Trying to steal a march on one nother, each capitalist overproduced which glutted the market. o a crash followed and then several years of slow, painful ecovery. This happened over and over again; in 1807, 1823, 831, 1837, 1848, 1857, 1873, 1884, 1893, 1907, 1914, 1921, 1929, 938, 1949, 1957, 1973.

As the old time socialists looked at this cycle of boom and ust it seemed imperative to them to put an end to it. But what ould end the boom and bust? Clearly, only the power of overnment which could administer the economy. In good times ıe government could hold the boom in check and in bad times it ould keep a floor under the bust. But to do that the government ould have to take over the economy and manage it. Administer .

Many socialists, particularly those from the higher classes, egan to think that they could persuade capital to let them run ıe economy more efficiently. No need, they said, to have a loody revolution. We'll show them that we socialists, with the cientific organization of society, can do such a good job that oth capital and labor will be better off. Collective capital, unlike ıe dog-eat-dog dynastic kind, had a ready answer, "Don't call s, we'll call you, we're quite ready and willing to introduce our wn scientific organization of society." And that's exactly what ıey've done.

That, in a nutshell, is the origin of the welfare state. It tries t compensate for the sins of capitalism. Instead now of having fu employment for everybody all the time we get unemploymen insurance—a good step but only a halfway measure. The sam thing is true of old age plans, health plans, social work plans, slu clearance and so forth. Collective capital taxes us for the mone to put band-aids on these problems. In so doing, it finds it has t take control of everything.

In our day it is clear that the main problem of the economy i not chaos but order. Our economy is deliberately controlled an managed by collective capital to advance its own interests. T substitute government ownership for corporate ownershi would change nothing. We'd still have a three class society. A the top, government officials would sit around like corporat officials do now and plan policy. Government middle elemen instead of a corporate middle element would carry out thos plans by administering us. We'd advance to where the Sovie Union is now. Some advance.

As for government ownership of this or that, those of us wh work for the government know that in some respects it is harde there for the worker than in private industry. Government bosse are much more difficult to get at than private ones. They don' need you when you work for them, you need them. If you strik they make it illegal and put you in jail while fining the pants o you.

Actually, many times the capitalists themselves call fo nationalization. This usually happens in two cases. If the worker in an industry are too militant, the private capitalist will be gla to get nationalized, provided the price is right. In this way thes demanding workers find they are no longer confronting th "rights of property" but "law and order," "public authority," " society of laws rather than of men." This is what happened to th British coal miners who, even with a Labour government i power, have to watch their step more than if the coal industry wa private. Don't forget here that in our country only the government can get away with using strike breakers anymore. Remember the postal strike a few years ago when they called in th National Guard to move the mail.

The other instance where the capitalists favor nationalization is when some company or industry is a dog, a loser. The they love to unload the company or the industry on the government at a fancy price, trading in their worthless stocks for new guaranteed interest-bearing bonds. That's how many of our cities acquired their rapid transit systems. The British steel industry was once palmed off in this way.

Socialists who call for government ownership of the means of production are really assuming that under socialism the workers will have less economic power than now but so much more political power that it will more than make up for it. Everyone knows it's hard to win a strike against government. It would be even harder to win one against a socialist government which would claim that it represented the working class and society, while the striking workers were being disruptive and greedy and a special interest. But, say our socialists, the working class would have such overwhelming political power that it could easily give up the right to strike.

I think that's the wrong approach. Socialism means getting new things, new rights, new freedoms, new privileges. It doesn't mean you give up what you already have. We give up no rights we now have. We only add new ones. In that sense, government ownership is a bad idea and we don't want it.

But if we don't want dynastic capital's chaos or the suffocation of collective capital or government, what do we want? Here again socialism isn't a utopian scheme. It merely clears the deck for the working class to solve these problems. Socialism says: Look, we know how lousy these old ways are, we know the kinds of problems they cause. Let's see if the experience and practical intelligence of our class can't solve the problems. We can't do worse because no vested interest in the working class has a stake in doing things worse. We can only do better. How much better? That depends on our intelligence, and ingenuity. Less than that we don't want, more than that we don't need.

How would industry be run under socialism? It would be run by the mass of workers in each plant rather than by a few managers. Workers, in meetings, would have to decide all questions of modern plant and industrial life. We would apply different ideas of usefulness to the items we produced. We'd aim at much higher quality levels. We'd make the health and safety of workers a top priority. We'd arrange production schedules to fit our family, personal and other needs. What would be similar to what we have now is that the economic system would have no central controlling apparatus. Recall that collective capital, because its interests are so bound up together, has no need of a central management committee. Tightly centralized at the level of policy and interests, the administrative setup can be quite decentralized. Just so for us. Once we have recognized standards of performance, agreed upon ideas about what is important and what is harmful, considerable latitude can be left to local management (that will also be us) to make decisions.

Running industry is no easy task and this little discussion hardly does justice to the subject. I really just wanted to make one main point: top-heavy central apparatus is not necessary to run industry. Collective capital already shows how an integrated, coordinated economy can be managed with considerable decentralization. Modern capitalists are right. They've proved that their way is superior to government ownership. We should be grateful for the lesson and press on to the next step, namely, how do we create workers' socialism, instead of the bureaucratic kind.

## 5. SOCIALISM IS NOT *A* HUMANE IDEAL

If you think about it, it's apparent that most of the men and women who ever lived had poor lives, lives of deprivation and unnecessary suffering. From the beginning of recorded history until several centuries after Christ, most people were slaves. Writers love to describe the glories of Greek civilization, for example, especially at Athens where democracy and art flourished. But that was for maybe two in ten. The other eight were slaves, chained for life to the naval galleys, subject to the whip, where death was a blessing. Athens' other slaves worked in the silver mines. Even today working in a mine is very dangerous. Imagine what it was like for slaves before there was modern equipment—ventilators and elevators—and before there was modern medicine to pick up some of the pieces for the callous mine owners.

For generation after generation for thousands of years, the vast majority of people who have ever lived were born in poverty and spent their lives working like donkeys so that a handful of parasites could live fat foolish lives. They were subject to the whip and chains, finally to die, often young, never having tasted much by way of accomplishment, never having lifted their heads in the pride of equality, never really having had full human lives.

'he problem with what I'm saying here is that I haven't exaggerated—slavery, serfdom, rural poverty, immigration, wage lavery—these have been the common lot of common people, ince the dawn of recorded history.

There are improvements now for many people in the indusrial countries. Life is better now but is still so much less rewardng than people deserve. I think most people are pretty admirble, they work hard and they mean well, they follow the path of uty which life imposes on them, and they don't complain all that nuch. But think about the people you've known. So and so loved o travel but never could, loved to read but worked so hard he ever had the time, loved the outdoors but was always shut up nside. This one was a natural leader but only her family had the enefit of her abilities, that one could have been a poet and this ne was a natural storyteller. I'm sure you've seen these things, ow much human talent and understanding people really have nd how little they're able to use.

Several years ago I was able to visit revolutionary Cuba. Being there underlined many of these things for me, especially he experience of meeting two or three particular individuals. One, a woman named I ________, came from an extremely vealthy family. Had there been no revolution in Cuba she would ave been brought up as a proper upper class girl, married off at he proper time in order to make children. Like so many other vomen of her class, that would have been all that was asked of er. Since no more was asked or permitted, she would have rown mentally listless and stupid, one of those women who, ecause no one listens to them, don't pay much attention to what hey say, chattering aimlessly or foolishly out of the emptiness nd frustration of their lives. But unlike other young women of er class I ________ had become active in the revolution and vhen I met her she had a number of responsibilities, not huge nes—she wasn't a big official—but her life was varied and hallenging. She was not without problems but they were the ind of problems from which she'd grow, not be defeated into umbness. Had there been no revolution and had I met ________, no doubt I would have thought, what an aimless, oolish person, lacking purpose to her life and destined to grow ver more aimless and foolish to the end of her days. Yet the very ame woman, by a change of circumstance, is today living a full and challenging life, contributing her talents and abilities to the vast changes now going on in her country.

I met another woman there who had been a prostitute in Havana. Not a fancy prostitute, but a streetwalker. When I met her she headed a construction gang at the other end of the island. As I talked to her I thought of the fate that probably would have been in store for her: drugs, disease, beatings, arrest: growing cynicism and depravity as the path of her life forced her into the lowest depths of Havana street life. Then a stabbing or an overdose or TB or an old age of begging and abuse. Instead she was wisecracking, bragging of her skill with the front end loader, proud of her hardhat and of the project she was working on.

For both of these women life was still difficult. It always is; if it's not one thing, it's another. But their lives were good lives. They were accomplishing things and enjoyed the pride of that accomplishment and the esteem that others had for them as a result of it. Even the difficulties of their lives were better because they were the kind of difficulties which called for new talent, new effort, new accomplishments. They weren't the kind of difficulties which defeat us and leave us numb with hopeless exhaustion.

Nowadays when I meet a foolish aimless person I often wonder about the other person inside them, the steady, thoughtful person who would be called forth from them if the circumstances of their lives were different. Every person has so much more to offer than ever will be asked of them.

The biggest unused resource of all is human talent and ability. Almost all of it is in the working class—the 80%—that group whose backs and hands are exploited and whose minds and souls are left to rot from neglect or abuse.

Capitalism, especially today's three class type—capitalist ruler, middle element manager, obedient worker—is the world's most inefficient system of using people. Worse, its whole point is not to use the humanity in people, the pool of talent, the reservoir of thoughtfulness, the sea of perception, the vast ocean of ingenuity and goodwill which people have. More and more a worker cannot be a human being except in the private moments of his or her life.

That's why I say socialism is not *a* humane ideal. It is *the* humane ideal. Kindness to animals is a humane ideal, wholesome food for all is a humane ideal, but socialism puts forward the notion that every single man and woman should lead a life of accomplishment, dignity and satisfaction. Again it's not the idea that everyone should have a chance at such a life but that they should actually have it.

There is many a slip twixt the cup and the lip. Having the ideal doesn't bring the reality. In our time, having socialism only means getting rid of the ideas, institutions and especially classes which cannot co-exist with people who use their god-given talents and abilities. A ruling class is a class which has a monopoly on rule; thinking, planning, and directing. The middle element is a class which has a monopoly on professional pursuits, on technical accomplishment and administering us with their ideas, machinery, processes, and systems. Our job is to work, do what we are told, keep our thoughts to ourselves, remain half-men, half-women, half-human. Socialism breaks that system down. It opens the way to replacing it with something better.

The vast infinite moral superiority of socialism over all other ideals is just this: only socialism says yes for everyone, the good life for everyone. Not just for some. And not just a chance.

In previous eras the socialist ideal was utopian—meaning it was impossible to realize. The slaves who revolted with Spartacus in ancient Rome had the socialist ideal but they could never have put it into practice. They needed a ruling class because their condition of life was such that they knew nothing about running a society. Similarly in the German peasant revolts of the early 1500's Thomas Munzer and his followers had the ideal but couldn't even run society in the old way, much less the new, more difficult way. The Communards in Paris one hundred years ago had the ideal but not the ability. Today's working class is different because collective capital has created our ability to rule. It has changed the utopian ideal of socialism into a practical reality.

# CHAPTER NINE
# WORKING CLASS SOCIALISM

We've already answered the question: what is socialism? It is the historical movement of the laboring people to understand and improve their own situation. In the present period it is the movement of the working class. It is a movement which grows out of the whole class and not from the brainstorms of a few gifted or privileged leaders. Its practical aim and ideal is to build a new revolutionary society conducive to a good life for each person. It rises or falls on the ability of the working class to shed its dependency on every other class and proceed directly to organize society in the interest of every person. If that's so, then where are all the socialists and in our country why are the people who call themselves socialists usually from another class?

The society built by collective capital is designed to be *worker-proof.* Every effort is made to prevent workers from even thinking that they can change things. Every effort is made to mock, distort, discredit, and misrepresent socialist ideas and the history of our own class. This effort is so effective that since World War I collective capital has been able to break the historical continuity of the working class and replace it with the radical isolation of the individual worker. But the moral force o socialist ideals is so strong that those classes which are permitte to experience them are often influenced by them. Young peopl of all classes have a natural love of justice. Many of them see th justice and humanity in the socialist tradition, especially as compares to the shallow, shoddy ideals of capitalist societ They find writers like Marx who are so imbued with a love of th people, and not just an elite few, that they have the most powe ful insights into the society. But workers are very mistrustful o other classes. When they see young people of the upper class o middle element attracted to Marx or Gramsci or Debs they ar turned off from Marx, Gramsci and Debs because it seems t confirm what they've been told, namely, that Marxism is a devic for the intelligentsia to manipulate workers. At the same time th class experience of these privileged young people is such tha they really miss the point of Marx and the others. They come t like his ideas more than the purposes those ideas were to serv They love the more philosophical and theoretical parts of Mar and they do not see him as a man who cared only for one singl thing: the emancipation of the working class. Often these youn people are attracted more to Lenin and his followers than t Marx and are flattered by Lenin's idea of the vanguard whic they take to be themselves, naturally.

## Who Are the Socialists?

If we want to find the socialists among working peopl they're not going to be walking around calling themselves socia ists. But their identity is apparent. The man or woman who love the working class and is loyal to it is a socialist. The ideas the have on the subject of socialism really don't matter at this poin all that matters is that a man or woman loves the working class, loyal to its interests, and wants or tries to improve the conditio of any part of it. On that basis they'll find it easy to recover th experiences and ideas of the socialist tradition. Without i impossible. Impossible.

I don't think I have ever worked in a place without meetin several people just like that. They were socialists though the didn't know it. Rarely, if ever, were they people who made radic noises, who spoke Marxist ideas or read socialist books. They' be the kind of person, familiar to all of us, who followed events in the paper or on t.v., who always seemed to see things from the angle of the working class, who was more thoughtful about these things than the average person. There are hundreds of thousands of these people around the country, perhaps even a million or more. They don't know about each other, they aren't working together, and they don't have that extra strength which comes from knowing that what you're doing is being indirectly helped by what I'm doing, he's doing, she's doing. One of the first practical imperatives for the coming movement of the working class is to start to get these people in touch with each other. These thousands upon thousands of working-class socialists have to come together in a spirit of "I'd like to meet you and share experiences with you and talk about our common problems."

Most, though not all of these people are in the labor movement. They're the ones who send out the meeting notices, set up the hall, make the coffee and clean up afterwards. They're the ones who take over the shop stewardship and work hard and well at it because they feel they owe it to other workers and to their class to do so. They're the ones who love the union because it represents an assertion of working-class intelligence and strength. They're the ones who are troubled over the declining strength of the unions and who spend the time and energy trying to improve and strengthen them. They're the ones who other workers respect because they see in them the sort of men and women all workers can be—thoughtful, class conscious, willing to stand up for their rights and the rights of others, willing to put some effort in rather than just complain.

They're only one in a hundred. But even so there's a quarter million of them. That's a very large group. They're spread by ones and twos through as many shops and locals in the country. They already have the respect of their fellow workers. They are *potentially* a very formidable group. There are at least another half-million men and women just like them but not in the labor movement. If the labor movement socialists ever began to come together and make their influence felt they would soon attract the other group to their banner. Then, capital would have something to worry about. And we'd have something to cheer about.

Many socialists think socialism is an ideal you hit upon only if you're well-educated. That's the "theory" idea of it which we've talked about. For them, as for Lenin, workers left to their own devices will at best just form trade unions, certainly never make socialism or a socialist revolution. This sort of socialist simply doesn't understand the true relation of socialism to the working class. Socialism is as natural to workers as cheating is to storekeepers. It is present in every worker, sometimes only in the dissatisfaction he or she feels with life, sometimes only in secret, or in distorted forms, which appear to be something else but which reveal their socialist content when you analyze them further.

In some circles it is fashionable to make fun, for example, of the patriotism so often found among workers. Now there is no doubt that we have some fatheads in our class who will rise to any flag waving bait offered them by a politician. They are the "my country right or wrong" people.

But people who dismiss all working class patriotism as being of this nature miss the fact that some of it is disguised class feeling and a form of equally disguised socialist sentiment. Remember that this country has been built by working people. Every brick that's been laid, every nail driven, every rivet, every piece of paper, every ounce of metal and plastic comes to us from the labor of our class and our people know that. For capitalists, the U.S.A. is a place to make a buck. They skip to Taiwan for higher profits, and the Mediterranean for vacations. For middle element people the situation is not so different, though they haven't the same opportunities to shop around for a desirable country to do this, that or the other thing in. But for the working class, the U.S. is where they'll stay—good times and bad, summer weather or sleet, high taxes or low. This, combined with the fact that they know they built up the country, makes for very deep feelings of patriotism among workers. They feel that the country is theirs by right if not in fact. That it is both their fate and their creation. Because our working class is socially and politically captive, underground, and has no visible or tangible movement to relate to, the symbols of our country—the flag, the land, the constitution—become the common symbols which bind workers together. In that sense patriotic sentiment mimics class sentiment and provides a socially acceptable vehicle for workers to feel unity and pride in themselves.

The key to understanding this is to recognize the workers'

atriotism is not the narrow arrogant kind of the flag wavers. It's ıore sentimental and even contains a feeling that our country wes it to other countries to behave well and generously.

Workers believe that people in other countries are normally ıisused by their governments and that, insofar as it is possible, ıe U.S. should stand on their side. They believe our country is so ɔrtunate that we should share our good fortune with others. 'hese sentiments are easily exploited for other purposes by oliticians and generals but that shouldn't mislead us as to their eal character.

I realize that some people have trouble accepting the idea hat patriotic sentiment among workers is often a form of isguised class sentiment and contains, in a hazy form, important ocialist sentiments. That's why it was so important earlier to tress that socialism is not a theory or an idea. It is a movement of he working people, a movement deeply imbedded in their utlook, certainly much more deeply imbedded than this or that onscious idea. The Italian Communist Gramsci points out that here really are only two broad philosophies that live among the ommon people of the world. One is religion. Among the uropean peoples it's Christianity. The Christianity of the ommon people is not the Pope's Christianity nor that of the heologians. It is a broad set of ideas and ideals about life and eath, about good and bad. It persists in spite of the fashions of he theologians, the corruption of the churches, or the edicts of he Pope. The other great philosophy which exists among the ommon people is socialism. This socialism emphasizes bringing he good life in the here and not the hereafter. Many of the other entiments and ideas are very similar to those of Christianity. ust as the simple, direct Christianity of the common people oexists with the elaborate theology, ritual, and bureaucracy of he organized churches, so too the socialist class sentiment of the orking class coexists with the official patriotism of the governıent and ruling class. Normally there's not too much of a roblem but when the common people feel betrayed by the uthorities, as occasionally they do, their deeper sentiment reaks forth and forces profound religious or social reforms.

When you understand this then you'll also come to undertand that the democratic sentiment among our people is also vidence of class feeling and is a barely disguised form of socialist ideas. In fact, the democratic feeling within the workin class—the feeling that everyone ought to have a say, that peopl have "rights," many more than you'll find in any constitutio that one person is as good as another—is the most direct an clear evidence of the socialist content buried within so muc working-class thinking. The most fundamental idea of socialisr is the democratic idea. Not the fancy arrangements and balance of liberal democracy but the deep-seated belief that the commo ordinary people should have a voice. This is the form in which th ideal of a classless society persists in our working class. Whe you consider that our working class has had no direct experienc of socialist ideas since the 1930's you will see how deep and pro found is the relation between the experience of the working clas and socialist ideals.

## The Benefit of a Movement

But the absence of a real socialist movement among ou working class for over 50 years now has taken its toll. Som consequences we've already met, some not. Probably the mos noticeable and least important is that it has allowed the socialis name and label to be taken over by the tiny grouplets of sectaria socialists, the people who push this or that narrow *ism* as the on true only *ism*, all contrary ideas being "counter-revolutionary. This has had some effect in driving workers to reject socialism i all its forms. But, as the Bible says, "by their fruits shall ye kno them." When we have a true socialist movement these groups wi be seen for the tiny nuisance they really are.

Much more serious is the fact that there is no universall recognized movement of workers which would attract to itse that large majority of men and women who would like to devot their lives to the betterment of their class. There are hundreds o thousands of fine, dedicated proletarians scattered over th country, their efforts isolated, or so ill-coordinated that the cancel each other out. Many of these people become discourage and cynical at the failure of their efforts and drop out of activ participation in the workers movement, leaving us all the poore

The lack of a broad socialist movement also makes it hard t concentrate on the problems of the whole working class. Insteac many people get caught up in trying to solve the problems c black workers alone, or women workers, or unionized workers o farm workers. Collectivized capital is a past master at deflecting these movements of part of the working class into special interests that prevent working-class unity and development.

Lacking recent experience of class-wide development and class-wide struggles with capital and the middle element, our class intelligence does not develop. Instead, shallow ideas about the invincibility of capital flourish, or workers are led to support false prophets such as George Wallace.

At one time in the history of our class we had a very lively cultural, intellectual, and moral life. Worker newspapers, orators, pamphleteers, and debaters flourished. The working class was home to new ideas about itself and about society. Young people stimulated by these discussions were led into a life of service to our class. The ordinary man or woman could, if they chose, shed much of the narrowness and ignorance forced upon them by their station in life. That cultural, moral and intellectual life does not go on now and we are much the poorer for it.

For the average worker who sees no tangible developing working class and who must face the overwhelming problems of his or her personal life without help from their class the result is very serious. They face demoralization, the idea that nothing can be done and that workers are the failures of our society.

In the more extreme cases this demoralization leads to the debasement of working-class life. People seek personal solutions in opportunistic schemes to make money, often at the expense of their fellow workers. Others go heavily into drink, drugs, sex, superstitious types of religion, horses and numbers, or anything that for the moment makes life seem more interesting or exciting.

It is a very different situation where there is a lively socialist movement. Aside from the benefits such a movement brings to our whole class, an individual man or woman who sees their class acting together with intelligence, idealism and courage draws enormous personal strength and satisfaction from that fact. It is one thing to think of yourself as a nobody in a nothing class, one of those people whose life cannot be composed into a satisfactory harmony of emotional, personal, vocational and spiritual activities, dragging through a frustrating adolescence to an adulthood of unremitting and unrewarding toil, only to spend your final years neglected by younger people and pushed around by social workers.

It is quite another to see yourself as a member of a class which contains within itself the seeds of a newer, higher, better human society, a society which the slaves of Rome dreamed of, that feudal peasants prayed for and for which the best men and women of all ages have worked for, sacrificed and often died for. Our class is the heir of Spartacus, the Gracchi, Munzer, Paine, Babeuf, Douglass, Debs, Marx, of Anna LaPizza, of John Ramy, of Jenny Curtis, of Elizabeth Gurley Flynn, of the Haymarket martyrs, of the Mollies and more importantly, of the nameless millions whose work has been distorted to produce the shoddy civilization we live in but who have laid the groundwork for the more humane civilization to come. We are members of the class which will unite all the members of the human family into one people. Of the class whose ideals have always stirred the best people and which has pushed society out of the barbarism of slavery and feudalism and soon will push it out of the barbarism of profit making and class society. This vision of the working class, true in all its details and more, calls forth the best qualities of our people.

## Socialism Today

What are the main characteristics of a working-class socialist movement today, the characteristics we have to design into our movement so that our fellow workers will recognize it as the genuine expression of the working class in this country?

First of all it will be a movement which clearly seeks to unite and embrace, on an equal basis, every part of the working class. As we have seen our working class is diverse. No one part of it can represent the rest, no one part of it is more vital than the rest, no one kind of oppression or mistreatment is more important than the rest. Not to see this is to fall into the standard trap of collectivized capital, the all-time expert at turning special protests into special interest divisions. But to unite ourselves on an equal basis does not mean to assume as many unconsciously do, that all workers are white males and have a union job in the corporate sector. The form of our class must be such that our unity will not smear over our different situations and problems. Neither should our differences lead us to place the interests of some of us before those of others.

Second, this means that we should seek to develop the broadest possible awareness of our many-sidedness and especialy of our inner contradictions, always encouraging a broad approach to the discussion and resolution of our problems. This is a much more important requirement than is apparent at first sight. Dynastic capital normally pushes the working class into some sort of unity—the unity of sheer poverty, of residential and social isolation, of neglect by society. Collectivized capital has the opposite tendency; it tends to capture parts of the working class—in this sector of the economy, of this race, in this alliance—and then use that capturing to pull the working class apart into different groups. Workers must be constantly aware of this. Our enemies today, collectivized capital and the middle element, are far wilier than their ancestors. They have a whole civilization full of tricks, devices, ideas, institutions, rewards, and privileges to fracture the working class along new lines. Only an active, thinking, discussing working class, on guard against precisely this, will be able to prevent new divisions of itself as a result even of its own revolutionary activity.

The third characteristic of the socialist movement is that it will place the interests of our whole class first. Right off the bat this means that everything must be tested by one test: is this a step toward uniting the working class, developing its power, and bringing it closer to the revolutionary step, to a society without classes? The socialist movement will be a revolutionary movement to its core. Not in the firebrand sense of riot, revolt, and insurrection, but in the serious sense of building the kind of society which is necessary for the interests of each worker.

Fourth, it is clear that capitalism will not die of its own accord, nor soon, nor easily. Capitalism will go to its eternal reward only when the overwhelming majority of our class have had it up to here with capital and are positively desirous of replacing it with something better. There will have to be a rich and very tangible understanding of what the new society will be like. That will take time. In Debs' day the workers movement took roughly 25 years to develop, from the founding of the Knights of Labor to the Pullman strike. Many things had to be tried and tested. Repeated failure is the price of success. The socialist movement must be organized to learn from its inevitable failures. It must be designed so as to be able to try sometimes simultaneously, many different ideas, programs, projects, stra tegies, you name it. Our movement will be as many-sided as ou class; it will be experimental in its outlook; it will expect failure but will learn how to learn the most from them.

Fifth, it will be a place for people who want to devote thei lives full-time, one hundred percent, to service to the workin class and to socialism. Almost any form of organization can d that but most do it badly and for reasons we can anticipate her and now. I've already commented on how much unused talen there is in our class. One problem with that, however, is tha many workers who plunge into activity in the workers movemen become competitive with one another. As workers, other ways t exert their abilities and gain esteem are closed; consequentl when they gain leadership positions they cling to them jealousl and view every other active person as a threat to themselves an their hard-won position. In this they mimic the dynastic capital ist of yore. We must find ways to build a collective, cooperativ leadership which views younger men and women who hav personal force and good ideas as comrades and not as deadl rivals. Only the collective talent of our class can outdo th collective talents and energies of modern capital.

Sixth, a genuine socialist movement is one in which th cultural, intellectual and spiritual development of the whol working class will be actively encouraged. It is a movement wher all topics and ideas are explored freely and openly as our clas tries to deepen its self-understanding as the surest path to it own emancipation. The task of the socialist movement o workers is an enormous one. It is nothing less than to prepare th men and women of our class to take over the entire direction o society for themselves and by themselves. To take over it technical life, its economic life, its social and cultural life government, law, police powers, education, health, everything The earmark of the socialist movement is the preparation of new ruling class of society, a ruling class not of one or two percen but made up, actively made up, of the great majority. This is th seventh and final and most important mark of the true socialis movement.

Many people think that in a classless society everyone woul be the same, or would have to be the same. What we want is ver different. We want a society where each man and woma normally leads a very varied and diverse life. In their work life they would work at jobs they found important and stimulating. They could vary their work because in the classless society work would be done for the benefit of the worker and not for the benefit of other classes. Individual workers would be called upon to participate in what we now think of as the work of management and of technical staff.

In social and political life, each man and woman would have to be well enough informed to make *responsible* decisions about community priorities. They would normally be called upon to serve in the government apparatus, somewhat in the manner in which people are now called to jury duty. We would try to bring up kids who would do all these things even better than we do ourselves. The point is that in a class society 80 out of 100 people must have most of their individuality choked off. They must produce. Their youth is devoted to preparation for that. Their adult years are spent producing a surplus. Afterwards, in their elderly years they're not worth anything so they're put on the shelf. A classless society would demand more out of us, not a choking grind of repetitive work but an intelligent participation in every kind of human activity. Each of us will be called upon to find talents and abilities we didn't even know we had—as a matter of course. For the first time in human history, the talents of every person will have to be developed and that will make us much more interesting and varied people than we could ever be when twenty out of a hundred hog most of the challenging areas of human activity. Certainly you're not going to have people sitting around munching on manna or drinking ambrosia, having everything they want, and not working a lick to get it. What you'll have is a society that really puts the pressure on us to be *human beings* and not donkeys.

Most adults know that happiness—a happy life not a happy moment—comes from just that, making an effort at things we believe are important, battling the difficulties, working hard at them and then having the sweet satisfaction of realizing we've done something well. When that sort of life is freely available to every man and woman, you have a classless society. And that is socialism.

## Four Things Which Won't Bring Socialism

As you can see bringing genuine workers socialism to the U.S. is going to be a gigantic task. So we have to consider what ways are open to us to do that—and just to improve things for the working class generally. There are four things, popular in one quarter or another, that won't help very much. We should have a brief look at them. They are:

a) correct ideology
b) a vanguard group, organization or party
c) trade unionism, pure and simple
d) coalitions with other classes

### a) Correct Ideology

There is a view, heavy with age in the working class movement, especially among certain socialists, that the working class in our country lacks ideology, Marxist ideology. Workers do not perceive their true interests and can be tricked by capital into division, inactivity and weakness. We are now in a position to see how shallow and thoughtless that view really is. No amount of ideology, that is, no amount of proof that capitalism is bad and that workers are screwed all the time, no amount of correct ideas from Marx or Lenin or Mao-tse-Tung can wash away the real, objective division in our class, or the alliances of necessity and convenience with other hostile classes. It would be nice if all workers were united around a common program against the ruling class and the other hostile classes. Union leaders in the corporate sector realize that. But they also realize that the bases for alliance with non-unionized workers are small, smaller even than those that now exist for an alliance with the corporate sector companies. To create new and stronger bases with unorganized workers would require union members to forestall wage increases, which, with inflation, means to suffer a sure loss in income in the hope that, later, a strengthened labor movement could make up those losses. It would mean swapping an easy peace with capital, with its occasional bone, for all-out war with capital, the two middle classes and the government on one side for sure and maybe organized and unorganized workers on the other. It would mean leaving a cozy nook in the Democratic Party for political isolation which, the ideologists tell us, would soon be overcome by a workers' political movement. Maybe that would work and maybe it wouldn't.

U.S. workers will never buy the ideology argument. Not because they "lack consciousness" but because they *are* conscious of the risky nature of the proposition. It offers a small likelihood of success and disaster in the event of defeat. Working-class people must be very conservative in their outlook of what is possible. As a captive class within a universally hostile system, we don't have all that much margin for error. When the CIO tried in the 1940's to adopt an aggressive pro-worker politics it had its wings clipped by the red scare and Taft-Hartley. I'm not trying to say nothing can be done or that the workers movement can't achieve greater unity. What I'm reacting to is the glib talk of certain left-wing ideologists who pass over the division of the working class as if it were just a misunderstanding that could be cleared up by reading a little more Marx, Lenin or Mao. I think we have to start differently, by taking the divisions and hostile alliances seriously and then going on to see if we can't work out a solid, well-thought out, conservative plan of action. A practical plan, not an ideological cureall.

### b) Vanguard Groups

Often the people who put forward the ideological patent medicines have another favorite cure. It's called a *vanguard.* Vanguardism is the idea that a relatively small group within the working class, or at least around its edges, is the best representative of the whole class. The rest of us are supposed to follow this group—supporting them, placing our own apparent interests second, and copying their ideas. In the recent past many different groups have been proposed as the vanguard. Such as the Communist Parties, either the one that favors Moscow, the one that favors Mao, or the various Trotsky supporters. Other candidates for the vanguard have included black people, black workers, black Marxist workers, hispanic Marxists, women, women workers, lesbians, homosexual men, workers in heavy industry, office and professional workers . . . The list goes on.

The main idea here is that some relatively small part of the working class is and should be the leader of the rest. Something in their situation makes them really representative of the interests of all the others. It's either the special intensity of their mistreatment at the hands of capital, or a special understanding which comes from their position in society, or in productio: Left-wingers spend much of their time thinking and fightir about the vanguard—who they are, how to tell. Some of th thinking and fighting is serious, and some of it is pretty frivolou

But that's not the point. The real issue is that there is r vanguard. The reason is, as we've seen, that our working class many-sided. It is very large and has many currents of opinion an experiences within it. The people who believe in the vanguar idea either don't see that or don't see that the variety an difference within our class is potentially its greatest strengt Instead of trying to erase its many-sidedness, we should be tryir to figure out how to end the conflict, hostility and competitic that they bring. Certainly there is no point trying to tell souther workers not to be southern, or trying to teach chicano workers t speak Harvard English, or women not to be female, or offic workers to get callouses. At a more fundamental level, each of th objections and hostilities one group of workers has to another- black vs. white, male vs. female, organized vs. unorganized, cra worker vs. part-timer—describes part of the real situation of ou class.

### c) Trade Unionism

Another thing which won't solve our fundamental problem is trade unionism as we now know it. There are two angles to th "won't," and they're different. To begin with, trade unior organized by craft *and* by industry are generally obsolete. Wher we already have them and where they are still effective—as i some construction work—fine. You never destroy a usefu workers organization. But as solutions for the more general an pressing problems of our class, no way. The plain and simpl truth is that a craft union— a union of all workers in a single craf such as carpentry,. is totally outclassed when it comes to dealin with big industry, big finance, big government axis, i.e., th collective ruling class. And industrial unions—unions of a workers in a single industry like steel or electrical—are ou classed too. The most successful modern corporations contrc their own prices and are thereby immune to our economic de mands. In addition they are diversified. That is, they act i several fields of industrial activity. They are also multi-nationa and have set up shop on several continents and scores of cour tries. To bring these giants to heel, workers must be organized o a broader basis. All the workers for Chrysler, both here and overseas, should be able to act together. All the workers for RCA, in manufacturing, publishing, military contract management, and real estate should be able to act together, to bring their unified power to bear on the company. I favor a class-wide worker organization. Certainly we should be thinking along those lines, talking it up, learning the difficulties in our way. But it may be that in the short run we'll have to have an RCA union, embracing every RCA worker, in every calling, and working with every RCA worker overseas. This is another question we have to come back to but one thing is for sure—the present bases of organization among workers—unions organized by craft, industry or nation—cannot contend with collective capital. *Cannot!*

There is a second angle from which to view trade unionism. We saw, in Chapter Two, how the corporation controlled the Critical Eight. This control is part of a larger picture in which collective capital lis a planning class. In our country the capitalist class exerts enough power and planning in government, the corporations and their supporting institutions, to control the broadest and most fundamental relationship in the economy, namely, the share of the product going to workers in the form of wages and the share going to the upper class and middle element in the form of profits, retained earnings, salaries and bonuses and publicly financed services, such as schools, or medicine. In the division of the surplus between the various classes, the U.S. has a controlled economy. From the economic, social and political standpoints, the working class cannot expect a general improvement in its condition unless it has the power and the organization to intervene in the decisions which shape the size of the surplus and apportion it among the various classes. The direct power of a union, any union, is not sufficient to do this. To our new, revamped, corporation-wide and class-wide unions we must add a workers' political party. As in Debs' time, and for exactly the sames reasons he discovered three-quarters of a century ago, we need a socialist party. But this party comes later in our story.

### d) Coalitions With Other Classes

In the past, our class has always sought alliances with other classes to fight the battle against the ruling class. The two classes generally approached for this alliance were entrepreneurial farmers and the middle class.

This strategy of class coalition was often well-founded. When the working class was still a minority of the population, and farmers were the majority, we could not hope to win anything except by a farmer-labor alliance. Of course, the interests of farmers and workers are so diverse that little really ever came of farmer-labor alliances.

Similarly, when the entrepreneurial middle class was numerous and powerful, and being torn to bits by capital, a small business-labor alliance made sense. And, even today, it still makes sense where small businessmen are dependent on working-class customers and hostile to big business.

Nowadays those particular class alliances are not a big issue. The entrepreneurial middle class is not so powerful as it was and it seems to have found a home to its liking in the conservative wing of the Republican Party. Similarly, the entrepreneurial farmers will no longer add much to an alliance. Here you have to separate the farmers from agricultural workers, either the low paid farm labor of the stoop and pick variety or the well paid operator of elaborate farm equipment for planting, harvesting, spraying, or processing. Both groups are workers, not farmers. They're important to us for both moral and practical reasons. But the entrepreneurial farmer isn't that important to us, and there isn't much advantage to be gained by allying with him.

The class coalition usually proposed nowadays is an alliance between the working class and the middle element. Its proponents argue that the working class plus the "progressive" part of the middle element plus the minorities plus the farmers should get together, gain control of the government and use it to check the power of big business. In fact, something like this goes on within the Democratic Party.

I want to stress there is absolutely no basis for a coalition between our class and the middle element. Invariably some individuals from that class will associate themselves with the workers movement and from time to time some disgruntled portion of that class will look for worker allies to pull its chestnuts from the fire. But no class alliance is possible. Why? First let's shoot down the arguments of those who propose such a coalition and then, with a clear deck, we can see why such an alliance is all wrong.

Right off the bat people will propose the coalition because of he numbers. In any fight it's better to have more people than ess. In elections, that's even truer. But we've already seen those umbers. Out of every 100 people who are eligible to vote 20 are f the middle classes, and about thwo-thirds, say 14, of these are iddle element. They generally vote, say, 12-2 for the more con-ervative position. Even if we could double the numbers who ote the more "liberal" ticket, we still lose the vote there 10-4. Ve are still dependent on worker votes to offset those middle lement votes. But if the question is over numbers, how about the 7 workers who voted for the conservative side? Doesn't it make ore sense to put the effort there? Or, even better, to try to get an xtra vote or two out of the 35 workers who didn't vote? The peo-le who stress getting extra votes for the progressive or liberal ide are trying to get the hardest possible votes. Doesn't it make nore sense to go after the 17 and the 35 and pay their price ather than go to the middle element 14 and pay their price for an xtra vote or two? If you are talking about numbers, the class oalition people can't even add.

"But," the fans of the Democratic Party coalition go on, there are parts of the middle element who have a direct interest n the government apparatus, to use it to defend their interests gainst the interests of big business. These are the middle ele-nent people who want better schools, and more government ser-ices." This is one of those cases where you start with an explana-ion and use it to create a "fact." Here, the explanation is the in-erest of middle element people in government services and this fact" is their opposition to big business.

Middle element people are very, very interested in schools, oads, public medical facilities and jobs within the government pparatus. As we've seen, the government expenditures are a rough where they feed unfairly on our taxes. They pay relatively ess and get relatively more. Their interest in controlling the overnment—local, state and federal—is not to prevent big usiness from getting its kids into the best schoolrooms but to revent ours; not to hog public payment to hospitals in compe-ition with the ruling class but in competition to us. The things overnment does in the social area are of immediate, pressing nd overwhelming concern to the middle element in defense of s privileges against the climbing part of the working class. The rice you pay for an alliance with the middle element is not to challenge those privileges. Nothing is free in this world, certainl not the middle element. They are in social competition with th working class and to get their support you have to give up tha competition. Black people found that out in the 1960's. Freedor now! Sure, we're for that, said the progressive middle elemen Votes for black Southerners. Sure, said the Northern middl element. School programs to help black kids get ahead. Sure—uhh—wait a minute; that's our bailiwick, said the middle ele ment. You niggers want everything; thank god, there's a Nixon t vote for.

As for controlling big business, it's a fact that big busines has done as well or better under the "liberal" governments c Theodore Roosevelt, Woodrow Wilson, FDR, Harry Trumar John Kennedy and Lyndon Johnson than they did under th "conservative" governments of Taft, Harding, Coolidge, Hoove Eisenhower, Nixon and Ford. That's a grand total of 75 year now and corresponds to the historical existence of collectiv capital.† But, for sure, the next "liberal" president will checl the power of big business. If wishes were horses . . .

The "fact" that liberals love to explain is this hostilit between the middle element and collective capital. But there i no "fact," only the fact that the middle element is closely tied t and dependent on big business. Some parts of the entrepre neurial middle class, such as the petit, or little, bourgeoisie, ar always resentful of big capital. But they're a fundamentall different class. The middle element is a salaried class; some of i is government salaries, but most is salaries from the corporat sector. It is a class which was brought into existence by capita and functions to control the working class. Economically it i dependent on capital, either directly through the surplus create and captured in the corporate sector or indirectly through the ta revenues generated by the corporate sector. Socially, it is th class which administers the working class—on the job, in school

† See Gerald Nash, *US OIL POLICY: 1890-1964* (Greenwood, 1968 for a good discussion of how the conservative Harding, Coolidge an Hoover administrations lacked understanding and sympathy towar the needs of the oil industry, and of how FDR's ultra-liberal administra tion promptly gave them what they wanted—a federally-controlle limit on domestic oil production.

in old age. Politcally it is therefore a class which has no real business being allied to the working class, except when the alliance is at the expense of the working class. Normally, about 85% of its votes are cast with the more conservative party. That 85% is much better evidence of its relation to collective capital than the "fact" of its hostility to big business.

Those people who propose, as the basis of our political activity, or economic activity or social activity, an alliance with the middle element, progressive or not, are foolish and misguided. They do not see plain reality. They do not see that the middle element is one of the prime beneficiaries of collective capital, nursed into existence, cuddled, rewarded, protected, and that is has the same interest in gains for the working class as the rabbit has in the eagle's dinner.

But the middle element is needed, say the class coalition people. Needed to keep the working class abreast of developments in politics, science, economics. Middle element leaders, being more articulate, can present our case better in courtrooms, Congress and the press. We need the cosmopolitcan outlook they bring to the workers movement, and we need their commitment to democratic procedures.

In fact, we need none of that from them. If, in our own class, we do not have intellectuals who can keep us abreast of the worlds of science, politics, the arts, or economics, which are now beyond our immediate class experience, workers who can lead us in the courts, Congress, and the press; if we have no love of the democratic way of doing things or the seeds of a cosmopolitan outlook we certainly won't get them from outside our class. I, for one, don't believe a single word of that. Nothing comes free inthis world. To the extent that we depend on the middle element for essential things—knowledge of politics, science, economics, the arts, etc.—we have to pay their price. And the middle element wants one and only one thing from the workers—docility. The manager wants to manage—us. That's a one-way street. The technical experts want to set up a system which determines—what we do. Another one-way street. And the professional wants to render an expert opinion to be followed by—us. Still one way. Coalition with the middle element means subservience to it and to its master which is collective capital.

Toward the beginning of the book I argued that the working

class had this profound impulse to run society, that it was the first laboring class ever to have such an impulse, and further, that the decent changes that make today's world different and better than olden times came from us and our arrogant impulse. Later I tried to show how much talent was lying around among workers, dormant and unused. The first and essential step for a revived workers movement is to rely on ourselves, in politics and everywhere else. Nobody can prove that we're now able to shed our reliance on the other classes in everything, though I believe we are. But the practical alternatives are clear. Either we do for ourselves, or no socialism. It's just that simple.

## Two Things That Are Needed

There are two imperatives for the working class today. First, we must create joint interests for our entire class.

The emphasis is on *create.* What's different and noteworthy between our situation and that of grandma and grandpa rests on that "create." Dynastic capital created joint, class-wide interests among workers by throwing them all in the slums, by grossly underpaying everybody, by treating all workers like cattle. (And it threw allies into the workers' laps by abusing the interests of farmers, small businessmen, government officials and intellectuals.) Collective capital doesn't do that. It naturally divides the workers and it naturally allies itself witht he middle element and the small business class. It naturally allies itself with different workers if they appear to get restless—with black people in the '60's, women today, manufacturing workers in the early '40's, and construction workers most of the time. So our task is to create joint interests among all the different kinds of workers and we'll have to do it in opposition to capital's always shrewd machinations. We'll look into ideas along these lines in Chapters Eleven and Twelve. But first, there's a problem we have to solve.

Today, the problem with proposing political or economic action by the working class is that there is no working class. In reality, as opposed to theory, hope and nostalgia, the working class is so divided that it does not act as a class and in fact isn't really a class. Thus, the second imperative is the formation of the working class.

What does it mean *to form a class?* At its simplest, a class is a roup of people who have the same spot in the productive elations of society—capitalist owners, middle element manaers, small entrepreneurs, entrepreneurial farmers, slaves, orkers. One of these groups forms into a class, not when they ecognize the similarity of their situation, but when they organize hemselves to assert their joint interests. Historically, the solated social life of the working class in the 19th century ermitted the growth of independent family-neighborhood networks. It was in this real community of experience that the nights made people aware of their identity as a working class nd of their common fate. An injury to one was a concern to all. ater, on that community basis, Debs and his associates were ble to build organizations within the working class—ARU, ocialist Party, IWW.

The key thing for the formation of our class then was the evelopment of the working-class community, independent of he ruling or middle classes. *We must create its equivalent for our wn time.* It won't be easy. We will have to do it against the social pposition of collective capital and its middle element. But the rmation of our class is, in fact, the fundamental step to ventual class emancipation.

Presently we are socially captive to capital and its allies. Our ocial form of organization is the nuclear family, a form which akes us socially dependent on a hostile social system and conomically overdependent on capitalist institutions. This amily arrangement fosters a particular kind of class consciousess in each one of us: "I am alone in society and can count only n my immediate family and friends. Provided I stay within aceptable channels I have some small chance to improve my peronal and family situation. Those channels are marked out by the uthorities and I must keep to them. The alternative, rebelousness, will bring me nothing positive and may well bring etribution from the authorities for whom I am easily identifiable. he working class does not exist for me save as weak or greedy nions, and a vague feeling that I get less than others in spite of reater effort on my part. I don't set any store by my class membership and have to work out personal and family solutions o my problems. This is the nature of the world I live in and I annot change it."

Note the features of such a consciousness. Personal or family isolation. Exposure to the authorities. Personal solutions or passivity. The working class appearing as a weak and/or shoddy force, or as something extremely abstract. Powerlessness.

The point I would make here is that these are not the ideas of the worker but his or her experience. Workers experience isolation, exposure, and powerlessness. You cannot debate with him or her to prove a consciousness of collective action because it doesn't have the force of experience behind it; the idea of interests shared by all workers is accepted in the abstract but is at the same time concretely refuted by the individual's experience of competing with and being harmed by other members of the class. A few workers are moved primarily by their ideas—but the average person wisely sticks to actual experience. Because the class is socially disorganized and weak, workers experience disorganization and weakness and their personal experience becomes more important.

It is here at the broadest level of class organization that we really can learn from our "betters," collective capital. As we saw, the corporate form of class organization evolved in order to overcome the internal rivalries which were destroying capitalism in the late 19th century. The corporate form enabled the propertied class to merge its formerly antagonistic interests into institutions which expressed joint interests and permitted the growth of a new, dependent middle element and a new type of society. The key thing here is the connection between class organization and interests. Under the family form, the joint interests of the rich were abstract and uncompelling. Each capitalist could say to himself—'yes, it's in the interest of the propertied class not to destroy each other,' but as soon as he saw a chance to make an extra buck he took it. The capitalist was experiencing things as an individual or a member of a dynastic family. J.P. Morgan's greatness was that he got beyond personal and family bias and saw class interests where most of his contemporaries couldn't see past their own noses.

The ideas people have are all tied up with the class they belong to and the way that class is organized. If it is well organized, the specific arrangements for pursuing joint interests will be relatively easy to design and build. That's the secret of modern capitalist class organization. The corporate form of organization is a form which easily and directly expresses the joint interests of collective capital and adapts easily to pursuing this and that specific interest. And behind that is a very simple fact. The capitalist class is organized in such a way that its members experience things through their corporate organizations, that is collectively, and not primarily through their own individual or family eyes.

How different it is with us. Class-wide interests and ideas have to fight their way through our individual experiences. Though our people see that class unity and class cooperation would be better than what we have, they also see that its truth is "in the long run" and that for now, we'd better push our international board for 10% more an hour, forgetting that it will hurt other workers, who will then turn around and hurt us.

It seems that we are caught in a bind. Because our class consciousness is consciousness of disorganization and weakness, our joint interests are not clearly and forcefully perceived. Because our joint interests are not clearly and forcefully perceived, our class consciousness remains a consciousness of disorganization and weakness. Again, I want to stress how the nature of the class struggle under the collective form of capital differs sharply from that of Marx's day. Dynastic capital created joint interests in its working class by attacking the physical existence of every worker. A working-class community evolved of necessity and without positive interference from capital. No longer. Collective capital does not normally attack the physical existence of the worker. In fact, the corporate wage yields an improved standard of living. Collective capital also takes positive social steps to prevent the formation of a working-class community—that's the significance of the Social System, the Welfare State, Equality of Opportunity, and so forth.

From a practical standpoint, we're in a dilemma. The working class will not spontaneously solve the dual problems. Collective capital is organized precisely to prevent a spontaneous solution. On the other hand, the Leninist or vanguard solution *could* work. An organized minority could create, by itself, enough strength to successfully pursue proletarian interests and thereby attract to itself a broader worker following. But to do so it must adapt to the working class itself the same relation as a ruling class has to a subject class. *In fact, that is the practical meaning of vanguard—a minority doing for a majority what it cannot do for itself.* (So, we've got a "price" question here.)

From our standpoint in the U.S., the vanguard solution is a very weak could. The Leninist party offers itself to the working class as a rival ruling group, a rival to the ruling class. But it isn't much of a rival, since the political, social, economic and cultural resources available to each of the rivals are totally unequal. On the one hand you have a class of a million people or so, with every advantage and resource. On the other hand, you have a tiny band with little beyond words and zeal to advance its fortunes. Not much of a contest, I'd say.

What other alternative is there, if neither an organized minority nor the spontaneous action of the majority are likely to work? And, how can anything be organized when workers lack the perception of joint interests?

I stress and even repeat these things because we must be clearer about what won't work. Over and over again in discussions on labor questions people attempt to escape one side of these dilemmas by adopting the other as if there were no other option. If they dislike vanguards, they opt for spontaneity, with a new wrinkle or different twist. Or, if they see that a spontaneous uprising won't occur they come forward with the old vanguard recipe in a new dish.

Similarly, people play games with the problem of lack of jointly perceived interests. It is plain to see that right now workers do not usually perceive themselves as a class and do not perceive that they have common specific interests. Certainly that's not the dominant perception they have of themselves. Yet the calls for trade union or political militancy which arise in various quarters appeal to worker unity and worker militancy to provide the motive and muscle to create—unity and militancy! All of this with a view to defending just those joint interests which workers don't perceive that they have.

Words really are deceptive. The dilemmas we've been discussing are verbal dilemmas which do not present the full range of alternatives. If our class is not well-knit and doesn't perceive its joint interests, that only means that we have to develop two things simultaneously and from scratch. We have to look for ways to build up the cohesiveness of our class. And we ave to begin to find and create interests which are in fact the nterests of a united class. The problems of *forming a class* and *oint interests* are connected problems, lacking one makes the ther worse, but you can work at both. The tent pole holds up the ent while the tent holds up the tent pole. That never stopped nyone from putting up a tent unless, like labor radicals, they nsisted on doing one first.

The same reasoning holds for the so-called dilemma that orkers will join and support organizations only if they share nterests upon which the organization is based. What we have to egin to think about are forms of organization which don't ssume that their members have perceived joint interests but hich are instead designed to draw out those interests. Here the istinction is made between organizations which are instruments o advance the already perceived interests of a group and rganizations which are designed to bring people together so hat they begin to perceive and express the joint interests which re concealed from them by their present social and economic fe. This is such an important subject that we will take it up in its wn right in the next chapter.

# CHAPTER X
# FORMING THE WORKING CLASS

Who represents the workers? How is it possible to represent the working class as it actually now is, divided in opinion and interests? What social form of class organization will provide the working class with the advantages which capital draws from its collectivized form, the corporate system? Is there any form of organization which is now appropriate to a divided class which will also be appropriate to it later when our diverse and opposed interests have been merged into a greater unity?

## Instrumental and Expressive Organizations

At first sight the answers to these questions are all "no!" Organizations are normally instrumental in character; they are social instruments. A group of people bands together to form an organization in order to achieve a common purpose—an election victory, representation before their employers, or to field an athletic team. The organization is meant to be an instrument for that purpose. Normally, the organization must make a series of decisions in pursuit of that purpose. If the purpose is an election victory, it must choose a platform, accept and reject candidates and planks, make fund raising strategy and expenditure decisions, and so on. In the process of making these decisions people generally expect that the principle of unity of action will hold. I'm for Brown but if Black wins the nomination, I'll go along with him or her and give my support. The idea is that the function of the organization is to unite everyone behind the purpose of the organization and the decisions made in pursuit of the purposes; unity of action is normally essential to the success of an organization.

But how can there be unity of action in the working class now? We are sharply divided, with opposing interests. The state of opinion in our class reflects that. There is no unity of opinion, there is not even the evidence that there is a will to unity of opinion. No single organization, imposing unity of action for any purpose could now truly represent the working class as it actually is.

This, of course, is precisely the point at which our old friends, the vanguard people, show up. See, they say, you don't like our pretense to speak for the whole class. But, as you've found out, the working class *cannot now speak for itself in a single voice*. Unless someone does it for them, with a view to leading them toward greater unity, it will never be done. Division and disunity will persist, capital will rule and socialism will be a distant and impossible dream. That's what it means to be a vanguard, to take the lead. Later, when the working class has gotten itself together, we'll have democracy, majority rule, the whole kit and kaboodle.

To me that view looks as if it's saying that the working class has to be led to freedom, hyped on socialism. For the sake of the argument let's go along with this view. Let's suppose the working-class grows on this basis and soon there is a single working-class organization including the vast majority of workers. It has our loyalty and support and the ability to make binding decisions in the pursuit of our objectives.

Such an organization *does not and cannot* represent our class. Today it cannot because we have diverse interests. But even farther down the road it cannot because our class is and should be as diverse in character as the broad humanity that makes it up. It is a distorted and bankrupt picture of socialism to epict it in this way. It would mean an organization in which our lass could be successful only at the price of substituting the ariety and diversity of our class with an arbitrary discipline. uch an authoritarian discipline would mean we sacrificed our iews and ideas in favor of some sort of unity of action.

But that discipline would be a democratic discipline, people etort. We'll vote on everything, everybody will be well-informed, verybody will participate, our organizational morality will be ery high, very principled. Every procedural and moral safe-uard will exist to protect the rights of minorities. The ıajority will truly rule justly and fairly, while respecting the ghts of the minority.

The problem with this line of argument is that it neglects verything we know about the nature of liberal democracy.

Organizations mimic the political state. In both tiny and ırge groups, 1 or 2% create a middle element or following of 20% r so. Adding their forces together they then attempt, usually uccessfully, to divide the majority and rule in their own ıterests. Such a state or organization will be democratic if the ıling group plus its following plus the fraction of the great ıajority it manages to "represent" is 51% or more. Otherwise it sn't democratic. But the democratic/non-democratic difference sn't a fundamental one. In both cases the minority really rules. d prefer the small gains by means of democracy to the "you get othing" of the non-democracy, but it's clear how really close ıey are. They differ by just that: one gives small gains, the other oesn't.

Socialism is not the promise of small gains. Either it is the romise of big gains, constant gains, qualitative improvement, etting rid of the classes which make problems and clearing the vay for our own intelligence. It is either that, or thank you, no, I'm ot interested, don't call me, I'll call you. So it is incompatible vith liberal democracy, even liberal democracy minus its warts.

No instrumental organization, enforcing unity of action, no ıatter how democratic, can bring the the working class to ocialism. Perhaps it can help along the way, but between ıstrumental organization and socialism there is and must be a ualitative break. Socialism is the rule of the whole working lass, in all its diversity, not that of a minority or even a majority equiring some sort of unity.

In traditional Marxist political theory, people understan the state and the society it governs to be radically different Society is everything, everything that people do and are. Accord ing to Marx the state is an organization over and above society. I is dominated by a single class which uses it to help rule an exploit other classes.

By the same token we should not confuse a class, which is sort of society, with an organization, which mimics a state. A stat claims sovereignty: that is, it claims that there is no authorit higher than itself. The only way for a state to settle its difference with another state is by force—war. And the only way to settl differences between a state and some part of society is to accep the state's word as final. So you either voluntarily give in t constituted authority or have force used against you, by cops o soldiers.

An instrumental organization mimics the state's sovereignt by claiming the right to unity of action over its member Normally that's harmless enough in an organization formed for specific purpose. If you accept the purpose it more or less make sense to go along with the decisions of the organization so long a they are likely to further that purpose, even if you would hav preferred an alternate way. But an organization representing th working class is not an organization formed for a specifi purpose.

Notice that I'm not saying that we don't need instrument type organizations. We need many, and then more, as many a are necessary to realize all our purposes. But the whole workin class, its interests, its variety, its socialist impulse can never b represented by molding its members to unity of action (c opinion) on behalf of the purpose or purposes of an instrument organization.

There are other forms of organization which are not instru mental in character. The one which comes most prominently t mind is a church. Not churches like the Catholic Church or th Methodist Church but churches which have what is called congregational form. Congregational churches are totally go erned, in all respects, by the congregation. Such a church is n primarily or even particularly instrumental in character. Peop don't join it or come to services with a view to join together some unity of action, to make their association function as a to or instrument. Their purposes are satisfied by coming together and engaging in non-instrumental activities. Things like the service itself, singing, fellowship, sharing the worship, or giving views, feelings and beliefs a social form. I would call such an organization an expressive organization. Its purpose is to express certain things which already exist between and among its members, not to impart a discipline in favor of a purpose. Most fraternal and sororal organizations have a similar function. Though the organizations seem to be formed for an instrumental purpose, such as getting a softball team together or holding a sewing bee, their real and obvious purpose is to let the members enjoy each other's company, or ideas, and to express, in a tangible way, the group feelings they have.

I've been around long enough to hear the gasps of some of my readers, especially the socialists out there. Religion, as everyone knows, is the opiate of the masses. No opinion is more favored among people on the left than anti-clericalism and a thoroughgoing contempt for churches and all their kin. Certainly this would have been my view in the past, which is to say I would have been triumphantly and proudly ignorant of something I should have known. Gramsci came to my aid on this point and perhaps he can help others too.

One aspect of Christianity expresses the superstition laid upon the people by priests, ministers and other clerics. But within Christianity there is something else going on, the expression of the spiritual and social needs of our people. This sort of Christianity, as a popular philosophy and cultural tradition, is in fact very close to socialism. Both are expressions of the laboring or working classes. It seemed to me logical therefore to look to see what organizational forms expressed that philosophy or culture and it is clear that it receives its purest and clearest expression in the churches, particularly the congregational type churches. So I accept the similarity between the need for an expression of popular Christianity and the need for an expression of popular socialism. In fact, I have used it to guide my thinking on the fundamental problem of the *social form of organization* for the working class or, more simply, the *formation* or *forming* of the working class.

The expressive form of organization is an attempt to unite people in all their fullness and diversity. In it the private world of our beliefs is made socially visible. We join with others to share our views and to enjoy the fellowship of those with whom we share important things. Unity of action, or opinion, is not required to satisfy its purposes. On the contrary, what results is a growing unity, fostered by shared experience and activity, discussion and fellowship, and the joys of human sociability and group life. The only unity required ahead of time for expressive organization is a general will to share, to discuss, and to enter into the company of others for mutual growth, support, and enjoyment. In this sense, expressive organization provides us with the general social form of organization of the working class because it solves the fundamental question we posed earlier about class organization: how can we unite people in an organization which does not assume unity of action or opinion as a prerequisite?

Very often when people discuss organizational questions they fight over the centralization/decentralization question. To what degree should leadership and decision-making be centralized: by district, by city, by nation; in the town meeting, the executive committee, the leader? But the issue of how far an organization should be centralized or decentralized has nothing to do with the expressive form of organization. Centralization/decentralization fights are about where decision-making should be located and about the degree or scope of unity of action. Expressive type organization is about other things. It is about people's general will to associate together, to make tangible such unity as they already have.

I want to make some proposals about adopting the expressive form of organization for the working class. But beforehand we might as well clear up the relation between expressive and instrumental forms of organization. To make it concrete, let's suppose that our class already had some general social form of expression, that it was forming—becoming socially visible and socially tangible. For ease of reference let's call the form The Workers' Society and suppose it was an actual society, with meetings, social events, and cultural programs. What would be the relation of the Workers' Society to our unions, political parties, commune groups, neighborhood associations and all those other instrumental groups?

First of all, there would be no necessary conflict between them. Whatever it was that people came together to do in the ociety, they didn't come together to decide on courses of action, hoose leaders, or determine priorities. Even by definition, the wo kinds of organizations have no conflict, provided, of course, hat nobody is of a mind to be a busybody or to try to turn one into he other. On the other hand, if we had both kinds of organiza-ion, we might see our way through to several powerful advan-ages. Three come easily to mind: the possibility of *reality testing* or our class, opportunities for *complementary activity*, and the evelopment of *functional concepts of leadership*. Let me explain hat those things mean and why it would be good to have them.

Let's say my union local has decided to put its main effort his year into health and safety issues. We believe that this will ring new workers who are now turned off into an active role in he union, that it will encourage our members to discuss and hink more seriously about their place in the industry, and that it ill provide a common meeting ground for various elements in he union who haven't been getting on so well in recent years.

Meanwhile, your local—maybe in the same industry, maybe ot—has decided to do something else. Perhaps rev up its olitical action committee or maybe start talking up the idea of lecting foremen. In both of our locals we've made an analysis of ur situation and decided that if we do such and such, a certain esult will follow. Maybe it will or maybe it won't. But it would be seful to have a place where people from our two locals could talk ut, in detail, what we are doing, why we decided to, and what esult we expect. It would be good if you pressed us, in a friendly ay, to be very clear on just what we think our situation is and hy we chose our course of action. It would be good for you if we imilarly pressed. We'd both learn something. And we'd not only et the benefit of each other's experience but we'd put each other n a position to learn more from our own experience.

That's a nice idea, you say, but a little idealistic. No, not dealistic. Necessary. The ruling class and the middle element ave schools, institutes, sociologists, production engineers, ersonnel managers, seminars, magazines and every other thing ou can think of to perfect their control of us—to study us etter, to keep abreast of what we're doing, to understand our deas and strategies, and to devise counter ideas and strategies o defeat us. Their class intelligence about us and about hemselves is already at a high level and is always increasing. We can't keep up with them, and we certainly can't beat them, if we keep on doing things the way we do them now. Today, what we do in our organization often reflects only what we did yesterday, the prejudice of a certain leader, the issue that Johnny-on-the-make has managed to get ahead with, or whim, intuition, or "experience." But what experience? In what situation? Some sort of Workers' Society could be used to quicken and deepen our class intelligence so that maybe we could start to take the boss to the cleaners once in a while.

I'm not talking, by the way, about a group of people coming into your union and laying a line on you, or about a caucus being organized in your union to push this or that idea. That is the old way that certain radicals and socialists, trying to "educate" the working class, managed to educate workers to distrust, dislike and ignore the very same radicals and socialists. So that's not what I want. What I want is to organize our class in such a way that you and I can learn from each other, and learn more by ourselves too, without getting in each other's hair. What I want is to improve the processes of self-learning in our class. All that is included in what I called "reality testing."

"Opportunities for complementary activity" is a little different. If the working class is ever to be free we are going to have to do a lot of things. We'll have to reorganize our concept of a union and then actually reorganize our unions. We'll have to get ourselves a workers political party. We need organizations to put our neighborhoods together, to bring up our kids with class pride and class intelligence, to help solve family problems, and so on. These things are complementary for the working class, meaning, by doing one of them you help out with the others. Being in a union makes workers vote more often and more consciously. Solving family problems would give young people more respect for our class and its organizations. The various things that build up our class are different but complementary. To free our class many things will have to be done—all of them necessary.

If the main organization of our class was instrumental we couldn't do all those things, or at least not well. An instrumental organization is ordinarily only able to do one thing well. I'm not sure exactly why. As good an explanation as any is that organizations are like people. If their mind is on one thing, it's not on another.

The more I think about this the more I realize the genius of the corporate system. The individual corporation is an instrumental organization. It has, usually, a single, focussed purpose: make cars, make money, make war, corral the intellectuals. But the corporate *system* is mainly an expressive organization. That way it enables capital to have many focuses and interests. If the system were formalized and set up as an instrumental organization some of the necessary activities of the ruling class would suffer.

We should consider this way of doing things for ourselves, since instrumental organizations are not always efficient. Suppose, for example, we had an organization of 100 people, all of them wanting to be active. But there's a difference of opinion. Some want to do one thing, let's call it A, and some want to do something different, let's call it B. There's a vote and the A's win 55-45. So now we're all supposed to do A. The 55 people who wanted to do A get all the money and resources of the organization and start to do A. But what about the 45 who wanted to do B? According to the theory of unity of action, they're all going to do A too. Maybe some will really pitch in and do A. Some will "just go along." They'll do A but in a half-hearted manner. And some, the ones who were the most committed to B, will sit on their hands, partly from pique but maybe because they were really convinced that A was a disaster for the organization. This sort of thing happens in organizations all the time. The majority wins and the minority has to go along. But without fail many are so convinced the majority view was wrong that they can't in good conscience work for it. This is just as important a factor as apathy in keeping most people from being active. In fact, we've seen that most majorities are made up of several minorities. After the minorities which pose as majorities get through winning the votes, an actual majority isn't really convinced by the so-called majority view. Instrumental organizations are very inefficient in this way. They can turn off as many, or more people than they unite.

This is the case where the expressive organization turns out to be more efficient. Maybe the 55 should do A and the 45 should do B, separating into two instrumental groups but keeping expressive ties to one another through the Workers' Society. A will be done by those who think it's very important; B will be done by those who think it's important too. The amount of resources going to A won't be much less than before, since not much effort was going to come out of the B people anyway.

Of course, this kind of division in groups isn't always appropriate. Sometimes unity of action is necessary. If A is a strike, the B's are scabs. If A means keeping some gangster out of union office, the B's may be gangsters. A and B may be totally incompatible, but that situation is very, very rare. Much rarer than most of us think. For example, one group in our organization is for day care. Another wants to push equal rights legislation. They have a huge row, spend a lot of time proving the other side is wrong, getting mad at each other—for what reason? Because day care and equal rights legislation are incompatible? Of course not! They're only incompatible if you are trying to get all the organization's resources to do one of them ("unity of action") and I'm trying to get all the resources to do the other. Here it isn't the two proposals that cause the incompatibility but the instrumental form of organization.

"Develop a functional concept of leadership," what's that all about? Start by asking yourself who are the leaders of our class? The answer is surprisingly easy to come by. The leaders are the men or women who are most successful at the internal politics of instrumental organizations. The man who's going to be the next president of your local is the person who's best at building a following in the local, picking the best issues to show himself to advantage and his rivals to disadvantage. Probably, he'll be a good speaker but certainly an excellent politician. He'll have a strong presence but be at least a little shifty in promising this or creating that impression, even though the two might not exactly square out. He'll be ambitious for office and—unless he's a saint—will covet the office at least partly for purely private reasons: pride, love of power, the desire to dominate others. He'll be better or worse partly by the luck of the draw and partly by the quality of the members. If you're lucky you'll have several first class leaders to choose from and if your members are pretty alert, they'll choose one of the better people offered to them.

Will this person help to develop the class consciousness of the members? Will she add to the stature of the union in the eyes of its members or of others? Will she be an able strategist? Will her presiding add something of permanent value to the union or to our movement? Will she merely be a good president, meaning, will she fill her office well? Maybe or maybe not. The plain fact is that the reasons leaders get elected don't have a particularly close connection with these *functional* (performance) aspects of the job. More likely a leader is elected because of certain things in the *internal* life of the union. But his or her worth in the job will depend on its *external* life. Sometimes those two things are closely connected. A very intelligent, alert membership will judge a leader more by the latter. But generally the connection isn't all that close between the internal power relations of the union and the external, instrumental purposes of the union.

At present, all the leaders of the working class are cut from the same mold. They are the type of man or woman who was successful at mastering the internal life of their union, by building a following, having a sponsor, or getting an inheritance. Within the pattern there are differences but they are variations on one and only one pattern. It's a dumb way to choose leaders, but short of the millenium there is no other way if we have such a narrow range of workers organizations, all of which are instrumental in form. I don't think our class needs a great leader. I know it doesn't. What it needs is many leaders, some good at this, some good at that. We need first class bureaucrats, first class thinkers, first class tacticians, first class strategists, first class speakers. We need leaders with their feet on the ground and leaders with their heads high enough in the air to get a little distance to their vision. We need some who are tough as nails, like John L. Lewis, and some who are sensitive. We need single minded leaders and experimental types. In other words, we need a corps of leaders so rich in skills and variety that we can always reach in and pluck out the one we need for the job at hand and then just put them back on reserve when the need is past. I think non-instrumental forms of organization will help us to develop such a corps of leaders.

Leaders are wonderful but also a pain in the butt. I've never met a leader, no matter how good, who didn't spend just a touch too much time worrying about his or her rivals. And I've never met a leader who didn't get a mite too much ego pleasure from being a leader. Maybe there are exceptions to my experience. As a rule, leaders are like mules. Both their excellent qualities and their dispositions are well-known. But unless a mule has a particularly bad disposition it's worth putting up with, even though it's rarely a pleasant experience.

The problem comes when you have two closely matche leaders. They'll spend too much of their time and your tim biting at one another. Each of them will swear to him or herself o a stack of *Capitals* that the other one is dangerous, irresponsibl or wrong. Being leaders, they'll convince the rest of us. A enormous amount of energy will be spent deciding who's i charge. And the result will be totally predictable. The defeate leader and his or her followers will either leave the organizatio leave off being active, or begin a perpetual conspiracy to win bac the organization. You lose a leader, a following, and a lot of tim and energy. It's a dumb set-up but it's forced upon us by ou notions of leadership which in turn are forced on us by the natu of instrumental organization. When you start to think abou using organization to test out options and ideas you start t figure out how to keep leaders out of one another's hai Similarly, the idea of complementary activities of the workin class, foregoing unnecessary unity of action, also begins t suggest a way of keeping leaders out of one another's hair. Th expressive form of organization leaves the way open to functional concept of leadership, that is, a concept whic acknowledges that there are many different types of leader whose activities can complement each other.

There is one other advantage of expressive organizatio which is very important. The way our class organizes itself no will have a decisive effect on the kind of socialist society we set u later. If our class is organized by a military-like communist part we're going to get a society run by a military-like communis party. The Soviet working class, who deserved so much more fo their pioneering efforts and sacrifices, fell before just such party. And today the Cuban and Chinese people are wrestling t keep their Communist parties from destroying the path t socialism.

Likewise, if we organize ourselves bureaucratically we'll ge a bureaucratic society. Now the point I would make is tha socialist society, in its broadest outlines, will be expressive organized. It will be organized to enable people to express the vitality, intelligence and good will. Within that larger expressiv framework various groups will come together to carry out this o that task, decide on this or that form of action, choose this or tha leader. But the general organizational form of the sociali society will be expressive in nature and not instrumental. The expressive form of organization could overcome the apparent contradiction between the means used to establish socialism and the nature of socialist society.

## The Workers' Societies — A Proposal

It is time to begin discussing proposals to improve the sorry state of our class. I have one here for your consideration. It is a proposal for an expressive organization—the Workers' Society. I've laid it out with the idea in mind that it would give us a general form of class organization good enough to take on and beat the corporate class form. That's the purpose of the proposal—the key design spec to which all the other specs are subordinate.

A person would have to be dumber—a whole lot dumber—than I actually am to believe that anyone could sit down now and work out a first class proposal for the working class. We don't have that much good experience yet. We haven't talked together enough. Even so, I'm going to push the proposal because proposals are needed to get us thinking and acting on our outstanding problems. Which is something we are not now doing. We have to start to apply an experimental attitude to our situation. And even if the proposal for Workers' Societies turns out wrong, we need something like them, or something designed for the same purposes.

The proposal is actually a very simple one. The traditional and universal type of organization of our class, the thing which pops up in every crisis of the working class, is simply a meeting of all concerned workers to discuss problems. In Russia they were called Soviets, in Italy *Consigli* (councils) and in our country they're called workers committees. Normally, these informal, unstructured groups meet and then go on to evolve into instrumental organizations: a representative or legislative Soviet, a works council, an organizing committee. The proposal is that even if that happens, the soviet, counsel or committees should not pass away but should become a permanent expressive organization of the working class. The idea is that these committees, say, called by the name The Workers' Society would evolve into regional and national link-ups, always having the same basic purpose, namely, to be a society which tries to give expression to our class—its existence, problems, and concerns.

The Workers' Society tries to express certain real but now invisible features of working-class life. We hope to find a social form to express these features, so that they will grow deeper and contribute to a better life for workers, as well as prepare us to become society's rulers.

The features of our class which we want to see expressed in a Society are:

A) the mutual dependency of workers on one another
B) their free association with one another
C) their fellowship with one another
D) the many sidedness of our class's life
E) its cultural, intellectual, spiritual and artistic life and, consequently, the generalized will of our class to greater social, moral, economic and political unity

A) Workers are dependent on one another. That's true and to a radical degree. I cannot live or do my work except for the work of other workers who provide heat, light, paper, pencil, food, transportation, health services and so forth. Collective capital, in what I've called social taylorism, tries to isolate every worker and to place him or her in an administered relation to the institutions of capital where the worker is dependent, identifiable and alone. Capital tries not only to control us but to create the lie in us that we are dependent for our life and well-being on capital and its institutions. But that's not true. We are dependent on the labor of one another. But by controlling that labor capital is able to hide its reality—the mutual dependency of our class—from each of us and create the impression that we draw our existence from capital alone. The Workers' Society aims to confront and defeat social taylorism by placing the individual worker in a definite, tangible relation to other workers, a relationship of intelligent discussion of mutual problems. In this way the reality and depth of our mutual dependency will emerge and begin to restore the social cohesion that social taylorism is pledged to destroy.

We are all dependent on one another in another way too. Your stupidity or wisdom affects me and mine affects you. If your union is being unconscionably neglectful of other workers' interests in its demands, or if my electioneering practices are hurting your community, then we need a place where the ıtelligence and general moral authority of our class can be rought to bear. Not to organize against you or me but to hold us ɔ a broad class standard by intelligent discussion and *moral* ıfluence.

B) Most of our associations with other people are, in a sense, ɔrced upon us. As they say, you can choose your friends but not our relatives. On the other hand most of the people we meet are ı some sense forced on us, not in a necessarily bad way, but ɔrced nonetheless. We work with someone, live near them, hop at the same store, happen to go to the same church.

In our private life things can be different. With a real friend, deep friend, our association has a free character. It is not ictated by anything external to the association, such as advan-age or convenience. So there is often a split between our public nd private selves. Yet association between and among workers s finally not based solely on mutual protection, advantage, or ecessity. At bottom, I believe, the social relations among 'orkers, the character of their association with one another, xpresses their broad humanity, not their special interest as a ɔmponent in the economy. That's not such a readily apparent ıct but it is implied by the history of the working class and of ıboring people generally. That history shows that the ideas hich spring spontaneously from the laboring people are always f a broad, generous, idealistic nature. When shopkeepers get ɔgether they talk about prices and give rise to ideas about price xing. When doctors get together they talk about malpractice ıits, livers and taxes and give rise to the narrow vision of the .M.A. When laboring people get together they probably talk bout circuses and football but they give rise to ideas of freedom, uman rights or the equality of peoples. In this sense workers are l friends because they don't seek advantage from each other. od knows, you'd never know it to listen to them. But in a rofound sense this is true and it is this historical friendship mong the lowly people of the earth that is the major realistic ope for a better world. The Workers' Society, as a free ssociation of men and women, should be conducive to ex-ressing this freedom, this friendship and profound streak of lealism.

C) The Workers' Societies should also provide comradeshi among workers. It should be a place where men and women ca go to enjoy the pleasure of associating with people of their ow class, people who share with them the broad outlines of a simila moral view. Here is where the parallel with the congregationa churches comes in. To be a class conscious worker in th movement, to join in a social expression of your moral vision i important for several reasons. It makes the tangible reality of ou class apparent, to us and to others. It establishes a social web c shared experience, associations, and fellowship among workers which contributes to the greater cohesion of our class. It break down the effects of social taylorism and gives visible evidence o a fundamentally different kind of social world. And, finally, it i pleasureable in itself.

D) Not only the inclination to unity, but also the many-side ness of our class should be found in the societies. The concerns c parents; of black people, of white people's apprehension ove black people (and vice versa); the problems of youth and old age of organized and disorganized workers; of unemployed peopl and unemployable people; of women and of men should b explored. The Workers' Societies should be places where ever aspect of working-class life is experienced and discussed, mad subject to the intelligence of working people. In that way, we ca transform oppressive facts and situations into occasions for th creative use of our intelligence and abilities.

E) Related to this, but important in its own right, is th development of the cultural life of the working class. It's a sham that so much of the recreational life of our class has to be found a the other end of the dollar, that to have fun you have to spen money. And it's a shame that organizations which are funda mentally hostile to our personal and class interests play such vital role in working-class life. I have in mind, the Legion Kiwanis, Little League, the superstitious churches, Police Ath letic Leagues, or the Salvation Army. These groups combin their hostility to our class with real service to it: youth activities recreation, social occasions, music, theater. We should be able t organize and carry out these things ourselves.

At the same time we need a way to encourage the cultura development of workers, as in the old time labor movemen

There should be cultural and political magazines, theater troupes, chess clubs, bands, and orchestras, specialized magazines, debates, lectures, forums, poetry circles, recitals. Everything. The Workers' Societies are a way to create them.

F) Finally, the Workers' Societies will contribute to the unity of the working class as a result of these other things. We start with a badly divided class. Unity is hidden, latent. The Workers' Societies is really a name and an organizational shell designed to discover and create greater unity among workers. In this they differ from many worker organizations which have a high degree of unity as a prerequisite. We need organizations which can start with a high degree of disunity and in an easy, natural manner contribute to a growing unity based on growing common experience and judgments.

It is clear from this description that the Workers' Societies should allow only working-class people as members. This class exclusiveness is very important. Both the old Knights of Labor and the IWW understood it. They prohibited as members: lawyers, capitalists, stock brokers, people in the liquor trade, i.e., people who were not workers. The Societies should express our conscious desire to exclude the outlook and moral biases of the other classes, to concentrate on understanding our own experience, and outlook. We have to develop that experience into a class consciousness free of the narrow and petty ideas and preferences of the other classes. In stressing this I am not trying to encourage a narrow class chauvinism, a proletarian hayseed outlook. The moral elevation of our class, the breadth and depth of its humane vision, the universality of its philosophy, all these are blocked by the influence of the other classes. In the last analysis, the various middle classes and the ruling class are, for all their pretense at civilization, merely a special interest in society. They are narrow, exclusive of the rights of the great majority, and morally akin to the real estate interest or cosmetics hucksters. By contrast, as the revolutionary hymn, the *International,* truly says, the working class will become the human race. The class is first crudely formed by our common experience as the captive class of capitalist society. That society is a school for workers but a school of negative lessons. We learn what is bad and unjust. But, justice, the full human life, is not merely a negative thing. Its content is not given to us by rejecting its opposite. The Workers' Societies should be the positive school of our class, where association and cooperation among workers and conscious attention to our situation gives rise to creative thinking and activity.

Several immediate functions of the Workers' Societies are worth comment here. We must develop explicit, conscious social relations within our class in order to counter the corrosive effects of social taylorism. Bourgeois writers on social science love to comment on the radical isolation of the individual in modern civilization. They even have names for it—*anomie,* mass society, consumerism, all of these they see as unavoidable diseases of modern society in general. But they are not unavoidable, they are not diseases, and they have nothing to do with modern society in general social taylorism is created by capital, supported by capital, defended by capital and, where possible, extended by capital. It is a policy of capital. It is not a disease which rises mysteriously. It is a wound inflicted upon us. Social taylorism can only be defeated by a positive policy of the working class, a conscious attempt to rebuild a community of interest, attention and effort.

The way to do this is to give conscious attention to *all* the problems which beset us, to have an institutionalized way of bringing to our collective attention every problem and concern of the working class. The Workers' Societies are not meant to be just one more organization of workers. They are intended to be the germ of the new workers society which must rise, develop and eventually replace the society in which we now live.

One of the most important functions of the Societies is to be the parent of instrumental organizations. The problems of the working class obviously can't just be talked about and we can't just experience togetherness. There is a point where discussion ends and action begins. The Societies are designed to be a place where people can discuss problems and solutions and, if 5, 10, or 1,000 feel sufficiently motivated and directed, they can go off to organize themselves for that purpose. The Societies are not the kind of place where you have to get 51% by hook or by crook in order to start working at some problem or start carrying out some projects. They're a place where people with good ideas can go to raise them with others. In that sense then they should be a font or matrix of various instrumental organizations, but retain no connection to the latter save this: the Societies should be the broadest embodiment of our class existence and intelligence. As such they should have a moral influence–nothing more but nothing less either—on the sort of things which are done or not done in the name of our class. They are the embodied voice of all workers, a recurring town meeting of the working class, a popular assembly of the proletariat.

## The Staff Association — A Proposal

So far nothing in the Workers' Societies proposal responds to the need for an organization to further the interests and purposes of the working class. Such an organization is badly needed and we should turn our attention to the problems and opportunities it offers.

I've written a lot about the problem of distracted majorities confronted by organized minorities. It is the general political form of the relation between a ruling and a ruled class. Not even the last word in liberal democracy was able to overcome the ability of organized minorities to get their way most of the time.

There is a sort of contradiction in human society here, much commented upon by all political and social writers. On the one hand organized minorities are needed in any movement, club or even in society itself. They take the lead; they're more consciously and instrumentally concerned to think and act; they have the ability to act in a coordinated way. In this sense, they often serve the majority and are in fact a necessary tool. But at the same time, every social, personal, and political factor favors their taking over and running things to their own taste and advantage. As I say, writers have commented on this problem from almost every point of view.

Except one. If the working class under collective capital is ready, or nearly ready, to assume the control of society, the problem of organized minorities and distracted majorities will have to be solved in a radically different way. Until now, people dealt with this apparent contradiction either by directly advocating the interests of the minority or by papering over the problem, which also favors the minority. In the first case, the minority has been the propertied minority. Historically, writers have tried, without success, to paper over the fact that democratic majorities are coalitions of minorities under the control o a small minority. In the interests of socialism a practical solutio is demanded.

The following proposal for a workers Staff Association is a attempt to confront and overcome the contradiction betwee organized minorities and distracted majorities. As in the pro posals for Workers' Societies, it is wrong to expect that thorough solution to the problem can be spun out of the thin air The Staff Association proposal is a beginning to get us thinkin about the problem.

In its broadest political terms the Staff Association proposa is based on the distinction between staff functions and leader ship functions. It is based on the difference between staff an line organizations in a big corporation. The idea is to create body of men and women organized, motivated and trained t perform essential technical staff functions for the worker movement without crossing over to become the commanders o that movement. Commanding must remain the prerogative of th average worker, or we have not found anything approaching th political form of socialism.

The general task of the Staff Association is to provid people who are able and willing to give staff services to th Workers' Societies and the instrumental organizations whic stem from the Societies. The services would run the full gamut o organizational activities: research help in agenda making, com munication, tactics and so on.

The hard part is the distinction between staff and leader ship. In a normal organization, all the key areas of the organiza tion's life fall gradually into the hands of leadership. With it following, the leadership then come to control the organization People may quibble with me that this doesn't *always* happen O.K. But it happens so frequently, and in so many different type of organizations, that it is certainly the kind of thing ever organization shoud be always on guard against.

One way of looking at the Staff Association is as a way o building an organized minority consciously committed not t become a leadership but trying at every turn to keep the rank an file sufficiently *technically* equipped to control their own organi zations. In a corporate or military body with a line-staff set-u the organization is broken down into functional line responsibi ities—army commanders, under them corps commanders, under them division commanders and under them eventually, platoon leaders. Commanders have authority over their subordinates and are subject to the orders of their superiors. But in a military organization there is another whole echelon of people who are called staff. They are neither under the command of the line officers nor do they command them. They provide technical services instead. Communications, supply, intelligence, transport, training, medical.

They supply the technical services at the request of the line commander but they're not part of the commander/subordinate set-up of the line organization. The analogy with the Staff Associaton is complete except that the commanders it is responsible to are not the organized minorities but the rank and file, the majority.

If we had such an Association it would have, practically speaking, three main roles. The first and most obvious would be to work in and around worker organizations to develop our capacity to do what we want to do well. Organizations are tools. But there are tools and there are tools and they can be in good repair or not. An unbalanced hammer or a dull chisel may do the job or maybe not. You can use a pipe wrench to loosen bolts but it may do more damage than good. In any workers organization it is useful to have a body of men and women working to keep it in good shape, alert, alive, apt to its purposes. At the same time, they are avoiding, for reasons of principle and long run class advantage, any interference in the leadership of the organization or any rivalry to its existing leaders. Second, Staff Associates should make their skills and abilities available to any organization of workers—any group, any cause, for any purpose—provided both the group and the purpose have the general moral sanction of the Workers' Societies. What that sanction would mean in practical terms we might borrow from the Quakers. Their "sense of the meeting" is not a legislative act of approval but refers more to the feeling of the whole body that what's proposed and discussed fits within the broadest framework of good and useful things to do.

Clearly this use of the Staff Association implies that associates are sometimes going to be helping groups of workers who are opposed to one another. That is important for it is the true and ultimate test of the staff nature of the Association. Our earlier discussion of an experimental attitude toward reality, of complementarity and of functional leadership makes sense of the Staff Association. It indicates that the apparently contradictory role it has will, in the long run, bring far more benefit to our class than its making choices about what is good or bad to do.

The third role of the Staff Association is to work within the Workers' Societies to further all their purposes. When an organization has one or a few purposes, it's not all that hard to make it effective. Most of us have some experience in unions, clubs and societies and we know some of the things that have to be done and some that have to be avoided. But the Workers' Societies are very, very different. They have to do many things, be concerned over everything, act as a vehicle for numerous undertakings. Yet they cannot become committed to any particular project to the prejudice of any other. It will take a very high political and organizational consciousness to make the Workers' Societies perform at all, much less perform well. A body of men and women is needed to try to help expressive organization work for our class.

It is already more or less clear what kind of people we want for the Staff Association. They should be people more concerned over the broad integral development of our many-sided class than with this or that specific idea or project. They should be people whose religion is the working class, prepared to give the class as much by way of self-less service as any believer. From the nature of the tasks which the Staff Association has to undertake, Associates should be a cut above the average in the moral virtues which workers think highly of: forthrightness in personal dealing, honesty about themselves, a demonstrated willingness to fight their own foibles and hang-ups, courage, and—this is really the least important—ability—trained skills and developed knowledge of their class. I say least important because anyone can pick up these things. It's only a matter of applying yourself. But character is a different story; it's a little bit rarer and deeper.

People should become members of the Staff Association only by being elected by a Workers' Society. There are several reasons for this. First of all, the Staff Association should not be a self-perpetuating organization. That's the sure path to becoming, eventually, a vanguard organization or another commanding minority. Second, like every movement against the present order of society, the workers movement will attract a wide variety of people. Some good, some bad, but a relatively large proportion of people with grudges, real and imagined, against society. Conservative writers are at least somewhat right, when they point out that anti-establishment movements attract large numbers of people who are disgruntled because of their own failure to make it in society. Of course, they exaggerate and, even so, not making it in society is a great awakening for many good people whom we want on our side. But people who are going to serve the workers movement should have more going for them than the fact that they dislike capitalism or the establishment. They should have a positive love of the working class and demonstrate that love in practical, useful ways.

In the Workers' Societies, we will find people who are valuable to the movement as a whole and who can be encouraged by their fellow workers to move on to a life of full time service to our class. The Workers' Societies should provide men and women for the movement, electing them to the Association and supporting them while they carry out the tasks of the movement.

Suppose, for example, an Associate goes out from his or her Society to work in a new area where our movement is not developed. It will be clear to the workers in that new area that this is not a self-appointed emissary, from god knows where, but a man or woman considered so outstanding by his or her own Society that they were elected to do movement work. We are a democratic people and the fact that an Associate is elected and responsible to the people who elected him or her, will give the Staff Associate a legitimacy, a standing, in the eyes of other workers which is obtainable in no other way.

We've already discussed how, in our organizations, the various leader types get into each other's hair, start rivaling one another until there's a clear winner and loser, and how our movement loses so much from that system. In the Workers' Societies these leader types should be selected out and exported, you might say, sent out to work as staff people elsewhere. The Society would benefit by keeping them from wasting everyone's time in rivalry and by clearing the decks for new people to get a chance at being leaders. The movement would benefit by a continuous supply of good people.

Finally, electing people to the Staff Association makes possible for us to get a greater variety of people into it than th types who are good only at administrative and political chore The best of every kind is needed—doers and dreamers, toug ones and soft ones, loud and quiet, writers and administrator

Ideally, in every Workers' Society everyone would feel tha it was important to keep their eye out for people who would b good Staff Associates. People themselves would vie with eac other to receive the honor of being named a useful, accom plished person worthy of the responsibilities. There would be feeling that everyone should want to be in the Association bu that only the most outstanding would be chosen or, mor accurately, that only by being outstanding could you be chose The Mormon Church and many of the smaller Protestant sect have the practice that everyone should at some time in their lif devote their full time to the work of the church. We should hav the same idea and the Staff Association is the way to carry it ou For young people this should be a great attraction to shed th sins of capitalism and take up the work of spreading the workin class gospel.

All in all, the Staff Association proposal is an attempt for ou class to get the advantage of a vanguard group with none of it disadvantages. It is also an attempt to get all the advantages of democratically elected leadership without its disadvantages. It an attempt to design an organization characterized by what w called, earlier, functional leadership.

## The Network

In their developed forms the Societies and the Association would form a very powerful Network of working-class relatior ships and organizations. Each Society would send off an support men and women to do work in the workers movemen This could be done by consultation between Societies c between the home Society and an association bureau set up fc this purpose. Between the home Society and the new Societ which arises, you create a real, living relationship. The tw Societies have to communicate with each other about the work c the Associate, whether he or she is ready for greater respons bilities, about his or her personal well-being. On a broad scal this arrangement would create a tough, vital Network of thousands of concrete relationships between Societies, Associates and instrumental projects. This Network would constitute an effective social form of organization of our class with far more latent economic, social, political and moral power than ever could be mustered by capital and its henchmen. Like the men and women of Debs' time we would have gone a step beyond capital in the development of our class. A step this time which capital wouldn't be able to make up.

The Network has other more immediate effects which are useful from an organizational standpoint. It gives us an organizational set-up which has many vital centers of initiative, all of which are linked up in such a way that the vitality of the parts will spread easily and naturally to the whole. At the same time, and for the same reason, the unity of our class will be a growing thing, growing out of the concrete advantages and stimulus of association. It won't be the kind of negative unity which stems from reacting to things, from having a line laid on you, from minority "democracy" or from an administrative-bureaucratic center.

Finally, I want to stress again that the Network would give to the members of the Staff Association a standing in the eyes of the workers everywhere which can only come from having been chosen for the honor by the working class itself. Workers are wisely distrustful of missionaries who come into their lives and organizations, promising improvements right and left. "This guy sounds good—but who is he." "Who does she think she is coming in here offering to help?" This defensive attitude of workers is necessary to prevent wholesale invasions of working-class activity by nuts, cops, company stooges, sectarian radicals, people on the make, and every other species of nuisance. Yet the same defensiveness also prevents necessary contact and communication between the isolated fragments of our class. The Network raises this as an important problem and tries to respond to it by respecting the democratic feeling of workers, especially in matters that pertain to the working class.

This combination of proposals—Workers' Societies, instrumental organizations and Staff Associations, which I've called the Network, doesn't in any way tell us what concrete problems we have to solve to build class strength and unity. It doesn't give us an economic social and political strategy or objectives. For the most part it is designed to provide a general social form of organization for our class. We'll have to take up the other questions later but for the moment there are one or two more points to be made on this subject.

When the workers movement begins once again to become active, it will predictably be attacked from two sides. The government will be looking always to tie its hands through the use of the law. Way, way back, at the beginning of the book we joked about the judge and the wildcat miner. Unfortunately the joke really isn't funny. The whole thrust of U.S. law has been for the courts to try to bring workers organizations under their jurisdiction so that they can force them to control their members. It is interesting that they are 500% timid about telling the corporations of capital what to do. Imagine if you will a judge telling a corporation to discipline its stockholders. Yet they routinely force union officers to discipline their members. Any organization of workers which claims to legally represent workers is subject to this sort of court tyranny. One of the features I tried to design into the Network was that it would have no responsible center of authority—no Board, no President, no central body which had any authority over the working class. If we have such an authority, the court would seize control of it with their writs and injunctions quicker than you could wink your eye. The Network is as impervious to this easy control by the legal system as you can get.

The other predators of workers organizations are the communist-type parties, our old vanguard friends. They pose a double problem for us: government influence and disruption. Of any kind of organization which the government finds it easy to get hold of, the vanguard groups lead the pack. Normally, they are very centralized so that if government agents manage to penetrate the leadership they can do untold damage. To be realistic, we should assume that they are under some government influence.

The people in these organizations often don't know they're under government influence. In the '50's a friend of mine was recruited to the Communist Party by a very good and militant member. In fact, there would have been no Party in that area, except for the member in question. Yet he was a government agent who later turned all his recruits in to the F.B.I., including ıy friend. Examples like this are very common. Some government agents give themselves away by acting as provocateurs to iolence and illegality. Those are the obvious ones. But the sleeping agent," the one who performs well and leaks informa-.on to the government is hard to discover. The only cure for this ort of agent is to avoid the vanguard form of organization.

On the other hand, we should not treat the members of these arties as undercover cops. Many, many excellent people join ıese sectarian groups, such as the Communist Party, Socialist Vorkers Party, or Revolutionary Youth League, because they ant to help our movement and nothing else is available. But the ıfluence of their organizations over us has to be checked and ıinimized.

Disruption comes about in the following way. The normal im of these vanguard organizations is to try to gain an influence ı worker organizations way out of proportion to their numbers. ometimes this will take the form of trying to provoke debate on ubjects they think are important, with a view to getting pportunities to repeat their views over and over again. Then hen they see who among the workers shares their views, they'll ry to recruit the person for their own organization. Anyone who bjects to them they call a "red-baiter."

They try to gain important posts within workers organiza-ions. From these they can exert more influence than either their umbers (usually small) or their views (usually narrow) would ntitle them. The Network style makes it hard for them to be lisruptive and to exert undue influence.

Nothing ever happens automatically in life and it is difficult o keep both the government and the sectarian political organiza-ions at bay. But the Network won't be an easy environment for nyone to work in who is trying to impose a view or a purpose on he working class.

In this context, finally, I think the Network poses a radically ew idea of what it means to be a leader of the workers novement. Traditionally, and under the influence of Marx and, specially, Lenin, the best leaders of the working class were lescribed as those people who had the most far-seeing political onsciousness and who, as leaders, would teach the rest of us vhile leading us in the correct direction. Very often this idea of eadership is coupled with Lenin's view that workers, left to their own devices, would never, ever advance beyond trade unionism and other defensive respones to capital. I've already commented enough on why I think that that is a false and dangerous view, a view which contains the seeds of the corrupt socialism of the Soviet Union.

Socialism is as natural to the working class as potatoes to an Irishman. The role of those men and women who now see and feel consciously the need for socialism is to try to clear a few boulders off the path and then stand aside because the working class will come tearing down that path hell-bent. It may be that the proposals for the Workers' Societies, instrumental organizations and the Staff Association aren't really workable. Maybe they're even way off base. But on one count they're right, namely that the broad mass of men and women must march the path to socialism because it represents for them the fullest expression of their qualities as sensitive, thinking human beings who want to build a life better and more worthwhile than is possible under capitalism. The Network assumes that as the basic fact around which the fundamental social organization of our class must be built. It assumes the desire for socialism is present very broadly and deeply in our class. It assumes the capacity for socialism has ripened in our class and that we have passed that critical point where we were still dependent on another class to rule over us and create a society for us, which we ourselves are unable to create.

# CHAPTER ELEVEN CLASS-WIDE INTERESTS IN TRADE UNIONS

The first imperative of the working class is to form itself into a class. The second imperative is to create shared, class-wide interests, especially economic and social ones. This will make political cooperation and unity possible.

## In the Trade Unions

The main economic instrument for workers is the trade union movement. But trade unions suffer from several mortal weaknesses. They are no longer able to wield any decisive economic power; they divide even the organized working class into economically competing groups; as a form of organization they are under terrible legal restraints from collective capital. Finally, they are presently much more a device for controlling workers than they are for workers to control themselves. We've already discussed why this is so, in chapter one. Here we need only recap the highlights.

In the corporate sector of the economy, which is the most heavily unionized, trade union organizations fail to control any of the Critical Eight factors. The result is that workers' economic gains are almost entirely illusory. Workers are failing and have failed for years even to keep their so-called share of the pie. As we saw from the table on p. 26 (chapter two), worker's share of the surplus (= value added) has fallen steadily. The pie gets bigger due to increased productivity but we do not share in it. More of us work harder than ever, yet our share in the economy continues to drop. The unions fail economically first because they cannot prevent the corporations from extracting an increasing share of the surplus from us by controlling the relation between productivity, wages and prices. Second they cannot influence the relations between what we pay in taxes (a lot) and the benefits we get (very little).

The trade unions face these two problems in the form of inflation and increased taxes. In its effort to keep up with rising prices and taxes, each union becomes a rival of every other and a rival to unorganized workers. In its public relations, each union says that its gains help the others to get their increases. But the plain corporate economics of the situation make each union compete against the others, changing the trade union movement from a cooperative endeavor to a form of class wide competition.

Our country officially believes in free enterprise in every area of the economy save one—the trade unions. Every aspect of trade union life is closely regulated by law or administrative fiat. In reality, we live in an economy closely controlled by collective capital, but the only place where this is admitted is the trade unions. What it boils down to is that what unions can legally do and what they can't legally do is closely controlled by government. By and large, they can do only those things which are ineffective at protecting worker interests and are prevented from doing those things which would be effective. I've exaggerated this thing a bit. Reality is rarely so clear-cut. But as a convenient short-hand it gives the main truth. Some lawyers who are on our side should sit down and spell out the whole sordid story of the one-sidedness of the law in dealing with worker organizations. But for now our characterization will suffice: the government allows or forces trade unions to do what is ineffective and prohibits them from doing what would be effective.

Finally, because the unions are getting weaker, and can't defend the economic interests of their members, the leadership becomes afraid that the members will get rebellious and take natters into their own hands. Thus union leadership joins with management to try to control the workers. Usually this happens where the rank and file is unhappy over something and wants to walk out in spite of the contract. The union leaders and management try together to prevent that. What really is happening is that the interests of union leaders and union members become opposed; the one has a career riding on the contract, the other feels the contract is lousy because it gives up too much to get some extra money. When this happens all the time, you soon have a situation where the union leader is as much or even more worried about fighting the members than about fighting the company. To a dangerous degree the trade unions now are devices to control the rebellious activities of workers. Wild cats, slow-downs, skippy, working to rule, sick-outs, and job-actions are good weapons in our armory for dealing with the boss. But on most of them, most of the time, the union leadership joins with the boss to try to prevent us.

The four fundamental problems, it seems to me, are that the trade unions:

1) lack a measure of decisive economic power
2) make workers compete against each other
3) are too easily legally restrained
4) capture and control the rebellious activities of workers.

Our first and most obvious response ought to be to create by trade union behavior class-wide economic interests. Sitting in a chair here I obviously am not going to tell anyone what to do. But it is pretty clear what kinds of things would create class-wide interests. Let me give some examples.

You'll recall that in our preliminary breakdown the GM car looked like this:

| Mat. & Mach. | | Wages | | Salaries | | Profits | | Taxes | = | Sale Price |
|---|---|---|---|---|---|---|---|---|---|---|
| | | | | | Value Added | | | | | |
| 1518 | + | 420 | + | 323 | + | 185 | + | 176 | = | 2622 |

GM controls the relative size of all those figures and uses it to defeat our efforts to increase real wages, i.e., our relative share of the value added. They simply add on wage increases to the final price, plus a little extra for themselves, so the rest of us get hopping mad at the auto workers and are forced to encourage our industry to do the same thing. We're walking on a treadmill.

The most obvious countermove on our part is for the auto workers to insist on two things—that annual increases in productivity go to lowering the price of the car, and that wages stay constant. Look at the figures for this. If productivity increases by about 2½% per year, throughout the economy (it does!), the price of the car should fall to about $2555, a difference of $65. If it doesn't come out of wages it will have to come out of the price GM pays to its suppliers, out of salaries or out of profits. By themselves, the auto workers do not have the power to force GM to do this. If they tried to, GM would scream bloody murder about free enterprise and the rights of management. The conservative press would see Bolshevists marching through the streets. But the auto workers would have a very powerful ally in such a scrap: the whole working class. By fighting for a lower price for the car they're putting $65 into your pocket and mine. More if you add in the inflation that would then not happen. We could say to ourselves, "Hey, those auto workers are thinking of the interests of our whole class, not just of themselves. They'll save the $65 too but it's a saving we'll share with them. We would have a direct economic stake—the $65—plus a moral stake—they're doing something not just for themselves but for all workers. Like the ARU in Pullman the auto workers would have a right to our moral and material support—strike assistance, "public opinion," hostility against GM products. It would also put the onus of inflation right where it belongs—on the company.

If all or many trade unions tried this tactic it would create broad working class interests. You and I would have a stake in it that we don't now have in the demands of this or that trade union. That's why I said earlier that trade unions *as we know them* are obsolete. There is life in the old dog yet—if we have the wit to put it there.

When you insist that productivity increases bring lower prices, wages remaining constant, you are in fact interfering with the rights of management. You are moving in on the Critical Eight by trying to influence the relationship between prices, wages and profit. When we do that we bring the overwhelming bulk and might of our class into the battle instead of having them sit on the side-lines saying "Screw all you S.O.B.'s. I've no interest in you and your selfish tricks."

All of us are for a shorter work week. It also is economically just. What with the steady increase in the relative size of the work force, meaning the number of people working as compared to the total population, we should be working fewer hours every year. If a big union was to insist on a shorter work week, say of 32 hours, wages and prices remaining the same they have an excellent case which you and I have a stake in too. It creates a class-wide shared interest so that we will be willing to support it. Spurred on by their example, we may start hollering for a shorter work week in our own industry.

When you get your head into thinking like this, other good ideas come along too. The consumer movement is a big thing now, not only because industry cheats so much on quality, dangerous substances, weight, phoney packaging and warrantees that would make a lawyer cross-eyed, but also because all of us have got to spend money on products we don't really know how to judge. As consumers, we buy and use the whole range of modern technology: electronics in our stereos, computers in our ignition systems, preservatives in everything, metallurgy and modern materials science (plastics, ceramics, new bonding agents) in most things. None of us can know enough about all of these things to get good buys for our money. Here's a new use for the union label. Why not use it to attest to the quality of the product? It was used for that in the days of the Knights. This is an idea whose time has returned. Right on the label there should be the name and address of the local which made the product. If possible the name and union card numbers of the workers who worked on it. Then, if you have a complaint you can complain right to the source. The AFL-CIO could set up a special Union Label Court, with *worker* judges, to keep records on complaints and to call to task locals who allow their companies to put crap on the market. I say "court" and "judges" because that court and those judges should be as reliable, high quality and free of political taint for our class as Federal judges are for theirs.

Of course, this idea infringes on the rights of management and of course they'll fight back. The local upstarts telling management that they can't produce the bicycles this way because any other way makes a safer product. You have to tell them, look, you can't put that stuff in the cookies because if you do we can't put a label on them and you're going to get sales resistance from union members and those unorganized workers who are smart enough to see what's happening. Obviously, management won't like it.

But when each one helps one you get unity. Many of the substances used in food preparation are even more dangerous to the worker who processes the food than they are to the worker who consumes it. The vinyl chloride used in wrapping meat and vegetables; the additives in food; the very fine fibre glass in air ducts. This new use of the union label involves consumer groups directly in health and safety issues on the job and ties our unions into consumer protection.

How different this approach is from the higher-wages-in-my-industry-and-everyone-else-be-damned approach the corporations have pushed us into. One creates a weak labor movement with an ineffective strategy and moral disrepute among all workers. The new approach creates unity among workers based on shared economic interests plus esteem for what our class does.

Every successful strategy idea for our class requires that we seize some definite economic power we don't have now. Every citadel of real power we seize from capital adds to our power, weakens theirs, and serves as a jumping off point for new initiatives and offensives. But the guiding principle must be the broad advantage of our class, not the narrow interest of our local, district or international. Each offensive must attack the so-called right of management to manage, i.e., the right of management to control us and to extract an ever increasing share of the surplus we create.

If the Critical Eight remain in management's hands, no amount of talk, no matter how militant and revolutionary it sounds, is worth a damn. We don't need what the old labor movement used to call Jawsmiths. We need power and to get it will take real knock-down bitter fights with management. It is almost a truism to say it, but if what we want doesn't make management get red in the face with rage, it probably isn't worth having.

Every industry is different; so is every shop. To get power in an industry or a shop, the workers in that industry have got to sit down and talk out what happens there. They have to find the best opportunities to get hold of the Critical Eight or any part of them. There's nothing that can replace workers' initiative on this score. Your initiative.

## Shop Meetings

It is easy to get caught in a rut and just keep doing things wrong today because that's the way you did them yesterday. If we had Workers' Societies and a Staff Association and I had any say in what anybody did, I'd argue that people in every shop in the country should get together once or twice a year to talk out their situation. Not the situation of the union. Put that aside for the moment—just the situation in the shop for the men and women who work there. The Women's Liberation Movement does something like this, called consciousness raising. They set up a session of maybe up to a dozen people who first just voice their complaints. The idea is that what people feel, they feel, and they should be able to say it—just as they feel it. Obviously a lot of bitterness and resentment is going to come out. But if other people listen sympathetically to it and take the anger and bitterness as being serious and worthy of respect, a change occurs. Very often what is bothering me is bothering you too. By ourselves we're so upset we just can't put our finger on it exactly. But when it comes out in someone else's piece, we may be able to recognize and grab hold of it. The thing is to listen. To use your ears to help the other person to hear him or herself and to be able to use theirs to hear yourself. Once several years ago I led such a session among some young, working class students in the New Bedford, Mass. area. At first they were very hesitant to do what I asked them, namely to speak of the bitterness in their lives, especially on the job and at school. Then one of them, normally a quiet person, began to speak. He talked about being hassled on the way to work by the police because he drove a beat-up car and looked poor. He spoke of losing his license because he talked back to the cops and they began laying for him. He talked about having to take the bus to work and how there were no decent wash-up facilities at his plant and how the people on the bus made him feel self-conscious because his hands and face had grease on them. As he continued, others in the group began to remember similar feelings in other settings or different feelings in the same settings. You know how people get into an absorbing discussion. They warm to the topic and before you know it they are really sharing how they feel. That was when I first began to realize there was an underground life to our class, a much, much richer underground life than most of us suspect. It made me realize that if I'm thinking something, someone else is too; if I'm bothered by something, so are others; that people know, fee understand and react more than they let on. Our class has a enormous resentment at the life it must lead and a profound developed sense of justice. But we're underground, and the firs step is to get it all out. So there is no substitute for shop meeting shop councils or Societies. They are the first and essential ste toward a revived workers movement. For our class, *bitterness* *truth,* no matter how one-sided, no matter how extreme. The firs step is to let that bitterness out. When people start to get conf dence in each other, begin to see that others will listen to ther even if they don't speak well or have an accent or a squeaky voic then enough of a group will exist to develop a balanced view an to talk about what can be done. But a group has to be formed firs and that requires a lot of trust and confidence in each othe Otherwise all you'll get is BS from those who like to run off at th mouth.

Another issue for the trade union movement is politics. It very important for the trade unions to enlarge and extend the freedom of action vis-a-vis the government. We should begin b clearing our minds of the idea that having a Democrat in th White House, State House or City Hall makes that muc difference. It's better to have a labor Democrat than th opposite. But that's not enough. Government, at all levels and i every way, is tied to the capitalist class. We saw that especially b analyzing the big stake government had in GM's surplus (th value added). There it ended up with $176 on every car. So it never neutral in a dispute between workers and capital. Neve Even the most far-out liberal Democrat never goes beyond wan ing social peace between labor and capital. By that he means "fair share" for the workers (at most a tiny bit more for us), an harmony (we can't ask for anything that steps on the toes capital and the middle element). As we've seen, liberal an conservative administrations don't affect the shares of th surplus going to capital and labor. Only one thing happen regardless of Democrats or Republicans—the workers' share the surplus falls. So there is no such thing as a neutral, thir party government. In any dispute between capital and us, th government is on the other side—maybe more, maybe less—bu on the other side.

It is foolish in the extreme for union members and officials to expect any change in this government behavior. If anything, government has been growing gradually more hostile to trade unions. Its attitude is getting harder on strikes, wild-cats, and wage increases. In the future it will use its power more and more to keep wage increases from keeping up with productivity.

People should explore the price we'd have to pay if we gave up the protection the government now gives the labor movement in exchange for its subservience. People with considerable knowledge of law and of NLRB procedure should raise this question because if the labor movement began to move in an independent direction the government would come down on it in two ways. New laws would be passed and old ones enforced to give us a hard time. We would lose NLRB protection for our organizing efforts and contracts. Employers would step up their harassment while the courts and the NLRB would look the other way. Even where we had 51% of the workers in a shop we might not be able to get the union legally recognized as the legitimate bargaining agent. We couldn't use arbitration and mediation services. The government might hold back contracts from employees who dealt with us just as FDR did to attack John L. Lewis in the early 40's. Probably, if we wanted to keep government and the courts out of our hair our agreements with management couldn't be legally binding contracts, but only "mutual understandings" not backed up by law.

On the other hand, we have experience in some of these things. In 1947, the government made a finding that several unions were Communist dominated and, by the terms of the Taft-Hartley law, excluded them from NLRB protection and services. The unions included the United Electrical Workers (UE), Mine, Mill and Smelter; and the Fur Workers. Of these UE was the most important and its experience is worth looking at. It was denied the protection and services of the NLRB. That meant that GE and the other employers could engage in any unfair labor practice they could think of. The government privately encouraged this and even used its power to hurt employers who continued to deal with UE. The CIO, then separate, organized a rival union to UE, the International Union of Electrical Workers (IUE), which, along with every other Tom, Dick, and Harry, raided UE every chance they could get.

Finally, the press and the Catholic hierarchy went after UE hammer and tong.

UE survived all this. Friends of mine in the union say that most of that government, CIO, IUE, press, employer and pulpit opposition didn't really hurt them that much. Where the locals were good and had built up loyalty among the workers they didn't crumble under the attacks. Marginal locals, locals with poor leadership or locals where the workers had been just yanked into the union without much say so on their part—those were the ones that went off with the raiding parties or collapsed.

If we could see our way to abandon the protection of the courts and the NLRB we'd gain several advantages. Take the strike, for example. Industry has learned to deal with strikes. It doesn't like them because, after all, they only make their money from our work. But industry can deal with strikes if it can anticipate them.

If they have a contract with us they know we can only strike at the expiration of the contract, which allows them to plan ahead. And, if the strike gets too "hot" for capital, the government can apply Taft-Hartley. We're "cooled off" or "cooled out" for 80 days while the company lays in extra production, builds up its inventories, forewarns its customers and does whatever else is necesary to sabotage our strike. Without government regulation, we might be in a position to make our strikes selective and unpredictable. We could develop the wild cat into an instrument of such precision and deftness that industry would really be up against it. We could extend our choice of issues. Except that if we started messing with the Critical Eight we might discover new barriers in our way, such as *administrative rulings* by government agencies saying that our messing around with the Critical Eight was an "unfair labor practice" and not within the legal bounds of a labor union's activities.

The point of this whole discussion was to see where and how we could restore and extend workers' freedom of action. The present situation of the unions is pretty much to the satisfaction of business. They can count on what we'll do, and have eight different ways to undo it. It's pretty much to the satisfaction of the government which has an enormous stake in the tax dollars that come out of uninterrupted production. And it's pretty much to the satisfaction of the international union leaders since the ystem puts all the power in their hands, and guarantees it by ıbor law and the edicts of bureaus like the NLRB.

The Industrial Workers of the World (IWW), a U.S. labor rganization which existed in the 1900-1920 period didn't like ontracts and government interference for the very reasons I've sted. But, they took a very extreme view. For them, an nderstanding between the workers and the company was only a emporary armed truce in the class struggle. Now the plain fact that perpetual, unending industrial warfare is not in our nterest. In fact, it can favor capital. For capital, industrial varfare is just an extra cost, not one they like to pay, but one they vill pay if necessary. They can hire help to do their dirty work— hether it's scabbing, strike-breaking, trouble-making, black-sting, provocation, goons, or espionage. For us to resist all that another story. Our strength is the intelligence, alertness and ıilitancy of the average man or woman. But the average man or voman can't devote 40 hours a week to union affairs. There are imes when workers are militant and spoiling for a fight and other imes when they have to tend to other things like work, family, or elaxing. The perpetual warfare the IWW engaged in demands hat workers have to spend enormous time and energy on union ctivities just to fight off the counter-attacks that management's ired hands were always launching. In the long run, perpetual varfare is not to our interest: what we need are "agreements" vhich are based on management's need for industrial predict-bility but which we are legally free to terminate for what we hink is good cause. To make this thing work we would have to be nuch more mature and thoughtful than the IWW was. The verage man or woman would have to be a strike tactician. They vould have to have crystal clear opinions about when it is best to ull management to sleep by their peaceableness and when we hould deliver blows that strike home. And they would have to nake this judgment over and over again, never provoking nanagers into all out class war, or providing incidents to rally public opinion" behind anti-labor sentiment, but always string-ng management along on the belief that "one more concession" vill bring industrial peace. We should always keep them guessing y neither going for total peace during the life of an agreement, as ve do now, nor total war as the IWW did.

The IWW didn't only talk industrial warfare. They practiced

it. They were very fond of talking about sabotage, the bomb, th gun and the club. Too much so, since their wild talk of thes things far exceeded the little bit they used them. But their tal just opened the door to wholesale violence against them. If yo speak of violence, sabotage and illegal action, you should alway remember that the very essence of government is that it alon reserves far more force and violence for its own use than it wi permit on the part of its subjects. People who talk of sabotag and other violent tactics should always be forced to answer tw questions right on the spot: are they prepared for civil wa immediately and is the working class prepared to wage i victoriously? The record is very clear on this. If we commi violence and can be identified, police and, if necessary, troop will be called in to suppress us. If we commit violence and canno be identified the authorities will commit random violence agains us and will encourage the goon element to prey violently on ou organizations, neighborhoods, leaders and people.

On the other hand, we must be prepared to be the victims c the outrageous use of law and publicly constituted authority Richard Olney's name should be engraved on our consciousnes for there are always new Olney's, Cleveland's, Walker's an Grosscup's to be found. There's not the slightest doubt in m mind that if we are at all successful in anything, that "anything will be attacked, hedged around and blunted by law. Certainly the attempt will be made by government and nine chances out o ten it will succeed.

## The Philosophy and Tactics of Non-Violence

The tenth chance is worth talking about. It's related to th sort of nonviolent tactics and philosophy worked out so bril liantly by the men, women and, especially, young people wh were associated with the late Dr. Martin Luther King. Nonviolen tactics are based on a profound truth, perhaps the most profoun truth to be found about human society: the love of justice amon the people is a mighty force in history. Our ideas of justice ma change from century to century but any time that the great mas of our people are animated by a positive idea of justice an identify a source of injustice, not even the heavens can help th mighty. History shudders and a new epoch begins.

This truth is based upon another great truth which is especially important for a captive class like our own. We are enslaved not by force but by our own ignorance, separateness and fear. When we overcome those three, when our intelligence binds us into class solidarity animated by courage, not even the force of huge armies can check our progress.

The second point is that the use of nonviolent measures to win change against the wishes of the authorities requires a much more conscious, disciplined people than violent measures. Under some circumstances, it isn't hard to get people stirred into violence. You know and I know that sometimes we want to break things or create a ruckus so that we need very little urging. It may not even be so dangerous for us since we're not likely to be singled out by the authorities if a big crowd is involved. By contrast, ask someone to engage in nonviolent tactics. It really puts them on the spot. You can't throw a brick and hide in a crowd. You've got to sit at the lunch counter, maybe alone, as hostile people crowd around. Maybe you just scrunch up as they work you over, or don't kick back as the cop aims his club for your face or groin. Alone, amidst people who are full of hysterical fear and hatred, you've got to discipline yourself by the cause you serve and not give in to your anger or defensive reactions. It takes great conviction, thoughtfulness, forethought, moral preparation and commitment to do that. Only the person with a deeply thought out conviction can participate in nonviolent struggles.

I am not a pacifist. There are times, I believe, when it is necessary to resort to violence, to strike back at unjust people or situations or institutions with physical violence and, in the last extreme, with arms in hand. On the other hand, all of us would like to see a world where fear, physical force, war, and all kinds of violence were near to extinction, a world where persuasion, cooperation and tolerance were as normal as their opposites are now. That's a human world, where injustice has the uphill fight, and would-be Caesars are routinely laughed down. The philosophy of nonviolence points our ideas to this more human world. It tends to blunt government's last resort against us—brutal force. All in all, nonviolent ideas and tactics as applied to industrial conflict is a subject that workers should explore further.

## Socialism in Industry

We need trade unions to defend our economic interests. But the ones we have are as much of a problem for workers as management itself is. We should confront that fact squarely, that it is S.O.P. for our trade unions to try to countrol us and keep us out of real conflict with management. I think the Workers' Societies and the Staff Association are really useful here. We should see them and use them as a complement to our unions, not as a rival. It would be of infinite value to our class if workers at every level—shop, city, county, state, district, region, nation—could meet periodically to talk about their grievances against the union. I don't mean a meeting run by union officers which really works as a safety valve, letting off steam in empty words, with the whole thing over at the final gavel. The reform of our unions and the attack against management have to go hand in hand—because the union leader and the manager are themselves too often holding hands. So, we just have to get things off our backs so we can stand up straight. There have to be big changes in our unions. But what kind of changes? To answer that question, we have to talk about socialism in industry.

If we had socialism in industry it might work something like this. Every couple of years worker representatives would come together in a National Economic Congress to decide the main outlines of the economy for the next period of time. That Congress would be the tail end of a process which involved just about every man and woman in the country in active discussion and debates about what sort of economic objectives should have first priority. For example, if a Congress was going on now some of the main questions people would have to answer would be:

> *How high should U.S. food be priced?* There is a world food shortage. Are the high prices we can get for our wheat or corn causing suffering to the less well-off people of our own country and to the poor of other lands? Can we price our food high enough to offset the cost of our imports, such as oil, or aluminum? Is it right to use our food as a lever to force other governments to cut back on arms and showcase industry, making them devote more of their resources to increasing their food

production? Should we refuse food to countries that mistreat their own people?

*What is the best way to bring the welfare population into the productive economy?* We all know that the present welfare set-up forces part of our population to live off the dole forever. How can we break this cycle? How much of our resources can we devote to providing good jobs for older people which don't over tax their health and energy? What are our priorities with respect to medical research, education, child care, basic science or transportation? What can we say to the people to whom we have to say No!?

*How can we develop a good energy program?* How much coal can we afford to use, balancing the dangers of coal mining to the miners and coal burning to the breathers with coal's cheapness to our economy? How much freedom of choice can we have on the number of private cars and the size of their engines? Questions of that sort.

Right now these questions are discussed and settled by men nd some women who are in all respects but one just like you and ne. They too don't always understand the issues. They too can et into trouble if they make a mistake. They too sometimes lose he forest for the trees. They are only different in that they are nembers of the ruling class and get a voice in these things. We're nembers of the working class and don't.

Under socialism the responsibility to make decisions on hose matters falls on us. After the experts get finished describ- ng the alternatives we'll have to decide. We would probably have o set aside a long period of time in every shop for workers to sit own together and begin batting these things back and forth. fter awhile we'd have to come to a decision on who were going to e our delegates to, say, a Congress of people in our industry. Ve'd have to instruct those delegates on major questions of ational policy. We'd have to instruct them on the needs of our wn shop. If we were miners they might report that any sudden ncrease in coal production could only be managed if we get this nd that piece of equipment, so much money for safety systems nd so many tens of thousands of new miner-trainees. If we were neighborhood and not a shop group we might instruct our delegates to hold out for extra money for housing repair and an increase in services to elderly people. Our goal is a working class with the time, intelligence, energy, information and power to set up the basic outlines for running the country and apply them to our shop and neighborhoods. That goal should guide the activity of the trade union movement. It means that we should be fighting for the right to have shop meetings to discuss whatever the people in that shop want to discuss. They should be held during regular work hours so everybody can be there and they should be free from management or union interference.

To keep the union and Society out of each other's hair, only the initial meetings should be Society meetings, the ones in which the workers express what they feel to one another. Meetings which decide on priorities and courses of action infringe on the purposes of the union. The two must be kept separate.

## Dual Unions

Where the union is too corrupt or too resistant to change it may be that some workers in the Society will branch off to create a rival union. The question of rival unions is a very old one in US labor history. It is often referred to as the issue of dual unions—meaning two or more unions competing for the allegiance of the same group of workers. The AFL itself was established in opposition and competition to the Knights of Labor. And, as we saw, Debs set up the American Railway Union because the Rail Brotherhoods were neglecting the interest of the great mass of railway workers.

Dual unionism is not a matter that can be settled by appeal to a vague principle, such as unity. It is a practical question, that has to be decided on the basis of its results. Rival unions may spend too much energy fighting and bad-mouthing one another or raiding the other's members. Naturally the boss likes that. He often sets up a company union of his own to "represent" the workers.

On the other hand, unions are notoriously undemocratic and there are times when the voice of the workers requires a new democratic organization to make itself heard. Competition between unions in the same shop or industry may divide and weaken the workers or it may put both unions on their toes so that the workers come out ahead. Something like this has happened in recent years in Italy. There you have Communist, Catholic and social democratic unions. At one time they fought each other bitterly but now they are by and large cooperating against capital. They work out joint demands and cooperative strategies.

In our country, specifically, the question of dual unions revolves around how you weigh two factors—the centralized power of the big union and the legal structure of collective bargaining. As we've had occasion to remark here and there, U.S. unions are very, very centralized and very, very resistant to change from below. Most unions have one master.Everyone else walks around on tip-toes. And that's mild compared to some unions. Tony Boyle of the Miners had Jock Yablonski killed because Yablonski dared to challenge him. Several years back the Carpenter's union was so beholden to one President that he was able to pass the office on to his son, as if he was owner of the business. This sort of one man rule or rule by a tiny unrepresentative crowd of insiders is one of the reasons—we've discussed some of the others—why the labor movement has been so blind to its own economic, social and political decline. On this basis alone, then, there are good arguments for rival unions to shake up the old ones so they'll do their job or, in some cases, to send them to deserved and blessed oblivion.

One factor against dual unionism is the U.S. legal system. The effect of the NLRB is to create union monopolies on workers. Mostly you hear about this from the employers who shed crocodile tears over the fact that 51% of their workers can force the other 49% to join the union, pay dues, and be covered by the contract. Employers love to say how unfair this is to minority rights. This is what Right to Work Campaigns are about. Unfortunately, all this employing class yowling about Right to Work covers up an other side of the NLRB coin. The 51%, whether they are a real majority or the kind of "put together" majority we talked about earlier, can force the 49% into a union and can keep them there even if the union is lousy. So many workers are captive in their unions. If they want, they can organize rival unions, but the legal system forces them to be members of the original union too. This is another area where workers may have to forego NLRB advantages for greater freedom of action.

If workers form a rival union they will have to cross difficult bridges. For starters, they'd normally form a new union only if the old one couldn't be, or wasn't worth, reforming. The old union has got to be pretty bad and maybe even near to useless. Still, it's important not to wage the kind of war against the old union and its leadership from which no good peace will come. War is really always waged for the sake of peace, but you can make war in such a way that peace is only a brief interlude of preparation for the next round. Unity in the working class will never come from merely defeating other workers, even if they really are bad guys. The thing is to win the other folks over even as you are defeating them. The ruling class does this well. Once they've taken you on and beaten you, they'll be nice to you, genuinely nice, because they genuinely don't want to have to fight you again. A new union, say, or a new slate in an older union isn't that much of an improvement if many of the old leadership or workers are so bitter and angry that they drop out or, worse yet, start to collaborate with management. No victory in any fight within the working class is really a victory unless it serves our long-run interests.

The plain fact is that the man or woman who is on the side of the angels today may be an ass tomorrow and the person who is full of wisdom tomorrow may be full of something else the next day. The traditional idea of fighting within the workers movement, both among trade union and radical types, is to commit mayhem on each other. The Christians have a doctrine of the forgiveness of sins but the workers movement never picked up on it. This makes our fights so bitter that people shy away from any fighting, figuring it's better to go along even with wrong policies rather than risk civil war among ourselves. It would be better to fight with one another more often but with less bitterness.

Right now the influence of the Kirkland's, Fitzsimmons', Shanker's and other conservative trade unionists is pretty negative. Clearly the socialist forces are going to have to fight with them in order to pull the labor movement out of the doldrums. Invariably, this means we have to challenge not only their ideas but also their power.

But what's the fight about? Conservative trade unionsts believe the labor movement is too weak to win its way. So they are timid before capital and to justify that to themselves they take arge doses of capitalist ideas into their heads. On the other hand, ve believe that a thorough reorganization of the workers novement can lead to socialism, that the power of the working lass is such that nothing really can withstand it. The different deas, policies, and programs all revolve around that difference.

Now the plain fact is that the conservatives have some truth o their argument. The workers movement is weak right now and here is no guarantee that it would win in a fundamental contest vith capital. In the long run, certainly, but in our life-time? So to ondemn our opponents is to condemn them for having a easonable view but one we believe is erroneous. The worst thing hat those people are is wrong. Not wildly wrong, maliciously vrong, or irresponsibly wrong. Just wrong and this in an area vhere there are good arguments on both sides.

I believe we should fight hard, to win. But the tactics, trategy, and ideas of that fight must, at the end of it, leave open he possibility of saying to more conservative people, "You too re part of our class, your views have merit too. Today you are vrong but perhaps tomorrow your judgment will be necessary nd good for us, therefore we want you to join with us and ontribute your special skill or insight to build up our movenent." That's a socialist position on conflict within our class, etter than the short-sighted, to-the-victor-belongs-the-spoils nentality we now have.

## imits of Trade Union Action

Imagine, if you will, that we'd achieved all our immediate oals in the labor movement. Class wide economic interests were apidly being created. Management control of the Critical Eight vas caving in. Workers were winning more and more freedom of ction in relation to government and also within the trade unions. Vonderful, but it isn't enough. Trade unions are the key to our conomic power. It depends on them whether we are well off or o hungry, whether we have common or opposed interests. Their uccess weakens the economic power of capital and reduces the esources capital has to fight us on other fronts. But, it is on those ther fronts that we too need power and resources, namely in the ocial world and in politics. We will turn to them now but first here's an item which needs our attention.

Throughout this book I've tried to keep the focus on our own country—the U.S. Clearly that was necessary because you've got to start in your own backyard. But capital is an international class. It believes that the corporation has no home-land and can operate as well across national borders as within them. Unless I'm way off base, international capital, under the leadership of the U.S., is now trying to build a truly international ruling class. The bases of this class are the multi-national corporations supplemented by the specialized international organs of capital such as the Common Market, the Organization for European Economic Cooperation, the Trilateral Commission, and various banks and law firms. The idea is to free the corporations from special identity with one country. Instead, they want every nationality on their payroll.

This raises the necessity of cooperation between the workers of the different countries. Even present union leaders see this and there has been an increase in discussions and even cooperation among the trade unionists of the various western countries. But international doesn't mean just the west. The only proper program for our class is to deliberately build ties with workers organizations of every country, whether the country is communist or capitalist, industrialized or non-industrialized, western or eastern. Hopefully, it will soon be a matter of course for the unions of all of say, GM's employees, in every country, to sit down together. If we don't do that we are, in effect, scabbing when British or Brazilian workers are on strike and vice versa. Over 100 years ago, on September 28, 1864, Marx led the founding of the International Working Men's Association to encourage cooperation between the various working classes. The International was actually a federation of various national organizations. Now, 100 years later we have to start to look toward, and plan for, an international organization of the working class.

# CHAPTER TWELVE
# CLASS-WIDE INTERESTS—IN THE NEIGHBORHOOD, THE COMMUNITY

Earlier in the book we discussed the functions of the family-neighborhood networks of the late 19th century, emphasizing the key role they played in the formation of our class. The inattention of the old workers movement allowed capital to move in and destroy those networks, replacing them with the administrative power of the Social System. Then we put forward the expressive organization as they key concept to use in forming our class once more, but this time on the basis of *forethought.* The result was the proposal for Workers' Societies. We should now look at the neighborhood-based Workers' Societies as we attempt to re-create our communities and neighborhoods and carry them beyond what they were in grandma's day.

## The Workers' Society in the Neighborhood

If we had Workers' Societies in our communities and neighborhoods, the uses to which they could be put are numerous. Certainly they'd be having continuous discussions of the neighborhood's problems and would be the setting in which people could get together to form instrumental organizations to solve those problems. Here are some areas which the Workers' Societies could help us to deal with. There are loads more.

*Community Services:* When the Social System deals with older people or ill people it really deals with them in the narrow spirit of their being the unproductive costs of production. Capital treats them like safety screens around dangerous machinery—something you have to spend money on but which won't bring a return. For older or infirm people the U.S. is one of the worst countries in the world to live in. The working class attitude is different to the degree that we shed the narrow views of life put on us by capital and the middle element. For us, the old and the infirm are us—people who, slowed down a little and having earned the right to an easier time of it, are still in every other respect just like ourselves. The problem of elderly people isn't that they're really old; the problem is that capital demands a uniform type of worker—healthy, moderately educated, obedient, moderately paid and able to work at a pace that only people in their physical prime can work at. When you get a step slower, or your eyes lose their edge, or you begin to be more susceptible to aging diseases, capital doesn't want you. This is not decided on an individual basis; instead a cut-off number of years is picked out—60-62-65. People are forced into a state of involuntary inactivity, with a restricted social life and low income. Age is a state of mind of capital.

Wonderful! Capital has given us an unending supply of the most valuable resource in the world—experienced, skilled, mature people. We are great fools if we don't take advantage of them. We want and need to rebuild our working class neighborhoods into places for good living. Let the Workers' Societies sit down and make a *social inventory* of the neighborhood. Start with the elderly. How many are there? How many sick? How many bed-ridden? What about their income and diet? What services are available to them, from government, churches, golden age groups, private agencies? How many of the older people are aware of the services? How many make use of them? Problems will begin to suggest themselves. The lack of a convenient place for old people to get together. Desperate problems of diet and nutrition, caused either by lack of money or lack of proper cooking facilities. When problems make themselves known, intelligent people figure out solutions to them.

But we are copying the idiocy of capital if we treat the elderly only as people who need our help. At a certain point there should be a meeting of the older people and the question put to them. Look, we want to rebuild this neighborhood into a really good place—what can you do as part of a common effort of all the working people? Maybe they could set up a canteen for the young children whose parents work. They could turn a few neighborhood lots into vegetable and flower gardens. Start a look-in service for people who are ill. All it takes is a little getting together.

The inventory of neighborhood services should also devote a session to teenagers. That's a very difficult time of life for all of us. We've been known, as a result, to make it difficult for everyone else too. Yet, teenagers are children becoming adults. That's what it means. They have enormous energy and an enormous will to prove themselves, to try themselves out. It's such a waste to allow that energy and talent to just "hang-out." The capitalist mistakenly tried to divert teenagers with sports, playgrounds or discos. The capitalist only sees dangerous energy, not an untried young person anxious to find his or her worth. Instead, let's admit teenagers as equals in our deliberations in the Societies. Sure their judgment is inexperienced but their energy and idealism will, if given a chance, more than compensate any error of judgment.

The inventory should continue: young children, working parents, neighborhood danger spots, the neighborhood's landlords. Any problem that concerns anyone should concern everyone.

In this way we make a revolutionary change in our ideas about living in a place. A neighborhood is an arrangement for living which involves a little society of people. It doesn't matter what chance threw them together. Socialism is working people running their own lives. It is most needed and most easily gotten right there in the neighborhood. You don't have to solve the energy crisis or win the White House. All you have to do is sit down with the neighbors and 1) gripe 2) analyze what's making everyone gripe and 3) try out one or two things to solve the problem.

*Neighborhood Employment:* In the course of a neighborhood inventory you're going to run across situations where people will want things done and are willing to pay for them. Maybe it's that canteen for young kids whose parents are working. Certainl there is somebody in the neighborhood who knows how t organize a big kitchen and cost things out. Maybe a neigh borhood owned co-op could be set up to run such a canteen. N reason to expect people to volunteer their service for fre Especially not when there are older people, teenagers, an unemployed adults who could use a few bucks a week extra. I many ways it would be better to pay people than expect volun teers. We still live in a capitalist society and are used to paying fo things we value. When something is free it's often not respecte More importantly, we want to create joint economic interest The teenager who's earning $50 a week at the canteen and th parent who's relieved to know that the children are being well fe and cared for at lunch time—they now have a joint interest whic will contribute to a deeper class outlook. With a volunteer, yo have an unequal relationship—a charity mentality, rather than we-are-all-equal-in-this mentality. Sometimes it's possible, yo see, to use capitalism to beat capitalism.

The canteen, or other neighbors working in the neighbor hood bring an extra advantage. These people begin to relate t the neighborhood not just as a place, but as a commuity. The notice and report who's sick, who is having money problems, o who the neighborhood bicycle thief is. When we now these things we can do something about them. This begins to knit togethe our neighborhood and our class.

The important idea here is for the working class to begin t learn more about its own problems and especially that it ca solve them itself, thereby making life much easier and bette than if we depend on capitalism and its social system. Earlie when I wrote about a National Workers' Congress it must hav seemed unreal to you. Can you imagine? Plunked into a meetin of 5,000 people and asked to solve the energy problem? We'd a be flubs. But if those 5,000 people had a couple of years experience in solving neighborhood problems and had gotte some confidence in their own judgment, a 5,000 person con ference could be taken in stride.

*Making Life Better and More Fun:* Life is not just problems We ought to be able to get more fun out of it. We should mak cultural inventories of the neighborhood. It must be that two ou of three people do something in their spare time that othe people would enjoy if they knew about it and could share it. Many people paint, sew, do crafts. There are all sorts of opportunities for shows, exhibits, demonstrations, classes. Maybe there's a retired cabinet-maker who could give classes in woodworking or, perhaps, someone in the neighborhood is a particularly good gardener, hunter, or pastry cook. In the old days of the family-neighborhood network these skills would be passed on just normally but now we have to deliberately make it happen.

A cultural inventory would include the neighborhood's aspiring musicians, actors, actresses and magicians. You have a natural set-up to put on a play, a musical, an operetta or a concert, to do a variety show. Nowadays we shoot $20 for a night at a bad film, followed by belly-bombs at some drive-in eatery. But we could have a better time right down the street. Block parties, May Festivities, Labor Day picnics, neighborhood softball or basketball, Polish Cooking Night, Bread Week. They're all so much fun it's hard to understand why we don't have more of them.

A few unions or communities have Forums, events where there are speakers, debates or discussions. As our movement grows there are going to be scads of topics that we'll have to get familiar with. Naturally a forum isn't just a dry-as-dust session. Most of the fun and most of the learning comes at the coffee hour that follows the formal meeting. This brings people together around a subject of mutual interest and gives us all a chance to get our ideas off our chest and to meet people in an easy, natural situation. At the same time, our class is learning and gaining assurance in our ability to have sensible opinions on subjects that are now the private preserve of the mighty.

## Dealing With Special Neighborhood Problems

At some point we have to talk frankly about racial problems and this is the place. When I think about racial conflict in our society I try to be careful to separate two very distinct components of our attitudes on race. At one level, all of us have negative racial attitudes. All of us, of all races. It's inevitable. We pick up these attitudes the way we pick up our language and we have no more choice in the matter than we had a choice of thinking in English. But we have to be aware of that and to try to fight its effects in ourselves. A white person steps on your foot in the bus or a black person doesn't hold the door at the movie entrance and you almost walk into it. Well, you think, you black/white so and so. That's wrong; seven chances out of ten color had nothing to do with it. If it did, reacting racially profits nobody anything. We're really stuck with our racial hostilities but we can positively and creatively resist them and we can make the attempt to think of and to treat people justly. At this level of the problem there's been a lot of improvement in racial relations in my lifetime. I think many people really are trying to get out from under their own racial attitudes and have been making good progress. That's not where the main problem is.

The problem of race is mainly elsewhere, namely in the *real* increase in conflict between the races over jobs, neighborhoods and schools. These are not attitudes, prejudices, or misunderstandings. These are real conflicts of interest. The most typical and most difficult case to deal with is when a white and a black neighborhood abut on one another.

On the next page is a drawing of a black neighborhood in a generally white district.

Now, it is simply amazing how directly we can characterize what's happening and how universally true it's going to be. Let's say the commercial downtown area is being torn down and renewed, with new shopping areas, theaters and, parking lots expanded. All of this comes out of the hide of the taxpayer and most of its goes into indirect subsidies for business and interest for the banks. At the same time the black (or Puerto Rican or Haitian or poor white) neighborhood is expanding. Some of this is due to population increase, most of it due to migration into the area. The commercial downtown is also expanding and since it has the city government behind it, it can nibble, nibble, nibble into the top or northern edge of the black neighborhood. Over to the left or west, that broad avenue forms a natural *barrier* to expansion of the black neighborhood. If the pressure in the black area builds up it may jump that barrier but, for reasons we'll see later, only if there is no other direction for expansion. Over to the east, the Park will also function as a barrier, so the black neighborhood will move south.

Notice on the south that the borderline between the two areas is not smooth. That's because of what's happening there.

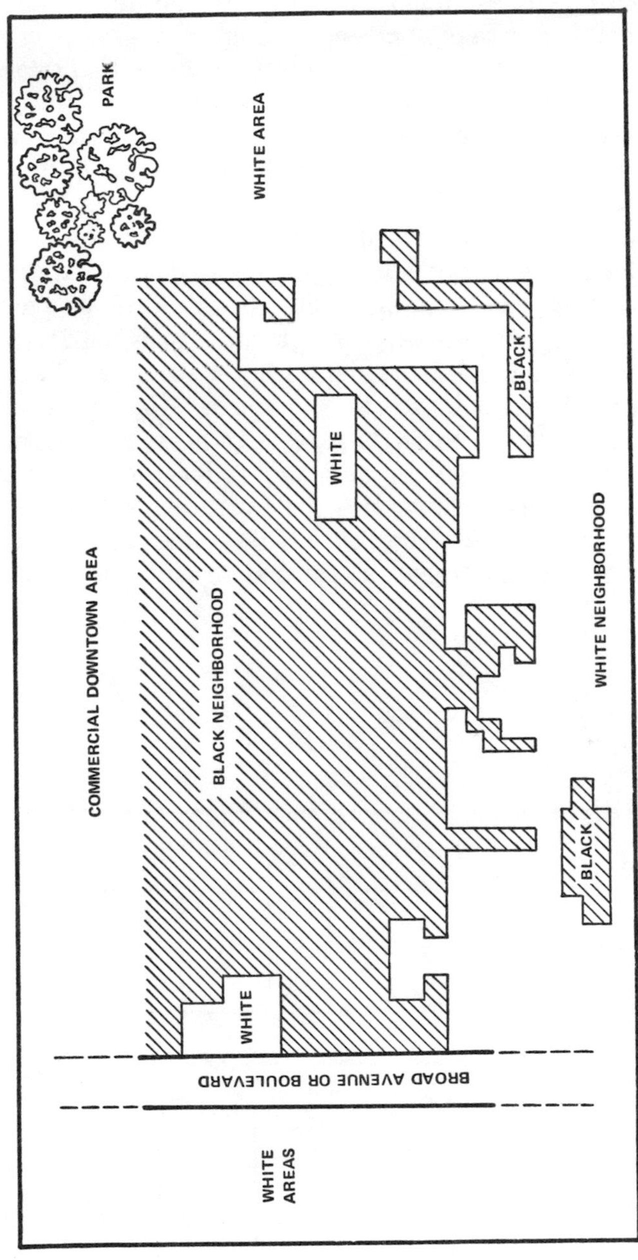
PARK
WHITE AREA
COMMERCIAL DOWNTOWN AREA
BLACK NEIGHBORHOOD
WHITE
BLACK
WHITE NEIGHBORHOOD
BLACK
WHITE
BROAD AVENUE OR BOULEVARD
WHITE AREAS

Mr. and Mrs. Jones, black, live in the middle of the black neighborhood. But they need more room. The area is crowded and run down so they can't find housing there. If they go way south housing discrimination will prevent them from buying or renting. But at the border and near it white families will be moving out so that that's where they'll go. Generally, the border isn't a clear line.

The Jones are involuntarily pawns in a process which, like so many other things in our society, is planned. Any experienced banker, realtor, city official, politician or observer can read what's going to happen when the commercial district pushes down on an expanding black neighborhood like ours. Therein lies a tale, because there is money to be made here like you never saw.

To begin with, up north there is the interest to the banks and the construction contracts and the federal grants and the condemnation proceedings and the tax subsidies and the law fees to grow fat on. To the south, there is a process of racial change to get fat on. Here's a street at or near the border.

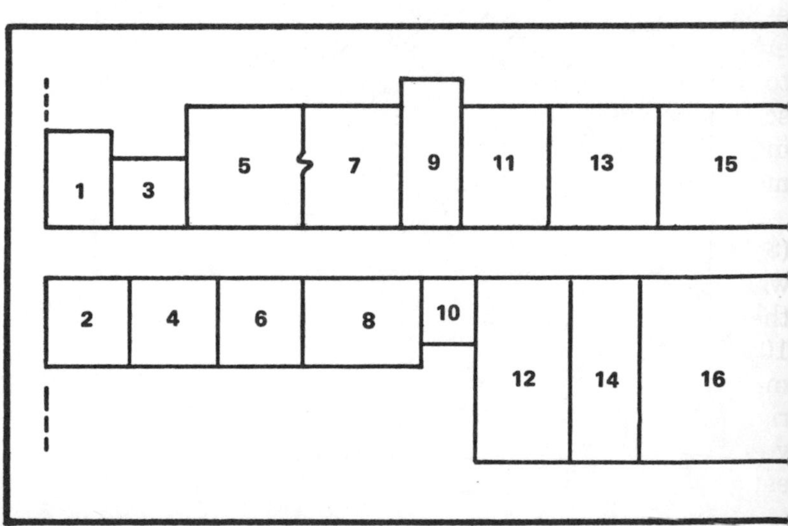

There are 16 houses there of various sizes. Let's say these are the fair prices of these houses:

#'s 2,3,4,6,10 are $25,000 each, give or take a few hundred.
#'s 1,7,9,11,13,15,8 are $30,000 each
#'s 5, 12, 14, are $35,000 each
# 16 is $45,000

If you add up all those values, you'll see that there's $485,000 of real estate here, nearly a half million on that one street alone. Normally, one or two of these houses change hands every year. At a certain point in time, as the black neighborhood gets closer, white buyers will be hard to come by. The banks will mark out the street as one of those where they're not inclined to give mortgages to white buyers. That will be conveyed to realtors who will discourage white families from looking there. The banking and real estate crowd knew this was going to happen or maybe even planned it from the day they decided to get federal renewal funds to build up the downtown area. They've been watching and waiting for the street to be ripe for a killing. Here's how it's picked.

House No. 10 is on the market. The Smith's who live there can't find a white buyer so they sell it the Jones family, black, at a stiff price—say $30,000, or $5,000 more than it's worth. The real estate people go to work on other people on the block, trying to encourage them to sell out. The people at No. 12 panic. They sell to a realty outfit for $30,000, $5,000 less than it's worth and scram out. A black family moves in at $40,000. There's $10,000 in someone's pocket, $5,000 out of a white pocket and $5,000 more from a black one.

Now the rush is on. Over the next year or two the remaining ($485,000 - $65,000) $420,000 worth of houses are sold by whites to real estate corporations. They go for 10% less than their value for a total of $380,000—and are sold, to blacks, for 10% more than their value or $460,000. Somebody in the middle made the difference ($460,000 - $380,000=). That's $80,000 right there. Add to that $80,000 the $10,000 we had earlier, you've got $90,000. But there's more. When $485,000 of real estate is sold there are also about $40,000 in legal fees and real estate commissions to be made. The shift of that one street from a white neighborhood to a black one yielded $130,00 in speculative profits and fees to the banking, lawyer and realty crowd. Meanwhile, all those white families, sixteen of them, have gone into the market for homes in other areas, so that another crowd of construction companies, construction unions (I'm sorry to say), help them get theirs. When all is said and done, the moving in of sixteen black families, and the moving out of sixteen white, adds *a quarter million dollars* to those parasites, who probably set the thing up to happen in the first place. The details of these neighborhood changes differ from here to there but the characteristics are everywhere similar. As always there's money to be made on the frontier—even if you have to create a new frontier to do it.

The blacks blame this situation on the whites, and in some sense they should. The blacks pay more, and get less because the whites won't live with them. The whites blame the blacks for pushing them out and for forcing them to pay high prices for the housing they're going into. Anyway you can't blame them.

The white families on the block who leave, and the black families who come in, have opposed interests. Even if all thirty-two families had amiable and positive racial attitudes, before all this happened, now they have good reason to be mad at each other. The whole transaction has cost everybody money. From the standpoint of people's private attitudes, the other side is to blame.

Meanwhile let's look at the border between the two neighborhoods. The trouble here is mainly young people, teenagers, mostly boys. There's hostility between the blacks and the whites. If the white neighborhood has lots of teenage boys there will be black/white gang fights. More often there won't be because the average age of people in the white neighborhood will be older than the black. Generally a neighborhood announces itself as ripe for picking by the parasites when its people get old. So the gang fights aren't as likely as other things.

The young black fellows will explore on the edges of their neighborhood and they'll find people—white—that they resent and don't like. Many of the whites will be older too, an easy mark for hand bag snatching, mugging or harassing. The kids will do this partly out of devilment, partly because they need the money and partly as a racial assertion, to get back at the whites.

Well before that, the first few black families who move into the all-white sections will be verbally harassed by young whites. Too often the black family will have its car, lawn or even house damaged. There have been several cases of fires being set to drive out the newcomers. While adults do these things too, the main problem, as before, is with groups of young men.

And you don't need many. An area of seven square blocks, say, can be terrorized by five or six boys. In that seven by seven area there might easily be over 6,000 people. But five or six boys can absolutely poison the already lousy relations between the races. And there will be a slightly higher than normal number of scraps between kids—over whose playground it is, over a smart aleck remark. The usual thing. Since many of them will be between white and black, they'll be racial incidents.

There's more. The city doesn't give very good service to black neighborhoods. So far as the city is concerned the border is a black area. Garbage pick-ups will get worse and the neighborhood will begin to decline visibly. There's a lot of petty crime and some really serious stuff in the black neighborhood as in any poor neighborhood. The people on the border will begin to experience this. They'll blame it on the blacks and it will support any harsh racial attitudes they have.

The neighborhoods of poorer people—any color, any race, any language—are noisier than the better off areas. More happens on the street. Radios are higher, people congregate on corners, cars get fixed at the curb. If it's been a quiet neighborhood before, the older residents will blame this too on the newcomers.

A captive class just suffers through these things. Black or white, you let events push you around and you try to arrange a private solution. You don't hear "nigger" when people say it, you put better locks on your doors, you keep the kids in front of the house, you move, you blame God for having you live poorly. A working class could deal with these things, if it had a mind to.

Near as I can make out the two or three things you've got to zero in on are the housing shift and those troublesome teenagers. You might start by discussing the problems of border areas in the Workers' Society. A parent's group, black and white, could form a neighborhood association. The first person who made a flowery speech about racial harmony would be told to sit down. The basis of this group is different. The white group is going to take responsibility for the whites and the black group for the black Both groups accept the fact that they have very little initi standing or support among their own people and that our black white council is going to fail unless they can show their ow people that they're more interested in delivering a good neigh borhood than in rhetoric and B.S.

To start with, the rate of racial change in the neighborhoo has got to be brought under control. People have got to sit dow and figure out what are the limits on the racial proportion of th neighborhood. Should it be 50/50? 70/30? 60/40? 40/60? The have to expose the parasites, letting people know throug neighborhood newspapers and meetings just what's happenin to the neighborhood. Then neighborhood pressure has to be pu on the parasites to get them to agree to the neighborhood's polic of change. Let's say Mr. Sharp the lawyer is in cahoots with Mr Edge the real estate woman and they won't accept working unde the guidelines of the black-white council. Everyone in th neighborhood could be informed about this with a view to makin sure that nobody will deal with them at all. Here the old boycot method of the Knights of Labor might be just the ticket. It can b nasty but in their quest to make a buck—or $130,000—M Sharp and Mrs. Edge have to be controlled. No way out of tha Now, if in the middle of this the Smith's put their house on Mr Edge's list or the Green's are using Sharp in a legal matter, the too have to be talked to and intelligent pressure, not bludgeon have to be used. The Green's and Smith's are of our class and w want to win their conviction, not their fear and enmity.

No neighborhood can remain lily-white. It is wrong for neighborhood to be lily-white. Every neighborhood should wan and work for a racial mix. True, people have a right to live in a on color neighborhood. Generally I'd respect their right even thoug I think they're wrong. But if push comes to shove, the right c someone else to live in a good house is more important. You don' have the right to all the water in your canteen if I'm dying c thirst.

The first job of the black-white council is to control the pac and character of neighborhood change. Let's say they decide on 40/60, black/white ratio and the neighborhood now is less tha 5% black. Then they should be recruiting both new young blac families and white families to come into the neighborhood. Yo have to aim at both because today's new families are tomorrow's neighborhoods. If you only recruit black, the average age of your white families will get older and older and you'll soon have an all black neighborhood. So you recruit both. That means the pace of neighborhood change will be very slow, too slow to solve the housing conflict between the races, unless we set generous, open-minded ratios. If your city is ⅓ black, your ratio should be more than ⅓, perhaps ½ or ⅔.

Setting a ratio is very, very important. To begin with, it asserts the fact that we are going to control the neighborhood, not impersonal forces. To the newcomers, it gives a commitment that people will work to make room for them and actually set a goal. To a person already in the neighborhood it guarantees that their old friends and neighbors are going to stay. That reinforces their will to deal with the problems of a racially mixed neighborhood.

The rambunctious boys and the petty thieves and the serious crime have got to be controlled. The police are of little use here. First of all, police activity doesn't stop crime. Putting lots of cops in our neighborhood just exports the crime to somewhere else. Or it drives the crime indoors. The police may be linked to the criminals, especially if drugs are involved. Moreover, the police will take sides, almost always with the whites. If it's racial harmony or peace that you want, you will try to keep the police out of as much as possible. Let them have the serious crime—rape,† murder, armed robbery. Make them get to it. But for the other stuff—harassment, purse snatching, scraps between kids, broken windows, or small scale housebreaking by

† However, this does not mean that neighborhood organizing cannot be done about violence against women. Several working-class communities across the U.S. have successfully made it safer for women to walk home at night by organizing "safe houses" (houses with green lights in the window and a woman home) where a woman who is threatened or physically harmed can seek refuge. Since most women are beaten, assaulted and raped (45% in their own homes in this country) in their own neighborhoods or homes, neighborhood-based organizing makes lots of sense. Experience in Cleveland and Boston has shown this is a much more effective method of curtailing rape than calling the police after the crime.

teenagers—only the working class can deal with it right. Those five or six boys have got to be identified. Their families have to be visited by the Council, or a committee of their own group. The boys have to be talked to, told exactly what's what. If they have a problem we can help out with—a job or something, fine. In any case what they're doing isn't going to be tolerated any more. That's the first time. If they continue to make trouble there has to be a neighborhood court. Moral force and social pressure are our preferred methods of dealing even with the most stubborn people but there are times when the threat of something more serious may be necessary.

That's vigilanteeism, a kangaroo court, you say. Perhaps, but it is absolutely necessary. There can be no racial peace in our class unless and until we get the authorities and their parasite friends out of the neighborhood and govern ourselves. It's not an empty phrase. If others do it they will divide, exploit and control us.

As I think you can see from our neighborhood analysis, the combination of lawyer, banker, realtor and local politician has no interest in our neighborhoods save to use us for other purposes. The police and the courts reflect that. Steal a radio you go to jail. Steal the neighborhood and they'll put you on the Real Estate Commission and make your lawyer a judge.

We can govern our neighborhoods, controlling their economic, social and moral development; controlling crime and violence, the parasites and the police. Everything hangs together. To the degree that the black/white council can develop neighborhood services and jobs, it can go to people and say, here is the best kind of neighborhood to go into, here people look out for one another, build good things together, and live a decent life. Our children grow up, not in the capitalist jungle, but in a environment in which they can see and understand the intelligence and creativity and morality of their parents. The class consciousness of the children will grow as fast as their feet. Even the worst racist will prefer to stay and live with the blacks rather than give up this neighborhood's advantages.

We've skipped over many things here. But the critical thing is that if we want to build a classless society we have to start building a classless working class. That means a working class governing its own essential life processes so far as is possible.

'hat means the whole working class, not just the men, or the mployed, not just the white ones, not just the people in their rime years. The whole class. Only this sort of preparation can ıake socialism so necessary for us, so positively desirous, such n expression of our full potential as human beings that we will ut capitalism aside as a trivial, inadequate way of doing things nd embrace socialism as the natural next step in our personal nd class development.

## 'he Social World of Women

Many of the old time socialists, like Engels, thought that vomen would become socially, economically, and politically qual with men when they were freed from traditional women's hores and were able to go out to work. These socialists felt that he narrow world of family and neighborhood made for narrow vomen and that an isolated woman, busy with babies, floors, tove and wash tub, lacked class feeling and therefore tended to e conservative in outlook. Her ideas were too dependent on nfluences of the local trades people and especially on the priest. They thought the cure was to send women out to work and to stablish communal facilities for laundry, sewing, child care and ven the feeding of the family.

All those things are fine and good so far as they go. Over half he adult women in our country work for a living outside the home nd are sorely in need of support services. Certainly, within our ıeighborhoods we should address the problems of women who re working outside the home or who would like to if they could ee their way clear to do so.

But what about the other women? The ones who, for vhatever reasons, feel that they have a special role to play at ıome and who are willing to sacrifice the extra dollars in order to lo things for their families that otherwise couldn't be done. We hould start out by shedding the old socialist idea that these vomen are "backward," "provincial," etc. The very point of mproving things for working people is that each worker, man or voman, will have more real choice of what kind of a person to be. f a woman wants to focus on her home and family then our job is o try to help her make that sort of life as rich as life is for the erson who goes off to the factory, school, or office.

There is more to this point of view than a choice of mora values. Collective capital has already absorbed a good part o family and neighborhood life into its productive arrangements Our families and neighborhoods have been invaded and dis rupted by the products of collective capital, such as the auto and by the administrative relations of the Social System. So ou attitude on women who stay at home isn't one of "let the littl dears have their own thing" but that these women have profoundly important job to do for our class. We must rebuild ou neighborhoods into real, human communities. The people wh can do that are the people who stay in the neighborhood namely the elderly people, the young people and the women wh work in the home or work outside only part-time, and, of course the unemployed of both sexes.

A table needs three legs to stand straight, and so does ou class. Economic activity based on the trade union is one of them Political activity is the second. And social activity based on th family and the neighborhood is the third. We shouldn't fall int the trap that Debs, Engels and others fell into by overlooking th third leg; in many ways it is the most important of all.

A second point follows from this view of the matter. Th well-being of women who stay at home is a class problem. Me should be as concerned about it as women. In fact, many are, bu this is disguised by the spheres of activity which they think ar important. Whether it's a so-called "woman's sphere" or "man' sphere" really doesn't matter. In our life time, a real reversal o roles between men and women will remain rare. You won't ofte see a man and woman arrange it so she follows her job or caree while he takes on the domestic responsibilities. But it wi happen occassionally and it will be good for our neighborhoods t have men around during the workday. Our children will grow u with broader ideas of what it means to be a man or a woman When we take responsibility as a class for home and neighbor hood we make it a little easier on those men and women who wan to break down the old, men-do-this, women-do-that idea of th sexes.

Workers, I know, tend to be somewhat conservative on th question of differences between men and women and much of th resistance to any change on that issue comes from our class Oddly enough it's also among workers that you find the me complaining most about the way women are and the women complaining most about the way men are. The reason, I think, is that we make our men and women into such different creatures that they have very little in common so they quickly get bored with one another. Friends have to have a lot in common to be friends. If men and women are to have much to do with one another, as I expect they will, they need common experience. If they are to be friends, it means we have to have less rigid ideas of what it is to be a man and what it is to be a woman.

Some people are afraid that the difference between men and women will disappear. They must have rocks in their heads. The two sexes are always going to have different reactions to the same things. You don't have to make laws and rules about that. If you're a socialist you want a situation where people are free of my prejudice and my preference on how they should think, act or feel. Socialism is a moral idea as much as a political or economic one. And its hold on us comes from the moral aspect, this demand for real, practical freedom for everyone in their everyday life. Of all the problems that face our class, the relations between the sexes, on all levels, is the one we are as yet least able to deal with. Too many working-class men are afraid of equality between the sexes, particularly sexual equality and moral equality, and so are too many working-class women. So this is an area where we have to make an extra effort and remember that we are building fundamentally new ways of doing things.

In the relations between the sexes, no less than between the races, we have to deal with our own dirty laundry. To ask the authorities to intervene is to ask them to sow the seeds of discord among us. The physical abuse of women by men is very common, as all of us know. So too is moral and economic abuse. Children are also victims here, sometimes of women. These abuses will become more common as traditional relations between the sexes are further broken down by capital. We must step in here, and establish reasonable standards of behavior between men and women and children. We must be willing to exercise moral and other pressure to enforce them. We will have to make *judicial* decisions, and have *court-like* bodies to do it.

Frankly, I am less afraid of injustice at the hands of fellow workers than of injustice at the hands of the authorities. You know they will do the wrong thing most of the time because their interests are opposed to ours. Sure we will make our own mistakes, but our inexperience and relative ignorance are correctable. Of course, we're talking here about a working class which is more thoughtful and more humane than the present ragtag chaotic collection of workers. But I'd just say here what I've said elsewhere: if we can't govern ourselves, we can't govern society. And if we can't break down the "class" difference among ourselves, based on age, sex, race, experience, or ability, how can we possibly so it in the country as a whole?

## Politics and Government

Under collective capital the main function of the government is to intervene into the life of the working class. The government tries to bring it under administrative control with a view to increasing its productivity and perfecting its captivity. Secondary functions include helping this or that capitalist make an extra buck or steering the surplus to the middle element.

The conservatives are right about the modern state. It is a devouring monster. Its wealth and power grow and grow without any reason—that is, any reason for us. (The reasons are clear to those who gain.) Its administrative form is hostile to the democratic spirit and suppresses our attempts at class independence. So how do we fight it?

The civil rights and antiwar movements of the 1960s have taught us a lot about how to deal with government. The tactic of civil disobedience, for example, is perfectly suited to resistance against administrative relations. We should talk about that a little bit.

People can be ruled by other people only as they morally accept the authority of others. That's true of the slave, or the prisoner in jail, and it's true of us. It isn't so obvious for the slave or prisoner but its true nevertheless. The slave can't be chained all the time, if he or she is to work and produce. Constant guard duty is too expensive. To control slaves you must show them that you have enough chains and guards to control them *individually* if they give you any reason to single out any one of them.

The thing the slaveholder must fear is the coming together of the slaves. Once they begin to realize that the force you have at your disposal can't control all the slaves acting together, you're n trouble. You prevent their coming together by convincing hem that your being the master and them being the slaves is ight. That it's in accordance with goodness or nature or god's vill. That's very important since it adds the chains of conscience, vhich never sleep, to the physical chains. So the slave cooperates n his or her own slavery. The mental slavery of the slave protects he slavemaster when the physical chains are down and the uards are dozing.

The working class of collective capital is a slave class. But he nature of their enslavement is very, very different than that of he chattel slave or the jail inmate. The elements of physical orce which bind us are much less important than the moral force. Ve are held by our moral acceptance of capitalism as the best vay to live, ordained by god, nature and human nature. The ourts, police, and jails play a much much less important role for is than they do for the slave. Because of the technical and social volution of society, capital has to depend to a much greater legree than formerly on our cooperation in our own captivity. You can watch a slave and beat her if she doesn't pick cotton fast nough or whip him if he doesn't pull the oars to rhythm. But hink of your own job. How well can they control what you do? On n assembly line—it's pretty easy, but in most other jobs they lepend on our conscience and our pride to make us do it right. The police depend on almost all of us driving near the speed imit. The one or two speeders are singled out. The IRS depends on most of us handing in an honest tax return so they can grab the ninority of cheats.

Civil disobedience exploits the authorities' dependence on our assent to their rules and laws. A mass of people refuse to go to he back of the bus. Thousands upon thousands refuse to be lrafted. The authorities are then faced with a clear alternative: each for force or make an accomodation. If they reach for force he situation could get worse since civil disobedience people, by heir courage and willingness to accept the consequences of the lisobedience, are the best possible advocates of their cause. They believe in a principle which they think is just. If there is any nerit to their view, they'll gain greater support since it is presented in the best, most dramatic and humanly persuasive ight.

Collective capital tries to run everything. It tries to introduce its productive relations everywhere. It tries to turn us into its products, that is, items whose behavior manifests the power authority and the will of capital. It seems to me that the line of defense against this sort of attempt is fairly direct and obvious. *We should become ungovernable.* We should try to remove every trace of acceptance of their moral right to rule from our minds. Every trace. We should assert as an absolute need—which it is—our right to govern ourselves. And we should act on that directly by universal disobedience. Everywhere and anywhere. Whenever it is to our advantage.

For example, we are exploited in the tax system for the benefit of the middle element. Everybody pays nearly the same percentage in taxes but the benefits given to them are two, three four or more times as much as those given to us. We want a dollar of service for every dollar of taxes. No more, no less. The reason taxes are so objectionable now is that we pay and pay and get little in return. We want equality of tax benefits and we will use every tactic of mass tax avoidance that the mind of man or woman can devise. That takes organization and mass determination. The earliest people who refuse to pay taxes—will be in trouble. But we know from earlier movements of civil disobedience that when large numbers of people disobey the authorities have to escalate or back down. Either way they lose.

In a shop or office being ungovernable means organizing an alternate work discipline. The work week is now too long. So maybe we encourage mass absenteeism on Monday or Friday. If large numbers of people refuse to work the authorities are faced with the same grim alternative—escalate or back down. If they do escalate, and fine or otherwise punish people, we have to be prepared to dig down deep to help those people. We don't need or want martyrs.

The strategy of being ungovernable was built into our idea for dealing with neighborhood change and social conflict. We—and not the parasites, realtors, banks, lawyers, courts, cops, or social workers—must control the neighborhood. Reapply that idea to the tax situation. We know that basically, the schools are taking resources from us and steering them to the middle element. Step One is for workers to intervene in the local school and insist on an accounting of where the money is spent. That will give us the awful truth in its ugly detail. Step Two may have to include mass refusal to pay school taxes and the setting up of an alternate school fund which we control directly. The government will respond with writs and injunctions. But that's good because then the question, of who benefits from what, will be fought out in public, not on the back stairs of the Board of Education building or in the meetings between Federal Education officials and the textbook manufacturers. If the court decisions are unsatisfactory then we go on to tax boycotts and school boycotts. In the not so long run we will make gains because they haven't got the physical force to compel us to obey. They do have enough force to compel me or you. And they'll use it. But when large numbers of our people resist they must yield.

Three things are necessary for a successful strategy of being ungovernable. First, the interests of all workers must be at stake. We cannot single out the special interests even of unjustly treated groups—women, black people, or old people. Every issue we fix upon to bring the government to its knees must be one in which every worker has a direct stake. They are experts at dividing us and we can't give them a handle to do this.

Second, the old kind of civil disobedience often tried to get the government to do something, to take some positive action. Civil rights people wanted the court to intervene and enforce the law. But the draft refusal and G.I. movements have a more instructive point. They tried to *prevent* the government from doing something—the war in Viet Nam—by refusing to have anything to do with it. The G.I. movement is interesting because it was made up mostly of workers' sons, not middle element students and it operated under the threat of military discipline. My impression of the G.I. movement is that they didn't refuse to fight, they merely *didn't fight.* They patrolled areas they knew were empty. They made local agreements with the other side not to shoot at one another. In an ambush site, they showed lights and made lots of noise to warn the other side. If we were to copy this tactic it would mean not getting involved in confrontation with government and the authorities but trying more to evade them, avoid them, mislead them, confuse them and keep them guessing. What we want, so to speak, is neither war nor peace with the authorities. War we'd lose, and peace is no good for us. Oblique attack and oblique defense is more the ticket.

The third thing is that we want to rebuild the life of our class, starting in the Workers Society and developing instrumental organizations. A positive workers' organization must create and then move into the vacuums of authority so we can better the lives, serve the interests, and express the desires of our class. With no movement to speak of now it's hard to figure out what's going to work. But I think the strategy of being ungovernable, seeking oblique and evasive forms of conflict and building up the governing power of our class is the best one for exploiting the weaknesses of collective capital.

## A Workers' Political Party

The last point is that there must be a workers' political party. You can reform the Democrats—to your heart's content—but whatever you do, it is worth nothing if our class remains politically allied with the capitalists. If we are to reform and not merely "reform" the Democrats we have to chase the other classes out—the capitalists, the middle element and the small businessmen. But it's easier to start our own party and to begin trying to get all 80 workers to vote—as a class. Let the other side have the 20—or, to be more exact, exploit the other side to get a couple of the 20 but pay no class price, concede none of our class interests, for their votes.

The formation of a workers' political party is not the first priority. You can't have a political party to represent your interests if you haven't got the interests. Formation of Societies, trade union reform, building the Staff Association—these have higher priority. But they should be a half step ahead—no more and no less.

Also, I don't believe in running campaigns to "educate the people," like many left groups do. Who's the educator? And what's the education? We should run candidates when our own people are strong enough and confident enough to "educate" the government and the authorities.

When we do organize a party only men and women who are workers should be allowed to join it. All its candidates should be workers. There are lots of people in our class who would make better Senators and Presidents than the ones we get.

The need for a party is very, very clear. Our economic strategy of seizing the Critical Eight and our social and political strategy of being ungovernable by any but our own class will put our movement into constant wrangles with the authorities. More often than not, we'll be at or over the edge of what's legal. There's no way out of that. We need a party and officeholders to fight the inside front of those battles. To prevent punitive legislation, to tie the hands of the police, to make the courts cautious. We don't want to be in Debs' position and be left open to a coup like Olney's.

The party also represents our commitment to the democratic process. We refuse to obey unjust and unfair authorities, true—regardless of majorities and minorities—but we do not propose to force anybody to do anything. We resist, we don't aggress. The party fights the public battle; the unions, the Societies and our other organizations fight best in the shadows. The party establishes the truth and lets people know what we are about, namely a society without classes, where human-ness is always first.

Our party—its a Socialist Party because that's what we're about—doesn't aim at the thing traditional parties aim at. We don't want to control the state in order to use it as an instrument of class rule, industrialization, social welfare or anything else. We understand the old socialist fallacy, namely you build-up the state today so you can destroy it tomorrow. We want to control the state so we can take positive progressive steps immediately to make it wither away, to get authority and power out into the society where it belongs.

Our general political strategy of a democratic and socialist workers' political party goes hand in hand with our economic and social strategies. They fit together; whether they'll work depends on us—alone.

> "Too long have the workers of the world waited for some Moses to lead them out of bondage. He has not come; he never will come. I would not lead you out if I could; for if you could be led out, you could be led back again. I would have you make up your minds that there is nothing that you cannot do for yourselves." (1905)
>
> — from *Eugene Debs Speaks*, Pathfinder Press, 1972, p. 124